TOWPATH GUIDE

To The

C&O CANAL

TOWPATH GUIDE

To The
C&O CANAL

by

Thomas F. Hahn

Revised Edition
edited by
Catherine Baldau

Harpers Ferry Historical Association
P.O. Box 197
Harpers Ferry, WV 25425
(304) 535-6881
hfha@earthlink.net
www.harpersferryhistory.org

The Harpers Ferry Historical Association is a non-profit cooperating association supporting the educational and interpretive programs of Harpers Ferry National Historical Park. All proceeds from the sale of this publication benefit National Park Service programs.

FIRST EDITION, April 1982
SECOND EDITION, October 1983
THIRD EDITION, September 1984
FOURTH EDITION, August 1985
FIFTH EDITION, June 1987
SIXTH EDITION, December 1988
SEVENTH EDITION, January 1990
EIGHTH EDITION, June 1990
NINTH EDITION, April 1991
NINTH EDITION, Second Printing, October 1991
TENTH EDITION, October 1992
ELEVENTH EDITION, June 1993
TWELFTH EDITION, March 1994
THIRTEENTH EDITION, January 1996
25TH ANNIVERSARY EDITION, 1997
FIFTEENTH EDITION, 1999
REVISED EDITION, 2015

ISBN 978-0-9674033-1-1

Library of Congress Control Number: 2015935399

Original maps by John Beck, National Park Service, 1974, updated and revised by Lisa Angstadt, 2014.

While every effort has been made to provide information, telephone numbers, and Internet addresses believed to be accurate at the time of publication, the publisher assumes no responsibility for errors or changes that occur after publication. The publisher does not have any control over and assumes no responsibility for third-party websites or their content.

Front cover: Lock 22 (*Image courtesy Steve Dean*); Back Cover: Monocacy Aqueduct, Interior Paw Paw Tunnel (*Images courtesy Steve Dean*); Georgetown level, canal boat couple (*Images courtesy of the National Park Service, Chesapeake and Ohio Canal National Historical Park*). Frontispiece: Big Slackwater, 2012 (*Image courtesy Steve Dean*)

The *Towpath Guide to the C&O Canal* provides towpath users with step-by-step descriptions of the canal, physical descriptions of canal structures, historical events which took place along the canal, and the presence of nature as seen and heard from the towpath. The guide is based on first-hand observations and historical documents.

For those who would like to know more about the history and descriptions of American (and international) canals and what is being done to restore them, visit www.americancanals.org or write to American Canal Society, 117 Main Street, Freemansburg, PA 18017.

For those particularly interested in the preservation and use of the C&O Canal or its volunteer opportunities, write or visit:

Chesapeake & Ohio Canal National Historical Park Headquarters Office
1850 Dual Highway, Suite 100
Hagerstown, MD 21740-6620
301-739-4200
www.nps.gov/choh or www.nps.gov/getinvolved/volunteer

C&O Canal Association   C&O Canal Trust
Box 366   1850 Dual Highway, Suite 100
Glen Echo, MD 20812   Hagerstown, MD 21740
301-983-0825   301-714-2233
inquiries@candocanal.org   www.canaltrust.org
www.candocanal.org

***Unless otherwise noted, all historic images in this book appear courtesy of the National Park Service, Chesapeake and Ohio Canal National Historical Park.

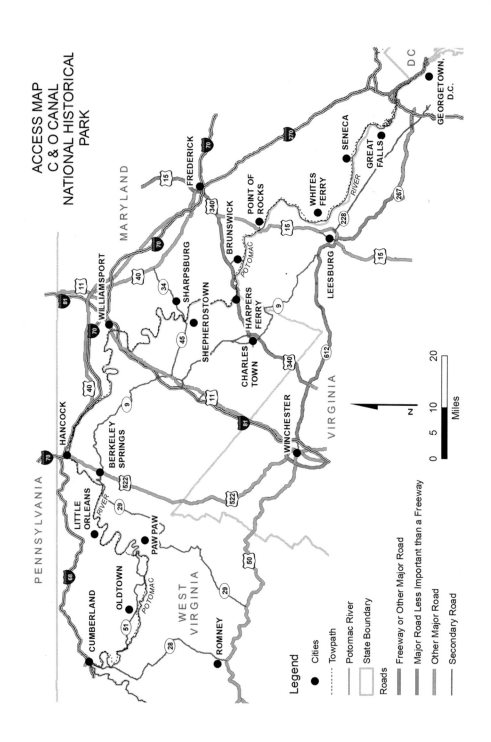

ACCESS MAP
C & O CANAL
NATIONAL HISTORICAL
PARK

Legend

Cities ●

Towpath ·······

Potomac River

State Boundary

Roads

Freeway or Other Major Road

Major Road Less Important than a Freeway

Other Major Road

Secondary Road

Contents

Acknowledgments

The revised edition of this book would not have been possible without the generous and enthusiastic help of volunteers who spent their free time, weekends, or vacation days on the towpath or in front of a computer. The Harpers Ferry Historical Association (HFHA) is deeply grateful for their time and efforts to bring this book back to life.

Before anything else, HFHA members Annette Keener-Farley, Frank Surdu, and Don Burgess accomplished the tedious task of converting the original text into a revisable electronic document. Special thanks to Don for scanning the book and maps and his work with the Canal Town Partnership.

From the National Park Service, Curt Gaul, former Supervisory Park Ranger for the park's Western Maryland District, and Historian Ahna Wilson helped inaugurate this project by leading HFHA to the C&O Canal Association (COCA). Ahna also assisted with gathering the historical photos that appear in this book. Additional support was provided by the Potomac Heritage National Scenic Trail Office, National Park Service.

Dr. Karen Gray of the COCA readily accepted the immense job of verifying much of the canal related technical and historical data in the book. HFHA is indebted to her hours of research and editing and the generous sharing of her knowledge and canal expertise.

COCA Level Walker Chairman Steve Dean spent countless hours on the towpath, offered his advice, support, and culvert expertise, and contributed stunning photos from his collection. Steve's infectious passion for all things C&O made this project a joy to work on. Most importantly, Steve helped recruit the COCA members and level walkers who walked the towpath and reported any discrepancies to the original text. Special gratitude is extended for the field work of Tom Aitken, Dick Ebersole, Bill Holdsworth, Pat Hopson, Jonnie Lefebure, Jim Lyons, Rod Mackler, Carl Pederson, Tom Perry, Paul Petkus, Dick Stoner, Susan VanHaften, Hilary Walsh, Stephen Williams, and Frank Wodarczyk. A special thank you to John Barnett for his personal Georgetown tour.

Some of these volunteers went beyond foot duty. Rod Mackler was the very first level walker to answer the call for volunteers and helped clarify facts along the dense Georgetown levels. Rod also loaned us his original *Towpath Guide* booklets as reference material for this book's introduction. In addition to verifying almost 26 miles of towpath, Pat Hopson provided insightful suggestions and ideas, double-checked facts when needed, and gave us her sharp eye in the review phases. Jim Lyons happily investigated any Western Maryland issues and enlisted Maria Keifer, whose beautiful photographs appear in this new volume.

In addition to his hours of editorial assistance, Bill Holdsworth contributed valuable research and new text. Special credit is owed to Bill, John Wheeler, and the COCA for their immense work gathering and formatting the towpath's GPS data. The Access Points page on the COCA website was a crucial tool for generating the driving directions in this book.

COCA member Dward Moore spent many hours of research compiling the book's glossary. Ed Kirkpatrick traveled all along the towpath to photograph the Canal Quarters lockhouses and offered his advice and expertise during the photo selection process. Historian Tim Snyder's dedicated research clarified and enhanced all of the Civil War facts in this book. Jenna Warrenfeltz of the C&O Canal Trust assisted with information and graphics for the Canal Quarters and Canal Towns.

Lisa Angstadt is another volunteer whose work and passion for this project were indispensable. Lisa took the 40-year-old maps, studied every road, creek and landmark, then applied her talent and skill to meticulously update them while maintaining their original look and feel. Her hours of work enriched each and every map.

Finally, special thanks are owed Chris Hahn and the Hahn family for their cooperation and support of this project. This book is dedicated to the memory of Thomas F. Swiftwater Hahn and all those—especially the above-mentioned volunteers—who follow his spirit along the towpath.

Capt. Thomas F. Swiftwater Hahn at age 72 in Shepherdstown, WV. *(Image courtesy Chris Hahn)*

Introduction

Footsteps from the nation's capital is a scenic trail acclaimed for its natural beauty and steeped in nearly two centuries of history. Today the Chesapeake and Ohio Canal belongs to a 20,000-acre national park visited by over five million people each year. Before it became a recreation area, it was a commercial waterway, an economic lifeline for small Potomac communities, and a home to locktenders and canallers, with an origin that traces back to our country's forefathers.

A young, enterprising George Washington was one of the first surveyors who envisioned a navigable trade route between the Potomac Tidewater region and the rich fur, timber, and agricultural resources of the Ohio Valley. In the 1780s his Patowmack Company first attempted this trade route by building a series of skirting canals around the river's falls, rapids, and other impediments, but the dangers of a capricious river still made Potomac River trade a hazardous endeavor. It would take a flatwater canal to open navigation and therefore commerce with the West.

The success of the Erie Canal, built 1817–25, spurred the states of Maryland, Virginia, and Pennsylvania to charter the Chesapeake and Ohio Canal Company. U.S. President John Quincy Adams inaugurated construction of the C&O Canal by turning the first shovel of dirt on July 4, 1828. It would take 22 years of financial struggles and setbacks—including work stoppages and riots among the immigrant laborers, a cholera epidemic, and a four-year legal battle—for the canal to reach Cumberland, Maryland, in 1850. By that time the Baltimore and Ohio Railroad had also stretched to Cumberland, and competition grew between the two freight carriers. Washington's vision of a navigable waterway to Ohio had only made it halfway; however, the completed 184.5 miles of the canal stood as a nineteenth century engineering feat.

Boats that departed the tide lock in Georgetown—towed by mules at a steady two-and-a-half to four miles per hour—traveled through 74 lift locks, across 11 stone aqueducts and more than 200 culverts, past seven supporting dams with inlets, and through the Paw Paw Tunnel (dug through 3,118′ of rock), rising 605′ to the terminus in Cumberland. Despite frequent flood damage, many army crossings during the Civil War, and competition from the paralleling railroad, the C&O carried freight (mainly coal, lumber, and agricultural products) for nearly a century. Following brief financial success in the 1870s, damage from the devastating 1889 flood sent the canal company into receivership with, ironically, the B&O in control. Another destructive flood in 1924 finally led to the canal's closure to navigation.

In 1938 the U.S. Government purchased the canal for $2 million. No longer conveying plodding mules, the nearly-flat towpath attracted naturalists, birdwatchers, fishermen, and history buffs. The National Park Service restored and re-watered the lower part of the canal as a recreation area, but plans to continue were halted during World War II. Congress's post-war proposal of a parkway modeled after Skyline Drive and the Blue Ridge Parkway received strong public approval. The best ally of conservationists was Associate Supreme Court Justice William O. Douglas—an outdoorsman, environmentalist, and frequent towpath hiker—who challenged editors of the *Washington Post* and *Evening Star* newspapers to hike with him from Cumberland to Georgetown to assess the canal's beauty and historical significance. Douglas argued, "It is a refuge, a place of retreat, a long stretch of quiet and peace at the Capitol's back door—a wilderness area where man can be alone with his thoughts, a sanctuary where he can commune with God and nature, a place not yet marred by the roar of wheels and the sound of horns." The journalists accepted the challenge.

The completion of the highly publicized eight-day "Douglas Hike" in March 1954 drew a massive crowd to Georgetown. Opinions began to sway. The NPS abandoned the parkway idea, but a 16-year battle ensued before the idea of saving the canal as a National Historical Park won the day. In 1961 President Dwight D. Eisenhower established the canal as a National Monument. Finally, in January 1971 the former commercial waterway—a landmark to nineteenth century engineering and a memorial to the lives of its builders and workers—became the C&O Canal National Historical Park.

Another early canal supporter was Orville Wright Crowder (1904–1974), a naturalist who circled the globe eight times, setting foot in all but five countries. Born in Baltimore, Maryland, Crowder first traveled in the 1920s, when his trip to the western United States initiated his great interest in hiking and mountain climbing. In 1937 he was the third person to hike the entire Appalachian Trail. He was founder of the World Nature Association and Crowder Nature Tours, which took tour groups around the world. Crowder also led frequent tours of the C&O Canal. Between 1957 and 1959 he pushed a surveyor's wheel from Georgetown to Cumberland, recording mileage measurements to 1/100 of a mile, and noting structures and natural features along the canal. He conceived the idea of a towpath guidebook but completed only a skeletal version of it.

Crowder was an active member of the early C&O Canal Association (COCA). He helped form and was first chairman of the level walkers, members who walked sections of the towpath and reported its conditions. Through the COCA, he found the person who would make his idea of a towpath guide a reality.

Thomas F. Swiftwater Hahn was born in Topeka, Kansas, in 1926. His maternal grandmother was of the Kansas Delaware (Lenape) Tribe, and Hahn remained closely connected with his Native American heritage—once serving as Chief of the Kansas Delaware Nation. After a semester at the University of Kansas in 1944, Hahn enlisted in the navy, a decision that eventually brought him to Washington D.C. and the C&O Canal.

A naval intelligence officer in Washington in 1948, Hahn went on several towpath nature walks led by NPS naturalists. Those early walks spurred his interest in the canal, but he found little literature on the subject. After two decades of active duty tours, including Korea, China, and Vietnam, Hahn's final assignment with the navy brought him to Ft. Meade, Maryland, and back to the canal.

Around 1969 Hahn began collecting C&O material. He was active with the COCA, chairman of the level walkers, and founding editor of its newsletter, *Along the Towpath*. With Orville Crowder's measurements, notes, and encouragement, Hahn published the first *Towpath Guide to the C&O Canal, Section One: Georgetown Tidelock to Seneca* in March 1971. Crowder's name appeared as co-author, but subsequent volumes were published by Hahn alone. Originally done as four booklets (with cover illustrations by Hahn's wife, Nathalie), the sections were later combined into one volume. In addition to Crowder, Hahn acknowledged many others for help in the book's early editions including several COCA level walkers, John Beck for the maps, Bill Shank of the Pennsylvania Canal Society, Grant Conway, and Bill Davies.

When Hahn retired as a navy captain in 1972, he went from being a canal "enthusiast" to a canal "professional." He was canal assistant for the George Washington Memorial Parkway, supervisory ranger of the C&O Canal, and a contract industrial archaeologist for the Denver Service Center on the C&O Canal Research Team. He was founding president of the American Canal Society and co-founder of the American Canal and Transportation Center, which published documents, maps, books, and drawings on the subject of early transportation history.

In 1976 Hahn moved his family to Shepherdstown, West Virginia, and furthered his education at Shepherd University and West Virginia University, earning several degrees, including a MA in history and PhD in industrial archaeology and education. He worked on canal restoration projects and published multiple canal books, the most popular being the *Towpath Guide*, which had 15 editions and sold over 100,000 copies. Over five decades of Hahn's research is now archived as the Thomas Hahn Chesapeake and Ohio Canal collection, 1939–1993, at the Special Collections Research Center, The Gelman Library, The George Washington University. Thirty boxes are filled with reference material, maps, correspondence, photographs, negatives, and slides.

Veteran, archaeologist, author, publisher, college professor, medicine man, Indian chief, husband, and father—Hahn wore many hats and had many accomplishments. He moved to Florida in 1999. When he passed away in May 2007, his Memorial Service and Life Celebration were held beside a river. Though the river was not the Potomac, where Hahn spent so much of his life, it was still fitting that he was remembered near a place his mentor Justice William Douglas may have called "a refuge, a place of retreat, a long stretch of quiet and peace."

About the Revised Edition

The Harpers Ferry Historical Association published the last edition of the *Towpath Guide* in 1999. In addition to an update on the physical conditions of the towpath and modifications to historical and structural data, technology has allowed the book a twenty-first century makeover, which incorporates features not available or common in the Hahn era. Changes to the original publication include:

Mileages This revised edition maintains Orville Crowder's original measurements to 1/100 of a mile. There are locations where these mileages differ from those used by the National Park Service (which were determined in a separate survey) in its literature and on its website. Significant differences between the Crowder and NPS mileages at landmarks (locks, aqueducts, campsites, etc.) are noted. Also, be advised that the distances between NPS mileposts are not always an exact mile. For example, the odometer reading between NPS mileposts 32 and 33 is 1.37 miles. An "x" in mileages (ex: 1.0x) denotes an estimated location.

Maps The classic maps created by John Beck in the early 1970s have been carefully revised and updated. Symbols for parking, restrooms, boat ramps, etc., were added, as well as new roads, interstate highways, and route numbers. Also, the map design was slightly modified to better distinguish rivers, major highways, bridges, etc.

Images Thomas Hahn's ca. 1970s "current" photos have been replaced with updated images that more accurately depict the canal's appearance in the twenty-first century. Most of the historical photos that appeared in the original books are included, though some have been replaced or omitted.

Sidebars Details or topics that stray too far from the mile-by-mile descriptions of the canal have been pulled from the main text and are treated instead as sidebars.

Links to Websites As websites are updated more easily and frequently than printed material, links to places, restaurants, organizations, etc., have been included. When traveling to C&O Visitor Centers or specific locations outside the park, it is always recommended to verify the operating hours prior to departure.

GPS Coordinates New driving directions and GPS coordinates were compiled utilizing Google Maps. As some GPS devices may not recognize the same roads/coordinates as Google Maps, it is recommended that visitors always confirm directions from their actual departure point prior to leaving for the towpath. Directions are given from the nearest highway or town. Note that some remote areas along the towpath, especially in Western Maryland, may not receive GPS satellite readings.

Geology Some of the names of geological periods and formations have been changed since the last publication of this guidebook. We have retained Hahn's original names. A good source for studying the geology along the C&O Canal is *Geology of the Chesapeake and Ohio Canal National Historical Park and Potomac River Corridor, District of Columbia, Maryland, West Virginia, and Virginia* by Scott Southworth, David K. Brezinski, Randall C. Orndorff, John E. Repetski, and Danielle M. Denenny (U.S. Geological Survey: Reston, VA, 2008), available at: pubs.usgs.gov/pp/1691/P1691.pdf.

Other additions to this revised edition include an overview of C&O NHP general information, indexes to canal features, vehicle parking access points, and campsites, and a glossary of common canal terms.

Most of the original references to wildflowers, trees, birds, etc., are now obsolete and therefore were removed. New sidebars with current nature information (including referrals to nature guidebooks and websites) have been added.

Many anecdotes in the original *Towpath Guide* were culled from oral histories passed down through the decades—the "big fish" stories where facts often became exaggerated or lost completely. These stories balanced the technical details of the guidebook with color and mirth and added to its popularity. Most of these stories have been retained in this revised edition, but if primary or secondary sources were unable to validate the facts, they have been labeled as legend or lore.

Despite the hard work many people invested in verifying and updating the physical conditions of the towpath and the technical and historical information in this revised edition, the fact remains that the Potomac River and its surrounding floodplain are organic, ever-changing entities. Continued research into the canal's structures and history may also uncover new information or facts contradictory to those presented here. Therefore, minor inconsistencies between the material in these pages and realities in the field should be expected.

C&O Canal National Historical Park
General Information

Park 24-hour Emergency Number: 1-866-677-6677
For all life-threatening emergencies, dial 911

Flooding, downed trees, rock slides, or maintenance may cause closures along the towpath. For up-to-date closures or park alerts call 301-739-4200 or visit: www.nps.gov/choh/planyourvisit/closures.htm.

The Chesapeake and Ohio Canal National Historical Park is open during daylight hours year round. See below for visitor center information and approximate mileage location along the towpath. Note that not all visitor centers are directly on the towpath. (Operating days and hours and park fees are subject to change; verify prior to visiting the park.) **All facilities are closed Thanksgiving Day, Christmas Day, and New Year's Day.**

14.30	Great Falls	(Fee area. Canal boat rides seasonally) 11710 MacArthur Blvd., Potomac, MD 20854, 301-767-3714, www.nps.gov/choh/planyourvisit/greatfallstavernvisitorcenter.htm
55.00	Brunswick	40 West Potomac St., Brunswick, MD 21716, 301-834-7100, www.nps.gov/choh/planyourvisit/brunswickvisitorcenter.htm
72.80	Ferry Hill	(Open seasonally) 16500 Shepherdstown Pike (MD-34), Sharpsburg, MD 21782, 301-582-0813, www.nps.gov/choh/historyculture/ferryhillplantation.htm
99.80	Williamsport	(Canal boat rides seasonally) 205 W. Potomac St., Williamsport, MD 21795, 301-582-0813, www.nps.gov/choh/planyourvisit/williamsportvisitorcenter.htm
122.85	Hancock	(Open Seasonally) 439 E. Main St., Hancock, MD 21750, 301-582-0813, www.nps.gov/choh/planyourvisit/hancockvisitorcenter.htm
184.50	Cumberland	Western Maryland Railway Station, Room 100, 13 Canal St., Cumberland, MD 21052, 301-722-8226, www.nps.gov/choh/planyourvisit/cumberlandvisitorcenter.htm

The following National Park Service recreational information is provided to give visitors a safe and enjoyable experience on the C&O Canal. For a complete list of park rules and regulations visit www.nps.gov/choh.

Biking

Bicycle riding in the park is permitted only on the towpath, not on any side or off trail. The surface of the towpath is for the most part an even hard-packed dirt trail. Cyclists should be cautious of tree roots on the towpath. The towpath can be very muddy following heavy rain. Bicyclists should carry tools for repairs; thin road tires are not recommended.

- Ride single file.
- Stay to the right except when passing.
- Yield right of way to all pedestrians, horses, and mules.
- Walk bikes over aqueducts.
- Sound devices (bell, horn, etc.) are required and should be sounded within 100' of approaching others.
- Helmets are recommended (children under 16 are required to wear helmets).
- There is a biking speed limit of 15 mph on the towpath.

Boating/Canoeing/Kayaking

Non-motorized boats are allowed in several watered sections of the canal: Georgetown to Violettes Lock (mile 0 to 22), Williamsport to Lock 44 (mile 99.8 to 99.30), Big Pool (mile 112 to 113), Little Pool (mile 120 to 121), Hancock (mile 124.1 to 124.7), and Oldtown to Town Creek (mile 162 to 167). Please note that these sections are watered seasonally and dependent upon the river's level. Canoeing on the Potomac should be done under the direct supervision of an experienced adult canoeist. Boat launch ramps are available along the canal.

- Boats need to be carried around lift locks.
- Gasoline and propane motorized vessels are prohibited within the park.
- Personal floatation devices must be used as required by the state of Maryland.

WARNING! THE FOLLOWING AREAS OF THE POTOMAC RIVER ARE EXTREMELY DANGEROUS:

- The entire stretch between Great Falls (mile 14.3) and Chain Bridge (mile 4.17), an area where many have drowned.
- Dam 2 (mile 22.15) at Seneca (low dam).
- Dam 3 (mile 62.27) above Harpers Ferry (low dam). Canoeing is not recommended between Dam 3 and the US-340 bridge downstream of Sandy Hook.
- Dam 4 (mile 84.4) near Downsville (portage on Maryland side).
- Power company dam (mile 99.59) at Williamsport (portage on West Virginia side).
- Dam 5 (mile 106.8) above Williamsport (high dam, must portage on either side).
- Low-water dam at North Branch (mile 175.5). Canoeists should put in at Spring Gap (mile 173.3).

Camping

Along the 184.5 miles of the C&O Canal National Historical Park are 31 hiker–biker campsites, five drive-in campsites, and two group campsites. Marsden Tract is the only campsite that requires a reservation and is reserved for organized scout or civic groups only. A permit can be obtained by calling the Great Falls Fee Office at 301-767-3731. All other campsites are on a first-come, first-served basis and do not require reservations. See www.nps.gov/choh/planyourvisit/camping.htm for current camping regulations. See page 267 for a complete index of campsites.

- Camping is allowed only in designated sites.
- A maximum of two tents and eight people per site except for group campsites. Hiker-biker stay is limited to one night per site, per trip.
- Groups with more than eight people need to use the group campsites or register for more than one site in the campsite.
- Group campsites are $20 per site, per night, with a maximum of 35 people. Stay is limited to 14 days between May 1 and October 1. Stay is limited to a total of 30 days for the entire calendar year. Fees as of January 1, 2015, are subject to change.
- Drive-in campsites are $10 per site, per night. (Senior Pass holders are entitled to a 50% discount.) Fees as of January 1, 2015, are subject to change.
- Draining or dumping refuse or body wastes from trailers or other vehicles is prohibited.
- Trailer length may not exceed 20'; no RV hookups.
- Antietam Creek and Paw Paw have adjacent parking, but visitors cannot park at the actual campsite.
- Recreational vehicles are allowed only at McCoys Ferry, Fifteenmile Creek, and Spring Gap campsites.
- All sites have a chemical toilet, water pump, picnic table, and grill. Please note: the water is often not potable and should be treated with water purification tablets. For the protection of drinking water, campers may not wash dishes, bathe, or clean fish near wells. **Water is turned off from November 15 to April 15 each year.**
- Quiet hours are between 10 p.m. and 6 a.m.
- Pets must be on a leash no longer than 6' or under other physical control at all times.
- Fires are restricted to the grills and fire rings provided or to portable grills positioned off the ground. Coals must be extinguished and removed from the park.
- Firewood may be collected from dead material on the ground but for use in campsites only. Do not remove wood from the campsites.
- Firewood cannot be brought into the park.

Dog Walking
Pets must be on a leash no longer than 6' at all times. Loose or feral pets often disturb or kill wildlife or their newborns. Protective wildlife parents can be aggressive and could harm you or your pet.
- Keep wildlife and your pets safe by observing the leash law.
- Dogs found harassing wildlife will be detained and appropriate action taken.
- Dogs are not allowed on the Billy Goat Trail Section A or on the overlook trail to Great Falls.
- All dog waste must be picked up and disposed of outside the park.

Firearm Regulations
Federal law allows people who can legally possess firearms under applicable federal, state, and local laws to carry firearms in the park. Federal law prohibits firearms in certain facilities in the park. Those places are marked with signs at all public entrances and include visitor centers and lockhouses. The actual use of firearms, including hunting, is prohibited inside the park.

Fishing

Fishing falls under the regulations of the respective state where the canal and Potomac River are located. The District of Columbia requires a license for persons 16–65. In Maryland, a person 16 years of age or older must have a valid license to fish that state's non-tidal waters. Virginia requires a license for persons 16 and older. West Virginia requires a license for ages 15–65.

Hiking

In addition to the 184.5 miles of towpath, there are additional side trails requiring various skill levels connected to the park, including 14 miles of trails in the Great Falls area and a two-mile trail at the Paw Paw Tunnel. Trail maps are available at visitor centers.

- Bring water and food.
- Wear sturdy footwear.
- Be prepared for changing weather conditions.
- Know your location.
- Share the towpath with other users.

Horseback Riding

Groups must obtain approval in writing for all club rides and trips lasting more than one day. Write to the Park Superintendent, C&O Canal NHP, 1850 Dual Highway Suite 100, Hagerstown, MD 21740-6620. Include an itinerary with dates and locations.

- Horseback riding is not allowed between Georgetown (mile 0) and Swains Lock (mile 16.6) or from Offutt Street (mile 181.8) to the canal terminus (mile 184.5).
- Horses are not allowed in the Paw Paw Tunnel. Riders must take the Tunnel Hill Trail at mile 154.85 (downstream portal), or 155.78 (upstream portal).
- Riders may not exceed the speed of a slow trot.
- Riders must dismount and walk their horses across aqueducts.
- Horses may not cross wooden footbridges, which are not designed to carry their weight.
- Trail riders are responsible for hauling manure away.
- No grazing is permitted in the park. Bring in feed for horses.
- Do not water, clean, or tether horses near park wells.
- Access from private property is prohibited.
- Horses are not allowed in drive-in campsites, picnic areas, or adjacent parking lots.
- Riders may camp at hiker–biker campsites but must tether horses at least 50' from the area's boundaries for sanitary and safety reasons.
- Owners must prevent horses from damaging trees or undergrowth.

Leave No Trace

The C&O Canal is a trash-free park, and trashcans are not provided. Trash must be picked up and the area left in a clean condition before departure. Trash bags are available at dispensers throughout the park.

Picnicking

Picnic tables are located at many of the visitor centers, campsites, and boat launch areas throughout the park. Fires may be built in established or portable grills only. ALL fires must be extinguished before leaving the park. Due to the emerald ash borer beetle infestation, firewood can NOT be brought into the park. Visitors may collect down and dead wood in the park.

Swimming

Swimming is not permitted in the canal or in the Potomac River bordering the District of Columbia and Montgomery County, Maryland. Swimming is not recommended in other areas of the river.

White Nose Syndrome

White Nose Syndrome (WNS), a disease responsible for the deaths of millions of bats in the eastern North America, has been observed in bat hibernaculum along the C&O Canal. The NPS continues to monitor these sites and may at times close to the public entrances to caves, tunnels, or mines. While humans are not at risk of contracting WNS, bats are known to carry other diseases such as rabies. If you see a dead, sick, or injured bat within the park, please notify the park at 301-714-2225.

Wildlife

Rabid animals are known to be found within park boundaries. All visitors are cautioned to avoid any contact with wild animals and to report any unusual behavior to park personnel. All wildlife, including animals, plants, and other organisms found within NPS boundaries, is protected by federal law. **It is illegal to pick, dig, or remove plants or other objects from a national park.**

Swimmers contemplating a dip at Lock 26 (Woods Lock), ca. 1900.
Swimming is no longer permitted in the canal.

Mile by Mile Guide

Georgetown
to
Cumberland

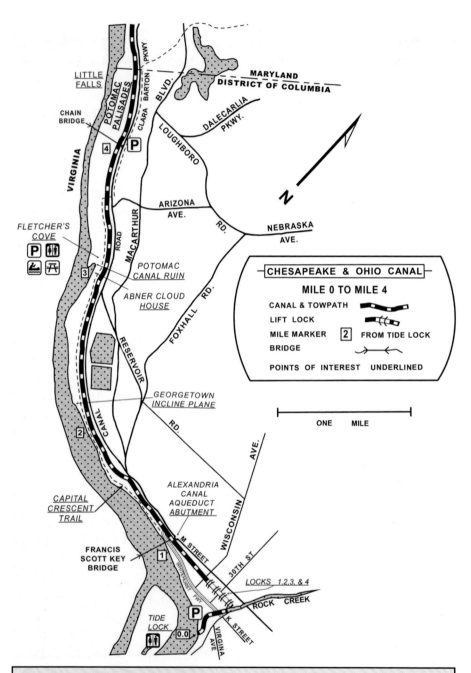

LITTLE FALLS

CHAIN BRIDGE

VIRGINIA

POTOMAC PALISADES

CLARA BARTON PKWY.

BLVD.

LOUGHBORO

DALECARLIA PKWY.

MARYLAND
DISTRICT OF COLUMBIA

4 P

ARIZONA AVE.

MACARTHUR ROAD

RD.

NEBRASKA AVE.

FLETCHER'S COVE

P

3

POTOMAC CANAL RUIN

ABNER CLOUD HOUSE

FOXHALL RD.

RESERVOIR

CANAL

GEORGETOWN INCLINE PLANE

RD.

2

AVE.

CAPITAL CRESCENT TRAIL

ALEXANDRIA CANAL AQUEDUCT ABUTMENT

WISCONSIN

FRANCIS SCOTT KEY BRIDGE

M STREET

1

WHITEHURST FWY.

30TH ST.

LOCKS 1,2,3, & 4

ROCK CREEK

TIDE LOCK

P

0.0

K STREET

VIRGINIA AVE.

CHESAPEAKE & OHIO CANAL

MILE 0 TO MILE 4

CANAL & TOWPATH

LIFT LOCK

MILE MARKER 2 FROM TIDE LOCK

BRIDGE

POINTS OF INTEREST   UNDERLINED

ONE   MILE

If you encounter a life-threatening emergency while visiting the park, please **call 911** or contact the Chesapeake and Ohio Canal National Historical Park's **Emergency Hotline 866-677-6677**.

GEORGETOWN TIDE LOCK

0.00 (38.901107, -77.057467) Access: The zero milestone terminus is one of two spots on the canal easily accessible from the Washington Metro subway. The Foggy Bottom/George Washington University station, 23rd and I Streets NW, is a half mile away: walk west on I St., turn left on New Hampshire Ave., turn right at Virginia Ave., and continue to the Thompson Boat Center. (The other Metro-accessible spot is at the Key Bridge. See mile 0.99 below.) The nearest food is at Washington Harbor, just over the footbridge upstream from the Thompson Boat Center.

The Thompson Boat Center parking lot is at the end of Virginia Avenue, on the west side of the Rock Creek and Potomac Parkway. Pay very close attention to the meters in the parking lot—most recently the meters had to be fed 5 a.m. to midnight, seven days a week. To reach the zero milestone from the parking lot, take the service road over the bridge and walk in front of the boat center to the tide lock on its downstream side. Thompson Boat Center offers canoe, kayak, rowing shell, and bike rentals. Thompson Boat Center, 2900 Virginia Ave. NW, Washington, DC 20007, 202-333-9543, www.thompsonboatcenter.com.

Tide lock (also known as an outlet lock) is the communication between the Rock Creek Basin and Potomac River. The silted-in lock has been damaged by floods. Lock walls have been partially restored. The lock has a lift of about 4', the difference between the normal level of the Rock Creek Basin and the mean level

Georgetown Tide Lock, "Mile Zero" of the C&O Canal ca. 1900. Note the dam across Rock Creek.

Washington Branch of the C&O Canal

The Washington Branch of the C&O Canal was a 1.2 mile tidal canal from Rock Creek Basin along the line of the Potomac River, to Tiber Creek at 17th Street and Constitution Avenue, NW, connecting with the Washington City Canal in 1833. Its purpose was "to facilitate a conveyance most advantageous to trading interests." It never lived up to its promise and by 1862 was described in a report to Congress as "nothing more nor less than a public nuisance." The filling in of the canal began in the 1870s. The small stone building at the southwest corner of 17th and Constitution, NW, was constructed as a lockhouse for the lock connecting the Washington City Canal with a branch of the C&O Canal from its Rock Creek terminus.

Hostelling International Washington, D.C. is located about a mile away from the canal at 1009 11th St. NW, Washington, D.C. 20001. 202-737-2333, http://hiwashingtondc.org.

Lockhouse B on the Washington Branch of the C&O Canal, ca. 1860. *(Library of Congress, Prints and Photographs Division, HABS, Reproduction Number HABS DC, WASH, 12--6)*

of the Potomac River at that location. The lock measures 91'4.5" between gate pockets. Some time after the canal closed in 1924, 12"-square creosoted timbers were installed vertically against the lock walls to stabilize them. The tide lock here may have been referred to as Tide Lock A to differentiate it from Tide Lock B at 17th Street and Constitution Avenue. Indications are that the towpath followed the west shore of Rock Creek from the tide lock to the point where the canal flowed into Rock Creek. Then the towpath was on the river side of the canal until Green Street (now 29th Street), where it crossed to the land side of the canal.

Tide lock is the "zero milestone" from which measurements on the canal are calculated. Those used in this guide were made by Orville Crowder, who pushed a measuring wheel 184.5 miles to Cumberland! The name, Chesapeake and Ohio Canal (rejected names were Potomac Canal & Union Canal), was chosen to represent the intended connection between the Ohio River and the Chesapeake Bay.

The tide lock represents the spot from which the canal departed from tidewater and headed upstream into a 100-year struggle with topography and the flooding river, with the frailties of man and the complexities of finance, never to reach the prize of Ohio River navigation. Its towpath passes through a mighty river valley, past rock cliffs and bottom land woods, through wild gorges and peaceful valleys, through virtual wilderness and the mountains, and beside, over, or through some of the nation's boldest engineering efforts of the nineteenth

Washington City Canal

Though quite a bit has been written about this canal, most accounts conflict or are vague in detail. A complete, clear picture does not exist today. A city canal was included in architect Pierre L'Enfant's plans for Washington, running from Tiber Creek to two branches south of the Capitol, one entering the Anacostia River near the Navy Yard, the other going southwest to James Creek. Though proposals for cutting a canal were received as early as September 1, 1791, the first sod of the Washington City Canal (Washington Canal/Municipal Canal) was turned by President James Madison on May 2, 1810. Engineer Benjamin Henry Latrobe and the canal company president, Elias B. Caldwell, were in attendance. The canal began at 17th and Constitution Avenue, NW, where there was a basin providing access to the river and a lock to the Washington Branch of the C&O Canal. From there it went to the vicinity of the Capitol, where it then turned south toward the Anacostia River near the old Navy Yard. Principal products carried were coal, flour, firewood, and building material. The canal fell into disuse after the Civil War. Possible remains of the C&O branch of the canal were exposed near the mouth of Rock Creek after Tropical Storm Agnes in 1972.

Tide Lock with the Watergate and the Kennedy Center in the background, 2012. *(Image courtesy Rod Mackler)*

century in the course of its 184.5 miles to Cumberland. Today it connects to the Great Allegheny Passage trail to Pittsburgh.

During the Civil War the tide lock was utilized by the Union army to lock canal boats into the river (where steam tugboats provided motive power) for a number of purposes, most prominently to deliver coal to the Washington Navy Yard, located on the Anacostia River (then known as the Eastern Branch of the Potomac). Today the tide lock is within sight of the Watergate complex and the Kennedy Center. Across the river is the wooded Theodore Roosevelt Island (managed by the National Park Service) and the high-rises of the Rosslyn section of Arlington.

ROCK CREEK BASIN

0.01 The terminus of the C&O Canal was the tide lock at the river end of the Rock Creek Basin, where Rock Creek flows into the Potomac River. The basin was formed by building the mole—a peninsula of land that extended Rock Creek from its original mouth in the K Street area to the present mouth of Rock Creek, where a dam was built beside the tide lock across the new mouth of Rock Creek. The dam impounded water 3' above the mean high tide. The mole formed an extensive wharf (or quay) for transshipment between the Rock Creek Basin and the

Potomac River. The length of the mole on the Potomac face was 840'. The 200' tumbling dam sent the surplus water of the creek into the Potomac River. The mole width varied from 160' at the Washington City end to 80' at the tide lock.

Originally, space in the center of the wharf was set aside for warehouses and stores as well as streets and landing places. Here goods were taken from canal boats and stored or transferred to coastal ships. A bridge above the tumbling dam connected the wharves on the Georgetown side with those on the Washington side. Georgetown wharves occupied the space where the Thompson Boat Center now sits. The Rock Creek face was protected by a well-laid dry wall that extended along both sides of the creek for a half mile.

The original dam seems to have been repaired and rebuilt on several occasions, altering both appearance and location. Only a few timbers and pieces of iron remain of the dam, across the current mouth of Rock Creek, just downstream from the tide lock.

There is no longer a towpath to follow from the tide lock to the first lift lock (Lock 1) in Georgetown 0.3 mile upstream. To reach Lock 1 take the sidewalk along the Rock Creek and Potomac Parkway.

Though most think the Watergate Complex across the parkway takes its name from the gates of the dam across Rock Creek or the tide lock, the complex likely was named for the floating concert stage (the Watergate Concert Barge) moored on the Potomac at the base of the steps behind the Lincoln Memorial for concerts that were played from 1935 to 1965. The dredging of the Potomac and building of Hains Point and the Tidal Basin in the early 1900s included watergates that regulated the movement of water to and from the basin as levels fluctuated in the river.

Across from the Watergate on Virginia Avenue sits a George Washington University dormitory. In 1972 this was the Howard Johnson Hotel, from which a White House Special Investigations Unit (nicknamed the "plumbers") monitored wiretaps they had placed in the Watergate office of the Democratic National Committee. This illegal activity ultimately led to the resignation of President Richard Nixon.

0.31 Godey Lime Kilns ruins. In the nineteenth century, lime manufacturing was an important local industry in Washington. The stone structures across the parkway are remains of lime kilns operated by the Godey family from 1864 to 1897, and by others until 1908. Limestone for the kiln came down the canal from quarries, including Knotts Quarry near Shepherdstown, West Virginia.

0.35 The canal enters Rock Creek Basin. Before the canal was built, navigation extended a half mile up Rock Creek to the P Street Bridge. Cross the footbridge and turn left to follow the asphalt towpath, next to which is a plaque erected in 1942 by the National Park Service and the Daughters of the American Revolution. It reads:

One of the best preserved and least altered of old American Canals, the Chesapeake and Ohio grew with Washington's vision of linking the valleys of the early west with the east by ties of communication. The Potomac Company fostered by Washington to improve navigation of the Potomac, transferred its rights in 1828 to the Chesapeake and Ohio Canal Company organized to connect the Ohio at Pittsburgh with Georgetown by a continuous canal. Today it is a memorial to national progress and the canal era.

LOCK 1, GEORGETOWN

0.38 (38.904167, -77.060133) Access: At 29th Street, one block south of M Street. Bus service along M Street and Pennsylvania Avenue connects Georgetown to 23rd Street one block above the Foggy Bottom Metro Station. There are parking garages in the area, for instance, on Thomas Jefferson Street, near K Street.

Lock 1 is the first of a picturesque series of four closely-spaced (less than a quarter mile) Georgetown locks separated by boat basins. The Georgetown locks rest on wooden piles and were built of freestone from Aquia Creek (a Potomac River tributary in Northern Virginia), with a granite rubble backing of the walls. Much of the lock walls have been rebuilt with granite, limestone, concrete, and brick. These locks had an 8' lift.

A turning basin adjoins the upper end of the lock on one end, and the canal empties into Rock Creek on the other. A modern cut-stone wall on the south of the lock hides any trace of the original towpath that was on the west side of Rock Creek from tide lock to Lock 1. Apparently tow animals (sometimes horses but usually mules) were unhitched from the towline and taken up to the Green Street Bridge, where they crossed the canal to the north bank and were taken down to the foot of the turning basin to be re-hitched to the towline. A mule rise of about 8' (like a gradual ramp) goes from just above the Rock Creek bridge to the lock. The towpath was on the north (land) side of canal from Lock 1 to Frederick Street (now 34th St.) until 1856. After that, the towpath stayed on the north (land) side from Lock 1 to a point above the Alexandria Aqueduct (above Key Bridge), where a mule crossover bridge was built to carry animals and the towpath back to the river side of the canal. Except for two stretches of slackwater operation in the river behind Dams 4 and 5, the towpath stays on the river side of the canal to Cumberland.

Note graffiti on the lock coping stones. Only the north lock wall coping stones show evidence of grooves called "rope burns" that have been worn by years of towropes catching and rubbing on the same place. The lock measures

Georgetown Locks 1 and 2 in the twenty-first century. *(Image courtesy Rod Mackler, 2012)*

90'3" between gate pockets. Above the lock is the boat basin (called a "pool" historically), 100' x 46', and evidence of former shallow side ponds.

Though there is no present evidence of lockhouses in Georgetown, records and the historical numbering system suggest there were two, perhaps acquired or leased, as records do not show money expended for construction of lockhouses here.

The 29th Street (formerly Green Street) Bridge, originally a low-arched stone bridge built 1830–31, was razed and replaced with an iron span in 1867. The present bridge is a concrete span with steel handrails. The federal government's West Heating Plant is on the river side of the canal. It provided heating to a number of government buildings in the northwest quadrant of the District of Columbia. In 2013 the government sold the plant to developers for $19.5 million.

LOCK 2, GEORGETOWN

0.42 Access: From 29th or 30th Streets. Bike rentals and bike repairs are available at Big Wheel Bikes at 1034 33rd Street NW, 202-337-0254, www.bigwheelbikes.com; Revolution Cycles, 3411 M Street NW, 202-965-3601, revolutioncycles.com; or Bicycle Pro Shop, 3403 M Street NW, 202-337-0311, bicycleproshop.com. All three bike shops are near the Georgetown end of the Key Bridge.

Lock 2 is the second of the four closely-spaced Georgetown locks. Basins between the locks in Georgetown were 46' wide, allowing a 15.5' clearance on each side, plus the 15' lock width in the middle. The boats could tie up on each side and have sufficient space for other boats to pass through, although the towpath side was probably kept clear for traffic and the river side of the canal was used for mooring and wharves. This basin is 120' long. Bridges were placed below downstream gates where it was possible to take advantage of the additional 8' clearance.

LOCK 3, GEORGETOWN

0.49 Access: At 30th Street or Thomas Jefferson Street, one street south of M Street.

A plaque in the open area notes the 1967 designation of the Georgetown Historic District as a National Historic Landmark. This is a favorite spot in Georgetown, with someone sunning, reading, or eating lunch on clear days in all seasons. The building on the south side of the lock was the Duvall Foundry, ca.1856. It provided veterinary services at a later date. Georgetown Inland Steel carefully preserved the exterior of this building during their construction here 1973–74.

The lower extension walls of Lock 3 underneath the 30th Street Bridge were part of the original stone bridge abutments. Culvert outflows are still open. Original transverse foundation timbers of the lock flooring (which appear to be hewn) and scraps of sheet pine planking can be seen mid-lock when the canal is drained. The original timber floor of the upper gate pocket has been replaced with concrete. All gate (or gooseneck) straps (curved metal bars anchored to stones—part of the mechanism which holds the lock gate in place) are slotted loops and appear old, though refitted with late period nuts and bolts.

Duvall Foundry (a veterinary hospital at the time of the photo) and Lock 3, Georgetown, ca. 1914.

How Does a C&O Canal Lock Work?

To overcome the increase in elevation between Georgetown and Cumberland, 74 lift locks were built along the C&O Canal with lifts of between 6' and 10' (8' on average) for a total lift of 609.693'. Twenty of these locks are found in the first 14.3 miles of the canal due to the Fall Line and rise from the Tidewater to the Piedmont.

The water channel of the canal is called a prism, as it is wider at the top than the bottom. The prism is 50'–60' wide and 6' deep. Locks are typically 90' to 100' long (between the miter sill of the upper gate and the miter sill of the lower gate), 15' wide, and average 16' deep.

Lift locks operate as follows: From approximately a quarter to a half mile from the lock, the boatman sounds a horn to alert the locktender of his approach. At the lock a crew member jumps ashore and wraps a heavy rope around a snubbing post to brake the boat. Boats moving downstream enter a fully-watered lock, the upper wooden lock gates are closed, and the locktender uses a large, wrench-like lock key to open small wicket (or paddle) gates located near the bottom of the lower lock gates. Once open, these gates allow water to be released from the lock. When the water level in the lock reaches that of the canal at the lower end, the lower lock gates are opened and the boat passes out.

The process is reversed for boats moving upstream, with the water level low when the boat enters, the lower gates closed, and water admitted to the lock from the small wicket gates in the bottom of the upper lock gates.

Locktenders normally opened the gates on the berm side (the side opposite the towpath), and the mule driver opened the gates on the towpath side. To balance the weight of the gates in the historic operating period, a rock-filled box was sometimes fastened on the free end of the balance beam (the large timber on top of and protruding from the lock gate). Lock gates on the locks between Georgetown and Violettes Lock (Lock 23) are modern replacements that generally replicate historic ones. Locks 1 through 25 were built originally with the upper gate on the breast wall, instead of full gates in front of the breast wall.

Each lock has a "mule rise" at the lower end of the lock, where the towpath gradually rises to meet the height of the lock's lift. This is the only place where the towpath is not level.

Most locks have bypass flumes (a type of channel) on the berm side of the lock to provide for a steady supply of water below the lock when it was in use, and to get rid of excess water. However, all but one of the locks through Lock 27 were originally built with masonry sidewall culverts that carried water from openings in the upper gate pockets to openings in the lock below the upper gates. The three outflows (openings) of the culverts are in the lower courses (rows of stones) of the lock walls, almost 9', 25', and 49' below the upper lock pockets on the berm side, and 13', 21', and 45.5' below on the towpath side. Later, bypass flumes were added to those locks for which there was room.

See the Glossary beginning on page 269 for more definitions and descriptions of lock components. Another source for reading about the engineering of the locks is *The Geology and Engineering Structures of the Chesapeake & Ohio Canal*, by William E. Davies (C&O Canal Association, 1999), available at www.candocanal.org/histdocs/Davies-book.pdf.

The Chesapeake and Ohio Canal NHP YouTube channel has a two-minute "Locking Through" video also worth viewing.

"Locking Through"

A locktender turns the lock keys to open wicket gates on the lower portion of the upper lock gates to release water and fill the lock.

A boat heading downstream enters a fully-watered lock. Ropes are secured to snubbing posts (left) to brake the boat and keep it in place. The upper lock gates are closed and the water is then drained through wicket gates on the lower lock gates.

Once the water level in the lock reaches that of the downstream portion of the canal, the lower lock gates are opened and the boat passes through. The process takes approximately 10 to 15 minutes.

11

0.53 The Old Masonic Lodge on the northwest corner of the Thomas Jefferson Street Bridge was used by the Potomac Lodge beginning ca. 1810. When Jefferson first arrived in the capital to be Secretary of State, he lived at 1047, south of the canal, in a block since razed of houses.

The National Park Service Georgetown Visitor Center was once located in the house at 1057 Thomas Jefferson Street. The canal boat *Georgetown* once offered rides but has now been retired.

> For towpath conditions on the C&O Canal, call Park Headquarters at 301-739-4200, Monday through Friday 8 a.m.–4:30 p.m. or visit www.nps.gov/choh/planyourvisit/closures.htm.

LOCK 4, GEORGETOWN

0.54 Access: Thomas Jefferson Street.

Uppermost of the four Georgetown locks. The Jefferson Street Bridge crosses over the lock extension walls. The original stone arch of the bridge did not have sufficient height to allow the towpath to pass under it. The tow rope was unhitched from the animals and passed under the bridge, while the animals followed the towpath over the north bridge approaches to be re-hitched on the other side. The lock is 89'10" between gate pockets. Lock walls are in relatively good alignment, and there are fewer stone substitutions than in Lock 3. A low dam of rubble stone (a unique feature) was laid just below the miter sill (timbers upon which the lock gate rests when closed). The towpath has rounded cobblestones to 31st Street, tying nearby houses and the old lock into a composition that has made this spot one of most photographed, sketched, and painted on the canal.

The Old Stone House, located at 3051 M Street, was built in 1765, making it the oldest standing building in Washington; it is operated by the NPS, and admission is free. See www.nps.gov/nr/travel/wash/dc17.htm. There are a number of small cafes and restaurants on the canal and within a block on the side streets of Georgetown.

0.59 31st Street (formerly Congress Street and Fishing Lane) Bridge. The original 1830 bridge was low arch stone with a 40' span, the first of four stone bridges to span the canal in Georgetown. The towpath probably went under the bridge. In an 1831 report by the U.S. Topographical Engineers, the original stone bridges were described as "very neat and substantial structures, faced with Aquia Creek freestone, well laid with hammered faces." Iron spans replaced the stone bridges in 1867 except for the Wisconsin Avenue Bridge. The present bridge was built in 1924. The next towpath access is at 34th Street.

Suter's Tavern (officially The Fountain Inn), built in the late 18th century, was located in the vicinity of 31st and K Streets and was operated by John Suter and his wife until 1896. George Washington met neighboring landowners there to negotiate the purchase of land for the "Federal City." At the end of a row of towpath residences at 31st Street were "Tow Path Apartments," built by the canal company in 1830 and used until the demise of the canal in 1924. The Canal Square building on the northwest corner is an interesting utilization of an old canal-side warehouse. Walk up M Street to take a hike around the historic sites in Georgetown.

0.61 One of many water intakes on the way to Key Bridge. The canal company sold water to various industries in Georgetown, and even after the canal closed to navigation in 1924, the section from Dam 1 was maintained to continue this revenue-producing activity.

0.68 Wisconsin Avenue (formerly High Street) Bridge. This bridge was originally built of Aquia freestone, 54' span, 11' rise. All of the other street bridges in Georgetown (29th, 30th, Thomas Jefferson, and 31st) have been rebuilt in recent years. The stone arch bridge carrying Wisconsin Avenue was rehabilitated with steel anchors. About 100' beyond the bridge, steps provide access to Wisconsin Avenue from the towpath.

Note the two stone plaques on the east spandrels of the bridge. Some of the legible names on the plaque on the south are: Thomas F. Purcell, Superintending Engineer; F. O. Williams, Assistant Engineer; Filbert Rodier, Assistant Engineer; Michael Corcoran; and Clement Smith, Treasurer Ches. & Ohio C. Co. The opposite plaque is dedicated to Andrew Jackson, President of the United States, and Charles F. Mercer, President of the Chesapeake and Ohio Canal Company. A rectangular stone on the west parapet between the keystone and the coping is inscribed to John Cox Mayor and James Dunlop Recorder. The keystone on the east side is inscribed "C. H. Dibble, Builder, 1831." The keystone on the west repeats the 1831 date.

Grace Episcopal Church, begun as a mission for canal boatmen and workers in the mid-1800s, stands on a hill on the river side of the canal. At the northwest corner of the bridge is an obelisk commemorating the beginning of work on the canal in 1828 and its completion to Cumberland in 1850.

0.79 Bridges passing overhead connected buildings of the Capital Traction Company, a streetcar company that had an imposing powerhouse on the waterfront in Georgetown. An attractive high stone wall limiting the width of the towpath was described in the 1831 report as a "specimen of good work."

0.80 Potomac Street Bridge. This bridge does not provide access to the towpath. The current Market House was built in 1865. When the canal was built, it went right under an earlier Market House begun in 1795.

0.81 A concrete intake on the river side of the canal admitted water to the Wilkins Rogers Mill company, which was established in 1913 when Howard Wilkins and Samuel Rogers purchased a flour mill from G. W. Cissell. It expanded to incorporate the milling of corn and operated until 1974, when the company relocated to Ellicott City, Maryland.

From the earliest days one of the unfailing sources of income to the canal company was water supplied to millers, founders, and textile manufacturers on the Georgetown Level. The mill buildings have been converted to condominiums and offices.

Another intake 40' to the west fed water to a flour mill built ca. 1831 by Col. George Bromford. It was destroyed by fire in 1844; a cotton mill was erected on the site ca. 1845. This mill was converted back to a flour mill in 1866, rebuilt in 1883, and in 1922 used for offices by Wilkins Rogers.

0.84 Steel footbridge. This bridge crosses the canal at 33rd (formerly Market) Street and provides no access to the towpath. A wooden bridge was built here in 1831 when the street was known as "Duck Lane" and the bridge as "Duck Lane Bridge." A concrete and brick water intake was on the berm at the PEPCO substation, 100' west of the bridge. Today the substation has one of the largest green roofs in the Washington area.

0.93 Crossover bridge at 34th (formerly Frederick) Street. This bridge carries the towpath from the berm to its usual location on the river side of the canal. While the mules walked up the ramp, across the bridge, and down the ramp on the other side, a crew member on the boat passing under the bridge would remove the tow rope from the cleat to which it had been fastened on the towpath side, and walk it around the bow, to be attached to the matching cleat on the new towpath side. The path directly ahead leads to M Street/Canal Road. This bridge is the site of the first wooden towpath crossover bridge built by the canal company in 1831 and used until 1856. Between 1857 and 1887, the towpath continued on the land side beyond the Alexandria Aqueduct, where another bridge carried the towpath to the river side beyond the aqueduct. The present bridge was built in 1954.

0.98 The frame building beside the towpath immediately below Key Bridge houses gate machinery for dual water intakes once used by Wilkins Rogers Mill.

0.99 Francis Scott Key Bridge. Access: Crossover bridge at 34th Street (mile 0.93).

The towpath passes under the concrete ramps of the Key Bridge, which replaced the Aqueduct Bridge and opened to the public on January 17, 1924. It is a concrete structure, 1,790'6" long, from the northern edge of the Georgetown approach to the southern edge of the Rosslyn approach. The bridge was built on bedrock 23'–25' below the mean level of the river. Upstream from the bridge is the Potomac Boat Club. The canal here is accessible from the Rosslyn Metro station, 0.7 mile across the Key Bridge.

Canal walls were extensively repaired in Georgetown between 1982 and 1983.

In 1805, Francis Scott Key moved to a house at the east end of the bridge at 3516 M Street. The house was razed in 1949 to make room for the Whitehurst Freeway. In that house Key is said to have first read "The Star Spangled Banner" before a meeting of his glee club. The Key family left the house in the late 1830s because the canal had come through the property, destroying gardens and fruit trees on terraces leading to the river. Key, an attorney, was active in social causes and civic affairs and was an early canal supporter until he learned it would pass through his Georgetown property. He also led a case to bring an injunction against the Alexandria Canal Company when clay and gravel were spilled outside cofferdams during the aqueduct construction, impeding navigation. (He lost his case.) A flag with 15 stars and 15 stripes flies over the small park now on the site.

1.0x Pass under the Whitehurst Freeway ramp. Steps lead up to Canal Road and down to Water (extension of K) Street giving access to the site of the former Alexandria Aqueduct.

POTOMAC AQUEDUCT (Alexandria Canal Aqueduct)

1.07 Access: From 34th Street, 0.14 mile below, or from stairway down from Whitehurst Freeway.

There are remains of the north abutment of the aqueduct above the Key Bridge, and the top of the south pier (one of eight) near the Virginia shore at Rosslyn is visible when the river is low.

Adjacent to the north aqueduct abutment is the boathouse of the Potomac Boat Club. Founded in 1869, it is the oldest surviving boat club along the Potomac River.

1.10 At this point, the character of the canal changes from town to country, in spite of the rush of traffic on Canal Road. There are fine views of the Potomac River, the towpath is pleasant, and an entirely different mood takes over. Traveling to the Potomac Valley from the Washington D.C. area today, one passes through five of the six great topographical sections of the eastern seaboard. From Tidewater in the District of Columbia through the Piedmont, the Blue Ridge, and the Great Valley, to the major Appalachian ridges, one may see every characteristic of the region and many native species of flora and fauna that are still extant.

Along this part of the canal boats stopped and waited for directions as to when and where they were to unload.

The former B&O Railroad right-of-way spur built in 1910 has been converted into a paved bicycle path, the Capital Crescent Trail (www.cctrail.org). The trail runs parallel to the towpath until the foot of Arizona Avenue, where it crosses the canal and Canal Road on a railroad trestle and continues to Bethesda, Maryland.

The Alexandria Canal And Potomac Aqueduct

The Alexandria Canal Company was chartered by Congress May 26, 1830, to construct an aqueduct across the Potomac River and to build a canal from the C&O Canal in Georgetown to the Alexandria, Virginia, waterfront. Construction began in 1833, and the canal cost $500,000 to build. The 7.24-mile canal formally opened to traffic on December 2, 1843. This canal operated 1843–86, bringing coal via the C&O

The Alexandria Canal's Potomac Aqueduct, ca. 1940. All piers but the one next to the Virginia shore were removed in 1962.

Canal to ships at the Alexandria wharves. The canal prism was 40' wide at the water surface and 28' at the bottom, with a towpath "of sufficient breadth to apply the power of horses to the navigation thereof." Excess or "waste water" was rented to various mills and plants along the line. The route of the canal is impossible to trace today. There were four lift locks at the Alexandria end of the canal that dropped it down to the river level. The outlet lock was excavated under the supervision of industrial archaeologist (and this guidebook's author) Thomas Hahn in 1982 and 1985, and it serves as the centerpiece of a reconstructed tide lock and basin at the northern end of Old Town Alexandria (66 Canal Center Plaza).

The outlet lock and part of the canal basin above were reconstructed between 1985 and 1987 as part of the Trans-Potomac Canal Center. See *The Alexandria Canal: Its History and Preservation* (West Virginia University Press, 1992) by Thomas Hahn and Emory Kemp.

The correct name for the aqueduct is the Potomac Aqueduct, but because it served the Alexandria Canal, it has come to be known as the Alexandria Aqueduct. The aqueduct was the chief feature of the Alexandria Canal and operated continuously until May 23, 1861. The north abutment remains, although one of two arches under it was enlarged to allow for the passage of trains on the Georgetown Branch of the B&O Railroad, which opened in 1910. The aqueduct, with eight piers and two abutments, was a wooden superstructure that carried a 1,100' wooden trunk 17' wide and 7' deep (heavily insured against fire), 29' above tidewater. The aqueduct itself was 28' wide, timber to timber. The width of its towpath was 5'. Stone for the aqueduct came from "a Quarry near Mason's Foundry, 1/2 m. west."

The aqueduct was originally planned to have 12 stone arches supported by 11 piers and two abutments, but because of a lack of funds, a 350' causeway was substituted for three arches at the south extremity. The remaining eight piers were 105' apart at high-water mark; two of them were abutment piers, each 21' thick, and six of them were support piers 12' thick at high-water mark, with circular wing walls of 13' average thickness at their base and 66' in length. The north abutment was built by the C&O Canal Company. Each of the support piers had icebreakers on the upstream end in the form of granite oblique cones sloping 45°, extending 5' below and 10' above the high-water mark. The downstream end of each pier was circular and had a slope, 1" to 1'. It cost $600,000. There was a towpath bridge across the

Potomac (Alexandria) Aqueduct, Georgetown, in the 1800s. Note the mule-crossover bridge in the foreground. The towpath remained on the berm side of the canal to Lock 1.

flume of the aqueduct until 1856 when the C&O towpath was moved to the north side of the canal. Slightly farther upstream the towpath was transferred back to the river side on a new crossover bridge.

During the Civil War the Union army considered the Potomac Aqueduct as a potential route by which Washington could be attacked and invaded by the Confederates. Accordingly, the army seized possession of it in late 1861–62, drained it, and converted it into a double-track wagon road, which denied the boatmen access to better port facilities at Alexandria, Virginia. Three forts were built to defend the southern approach to the aqueduct, which during the war was referred to as the "aqueduct bridge."

After July 27, 1868, a new aqueduct trunk was built out of North Carolina timber, and a toll-road bridge was built over the water-filled trough. For many years the structure served both vehicular and canal traffic. But usage of the Alexandria Canal diminished when the Georgetown bridges were raised, the Rock Creek Basin was improved, and tugboats were available to take canal boats exiting through the tide lock at the mouth of Rock Creek to wharves up and down the river. The Alexandria Canal was closed, and the aqueduct was purchased by the federal government in 1886, at which time the wooden structures were removed and an iron truss bridge 24' wide with 3' sidewalks was built on the old stone piers. In 1894, it was known as the "Free Bridge." In 1906 the Great Falls and Old Dominion Railroad built a track across the bridge from Rosslyn to a terminal adjacent to the still-standing Georgetown Car Barn. Rail service across the bridge continued until 1923. The original Aqueduct Bridge was replaced by the Key Bridge in 1924, but it was not torn down until 1934. In August 1962 all piers but one next to the Virginia shore were removed.

Capital Crescent Trail

The Capital Crescent Trail is a 10-mile-long link that connects Georgetown and Silver Spring, Maryland, using the former right-of-way of the Baltimore & Ohio Railroad's Georgetown Branch. The trail begins at the end of Water Street, the western extension of K Street, in Georgetown. For 2.6 miles, the paved path runs parallel to the C&O Canal, between the towpath and the Potomac River. At Arizona Avenue, the CCT uses a former railroad bridge to cross over the canal and Canal Road. The paved path continues another 4.6 miles to Wisconsin Avenue, three blocks south of the Bethesda Metro station. The trail surface changes to crushed stone for the final 2.9 miles of the CCT between Bethesda and Stewart Avenue in Silver Spring. This section is also known as the Georgetown Branch Trail. A 1.6-mile, on-street bike route guides riders from Stewart Avenue to downtown Silver Spring and its Metro station.

The Capital Crescent Trail features some interesting engineering works. The 321'-long Arizona Avenue bridge consists of two steel truss spans. The 341'-long, brick-lined Dalecarlia Tunnel takes the trail underneath MacArthur Boulevard. A 241'-long trestle towers 67' above Rock Creek with an observation platform in the middle. Here the CCT connects with Rock Creek Trail, which leads back to Georgetown, allowing a 22-mile circular trip.

The B&O began construction of the Georgetown Branch in 1909 and started operations in 1910. Freight trains brought coal and construction materials to customers along the route. There was never any passenger service. The last train ran in 1985. The last customer was the General Services Administration heating plant in Georgetown. In 1988 Montgomery County acquired the right-of-way from the Maryland–District line to Silver Spring. In 1990 the NPS purchased the right-of-way between Georgetown and the Maryland–District line. The CCT opened in sections between 1991 and 2003, with the rehabilitation of the Rock Creek trestle completing the route.

Trains could return to the CCT in the future. The CCT section between Bethesda and Silver Spring is part of the proposed alignment for the Washington Metro's Purple Line light rail route. Proposals would rebuild the trail adjacent to the new light rail tracks.

1.30 Streetcar trestle ruins, which served the Washington and Great Falls Electric Railway trolley line to Glen Echo and Cabin John, are visible in the cleft in the hillside above Canal Road. This was surely one of the most scenic rides ever to be taken, paralleling the canal and river for much of its distance. In the winter, the views were incomparable. The last trolley ran in January 1960.

1.35 A mission on the towpath was established in 1894 by Mrs. S. E. Safford, who lived across the road from the canal, an area since cleared of buildings. A 1905 news story described the mission as a small brick house where children were taught to read and write, and adults were instructed in industrial arts and assisted in finding housing in the winter, when very few lived in canal boats. The mission reportedly closed in December 1913 and moved to a building on the site of the former Foxhall Foundry (see mile 1.48).

On the Georgetown waterfront were four ice companies: Barker Brothers, Great Falls, Kennebec, and Knickerbocker. They shipped ice from Maine and carried coal north on the return trip, in what was known as the coal–ice trade. Between 1880 and 1900, seven percent of Maine's ice came to Washington, D.C.

1.48 The Foundry Branch takes its name from the Columbia (Foxhall) Foundry (1799–1849), which covered a five-acre tract along the river and extended across the present Canal Road. The four-story stone cannon-boring mill and the shot tower were operated by Henry Foxhall. Located above the canal, the mill was powered by an overshot wheel on Foundry Branch. Later, power was supplied by the canal under the foundry operation of Gen. John Mason of Analostan Island (now Roosevelt Island). Workers bore large numbers of cannon here and during maximum production produced 30,000 shot annually. Commodore Perry delayed the Battle of Lake Erie until his ship could be rigged with Foxhall-bored cannon hauled overland by 12-ox teams. British soldiers dispatched to destroy the ordnance plant in 1812 encountered a violent storm and turned back to Rock Creek. The site of the foundry has been used since 1849 as a flour mill, distillery, brewery, ice storage warehouse, summer resort, and a boat yard. There is a vestige of a stone foundation remaining.

Foundry Branch culvert (22' span, 10' rise) served as a road culvert. Although it is now blocked to vehicles, it still provides access to the towpath from Canal Road.

1.51 Concrete spillway. This type of spillway was also known as a "mule drink," as they were one of the few places a mule could drink with ease.

Georgetown Level, boats in port, ca. 1900.

1.52 Two closely spaced historic waste weirs. The lower one is filled in, while the upper one is of a late design with screw-type lift gates, typical of most waste weirs on this canal. In the canal operating period the weirs permitted the draining of the canal in the winter to prevent ice damage and to carry out seasonal repair and cleanup of the canal. The waste weirs and spillway discharges are confined by concrete walls and carried under the Capital Crescent Trail in a concrete culvert.

The Georgetown level extends 4.5 miles between Locks 4 and 5. The canal level above the aqueduct was 80' wide, 6' deep in this area. The level is generally watered, fed by Inlet Lock 1 at mile 5.02.

1.63 The Three Sisters Islands in the Potomac were bought in 1951 by the U.S. Government for $1,200 from the Stone family of Bethesda, Maryland. The islands were originally given to contractor John Moore as part of his payment for building several locks on the canal. At one time there was soil on the islands, but over the years the changing course of the Potomac has left little but barren rocks above water.

It is interesting to note that a river crossing here is not a new idea. In a March 26, 1791 report, Pierre L'Enfant recommended to President Washington, "Georgetown itself being situated at the head of grand navigation of the Potowmack should be favored with the same advantage of better Communication with the Southern by having also a bridge erected over the Potowmack at the place of the two sisters where nature would effectively favour the undertaking."

2.18 Stop gate remains are visible when the water is low.

GEORGETOWN CANAL INCLINE (Inclined Plane)

2.26 Access: From 34th Street crossover bridge (mile 0.93), or road culvert at Fletcher's Cove (3.21).

The Georgetown Canal Incline (also known as the Old Boat Incline, Georgetown Inclined Plane, and Outlet Lock), ca. 1874, has a few remains next to the towpath near the bike path and at river level. The first boat to use the incline (designed and engineered by William R. Hutton) went from the canal to the river (a fall of 40') on June 29, 1876. In 1878—the first year in which a record was kept of boats passing over the incline—1,918 boats used it. It was the largest incline in the world at the time, and a model was exhibited at the Paris World's Fair of 1878 as one of the United States' best efforts in the field of civil engineering. Hutton was also chief engineer of the canal company from 1869 to 1872, and consulting engineer until 1881.

Boats went through a double gate (canal's and caisson's) at the upper level into a wooden caisson mounted on wheels designed to keep the caisson level as it descended. The caisson was 112' long, 16'9" wide and 7'10" high. It rested on six, six-wheeled trucks that were fitted to four iron rails 600' long on a 1:10 slope.

Remains of the Georgetown Inclined Plane ca. 2012. *(Image courtesy Rod Mackler)*

The caisson was held tight by a clamping device, which reduced leakage of water when the canal gate and caisson gates were opened for the boat to move through, after which the gates were closed and the caisson prepared for lowering. Through a pulley arrangement, stone counterweights traveled only half as far as the caisson, which entered the river at the bottom where gates at the river end of the caisson would be opened to allow the boat to enter a basin from where tug boats would take it to wharves downstream. The incline was originally built to operate on canal water power from a turbine.

Use of the incline declined after 1879. In May 1877 a failure of the counterweight pulley system killed three men. Subsequently, the caisson was drained after boats entered, and it was lowered without water in it. The incline was not repaired after the 1889 flood. In 1908 the incline was dismantled and the area was dramatically changed for the right-of-way for the Georgetown Branch of the B&O Railroad. (Between 1906 and 1909, the railroad branch from Potomac Palisades to Georgetown was constructed as the Washington and Western Maryland Railroad—a B&O subsidiary.)

2.36 Floodplain broadens; from here onward it becomes a fine, in-town wildflower display, especially in spring.

3.13 Abner Cloud House. Access: From Canal Road at intersection with Reservoir Road. This site is of historical significance because it stands near the lower end of the former Little Falls Skirting Canal, and because the ca. 1801 house is the oldest existing building on the canal.

Abner Cloud House

The site of the Abner Cloud House was included in the original patent of land dating back to 1689. On December 10, 1794, John Threlkeld, a prominent landowner in Georgetown, owned the title. Threlkeld deeded the land to his brother-in-law, Abner Cloud, Jr., on October 19, 1795. Another source says Abner Cloud acquired 195 acres from Richard Arell in 1795. Abner Cloud came from a Quaker family in Pennsylvania. When he took up arms for the Revolutionary cause, he was disowned by his family, and he settled in Washington after the Revolutionary War.

The Abner Cloud House (seen here in 2012) is the oldest existing building on the canal. *(Image courtesy Rod Mackler)*

Cloud built the house and the mill that bears his name in 1801, and lived there with his family until his death in 1812. Italian stonemasons helped build the house. The initials A. C. and the date 1801 can be seen on the stone in the upper portion of the chimney. During this period Cloud used the basement that now fronts the canal for the storage of the grain and flour he milled. His widow, Susan, continued to live here until 1852.

The mill built by Cloud was located near the outlet of the Patowmack Company's Little Falls Skirting Canal above the road culvert. Two other mills (one of which may have been named "Old Locks Mill") and a distillery were located above this mill on the Patowmack Canal. Isaac Peirce married a daughter of Abner Cloud and constructed the Peirce Mill on Rock Creek in 1801. The property was sold to John B. (Bull) Frizzel in 1852. Frizzel, who lived at the site and operated the mill, was the great-grandfather of Julius Fletcher, owner of Fletcher's Boat House. Sometime in the 1860s, the property was owned by William A. Edes, a Georgetown miller who operated the mill as the Cloud-Edes Mill. In 1869 D. L. Shoemaker, member of a prominent Georgetown family, probably owned the property and milled locally the popular Evermay brand flour. Ownership is sketchy for 75 years thereafter. James C. Copperthite probably resided here and was owner in 1939. Mrs. Helen Redmon owned the house in 1957, when it was purchased by the U.S. government. The house is currently used as a chapter house by the Colonial Dames of America.

The house is described by architects as a "simple" random rubble stone house with stone gables at the east and west ends. The house stands on a hillside sloping down to the canal. It has a wood frame interior with plaster walls and ceiling. The roof was originally wood shingles. It is regarded as an "ordinary" house of the period. There have been several structural changes in the building. At some later period a porch was added, but it was badly damaged and removed in 1962.

The Abner Cloud House is a property of the C&O Canal National Historic Park, but it was restored with the assistance of the Colonial Dames of America, Chapter III, was furnished by the Colonial Dames, and is operated by them. The house is open and free to the public one day a month, usually the first Sunday (except January and February), from noon to 5:00 pm. For information, search "Abner Cloud" on the park web site, http://www.nps.gov/choh/.

LITTLE FALLS SKIRTING CANAL

3.14 Fletcher's Cove (38.918691, -77.102019) Access: From downtown Washington take M St. west to Key Bridge, and continue straight, now on Canal Rd. After 0.5 mi, turn left at the first traffic light to continue on Canal Rd. (straight ahead becomes Foxhall Rd.). Go 1.6 miles and turn left into Fletcher's Cove.

From the Capital Beltway (I-495) in Maryland take Exit 40, Cabin John Parkway/Glen Echo. Go 1.7 miles and merge onto the Clara Barton Pkwy. Go 4.5 miles to the entrance to Fletcher's Cove, but do not attempt to turn right—it is a dangerous hairpin turn into a narrow road. Instead, continue about 50 yards and turn left onto Reservoir Rd. (You cannot turn onto Reservoir Rd. Mon.–Fri. 2:45 p.m. to 7:15 p.m. except federal holidays.) Turn left onto MacArthur Blvd., left again back onto Reservoir Rd., right onto Canal Rd. and left into Fletcher's Cove (yielding to inbound traffic).

CAUTION! When accessing points of interests by vehicle via Clara Barton Parkway and Canal Road, please note vehicle direction restrictions: Mon.–Fri. 6:15 a.m. to 10 a.m. inbound to Washington traffic only, and 2:45 p.m. to 7:15 p.m., outbound to Maryland traffic only. These restrictions are not in effect on federal holidays.

The Boathouse at Fletcher's Cove rents rowboats for use on the river, canoes for the canal, and bikes for the towpath. Picnic tables, refreshments, fishing supplies, and toilets are available. The river here is a favorite fishing location, especially during spring herring and shad runs. 4940 Canal Rd. NW, Washington D.C. 20007, 202-244-0461, www.fletcherscove.com.

From near this point and up to Lock 5 (mile 5.02), the C&O Canal was built on the line of the old Little Falls Skirting Canal, a segment the Patowmack Company built to avoid the Little Falls of the Potomac. George Washington was a primary promoter and the first president of the Patowmack Company. The canal was 3,814 yards long. Other skirting canals of the Patowmack Company were built at Great Falls, Seneca, and above and below Harpers Ferry. Originally, three wooden locks were built at Fletcher's (Garrisons/Lock Cove/Lock Harbor), completing the Little Falls Canal in 1795. The wooden locks were replaced in 1817 by four stone locks with a combined lift of 37'.

3.18 Battery Kemble culvert, 14' span. The outflow was extended to permit passage under the railroad.

3.21 The span of the road culvert at Fletcher's was historically 15'3" with a 9'6" rise at the outflow. It was extensively used to provide access to the towpath and Fletcher's Cove.

3.23 Third waste weir on this level, believed to have served Edes Mill.

3.64 The Capital Crescent Trail crosses the canal on the former railroad bridge at the intersection of Canal Road and Arizona Avenue. The bridge has a 13'6" clearance over the towpath (10' clear width between abutment and canal side of the towpath).

3.86 Spillway 2 is the longest on the canal, 354' long and 18" below towpath level, built by the NPS in 1936 to relieve the canal of surplus water. The spillway was rebuilt a year after the damaging June 1972 flood.

CHAIN BRIDGE

4.17 (38.932652, -77.113304) Access: From the Capital Beltway (I-495) in Maryland take Exit 40, Cabin John Parkway/Glen Echo. Go 1.7 miles and merge onto the Clara Barton Pkwy. Follow the parkway inbound approximately 3.2 miles to parking on right, about 0.3 mile before Chain Bridge. The path across the road goes to a bus stop on MacArthur Boulevard.

WARNING! Canoeists should avoid the section of the river between Chain Bridge and Great Falls because of the many rapids creating hazardous river conditions.

The Clara Barton Parkway was renamed from the George Washington Memorial Parkway in 1989—a change that prevents confusion with the George Washington Memorial Parkway on the Virginia side of the river. A ferry operated here from ca. 1737 to (probably) the building of the first bridge in 1797, which was a covered structure that collapsed in 1804. The first "chain" bridge was built in 1808, its roadway suspended from huge chains anchored from stone

Union soldiers patrol the Chain Bridge during the Civil War. (*Library of Congress, Prints and Photographs Online Catalog*)

abutments. Flood waters swept it away in 1810. It was rebuilt around 1811 and lasted until 1852, when it was severely damaged by a flood. The next bridge was built in 1854, although the form of the structure is not clear. There are Mathew Brady Civil War photos showing a bridge of timbered truss construction on the same masonry piers that exist today. A Howe truss bridge (eight iron trusses) 1,350' long, was built in 1874, with the timber floor laid on the old stone abutments. That bridge collapsed in a 1936 flood and was replaced by the present steel cantilever girder structure.

The first Union army sentinel to be court-martialed for sleeping at his post in the Civil War had fallen asleep on the District end of the bridge. (Lincoln saved him from execution.) On June 12, 1861, 90-day volunteers from the District of Columbia advanced up the canal towpath from the Chain Bridge, using two canal boats for their supplies. They were part of Col. Charles P. Stone's Rockville Expedition, which placed the first Union pickets along the Potomac above Washington.

4.54 Unused Dalecarlia hydroelectric plant and culvert under the canal with deeply-cut outflow in a straight line to the river 300 yards away. This area of the river was used by the Army Corps of Engineers for a supplemental source of water from the tidal estuary of the Potomac River (water coming up river by tidal action rather than down river by gravity).

4.72 Cross the District of Columbia–Montgomery County, Maryland line, the upper limit of tidewater. A Maryland fishing license is required above this point.

4.76 A large modern concrete culvert carries Little Falls Branch.

Angling Along The C&O

The Potomac River and watered parts of the canal have been attracting anglers for decades. A 2002 survey recorded 49 species of fish, both introduced and native. According to the *Chesapeake and Ohio Canal: A Guide to Chesapeake and Ohio Canal National Historical Park, Maryland, District of Columbia, and West Virginia* (U.S. Government Printing Office, 1991):

Introduced species are smallmouth and largemouth bass, bluegill sunfish, blue catfish, and rock bass. Brown and rainbow trout are stocked in some of the mountain tributaries. Native fish include black and white crappies, chain pickerel, yellow perch, pumpkinseed, white cat, channel cat, and American eel. Brook trout are native to a few headwater streams. . . . Blue and channel catfish, carp, several sunfish species, and pickerel predominate, with here and there occasional bass.

The Fletcher's Cove and Chain Bridge areas are most popular with fishermen during the spring spawning runs of herring, shad, white perch, and rockfish that follow the herring up the Chesapeake Bay to the tidal Potomac. Fletcher's offers current fishing reports at 202-244-0461 or www.fletcherscove.com.

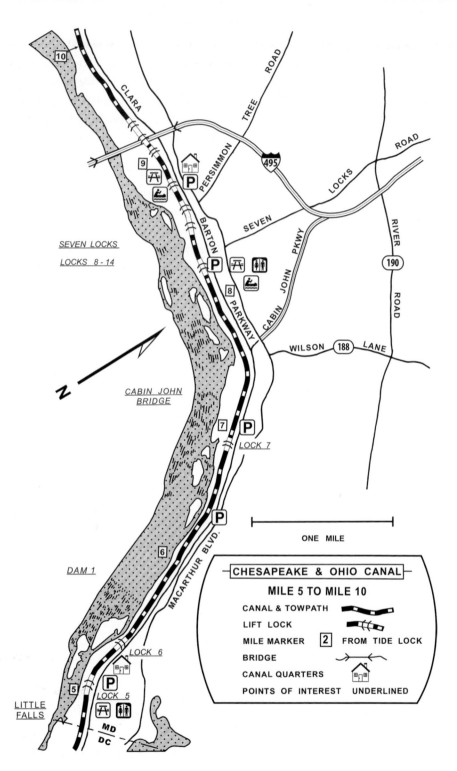

SEVEN LOCKS
LOCKS 8 - 14

CABIN JOHN
BRIDGE

N

DAM 1

LITTLE
FALLS

LOCK 7

LOCK 6

LOCK 5

MD
DC

CLARA

PERSIMMON

TREE ROAD

495

SEVEN LOCKS ROAD

CABIN JOHN PKWY

BARTON PARKWAY

MACARTHUR BLVD.

RIVER ROAD

190

WILSON 188 LANE

ONE MILE

CHESAPEAKE & OHIO CANAL

MILE 5 TO MILE 10

CANAL & TOWPATH

LIFT LOCK

MILE MARKER   2   FROM TIDE LOCK

BRIDGE

CANAL QUARTERS

POINTS OF INTEREST   UNDERLINED

LOCK 5, BROOKMONT, AND INLET LOCK 1

5.02 For vehicle access see mile 5.40. Access is available on foot from Brookmont, which offers Montgomery County Ride On bus service. There is a footpath on Ridge Dr. about 150' south of 61st St. Take the path about 0.1 mile downhill to the spiraling concrete footbridge over the parkway, which brings you to the downstream end of the picnic area on the berm side of the canal. There are portable toilets, a picnic table, and a bench in the picnic area.

The cornerstone of Lock 5 was laid by President John Quincy Adams in 1829. The two-story frame lockhouse was torn down in 1957. In the late operating period the lock was known as "Willards Lock" for the locktender.

Just below Lock 5, the C&O Canal turns inland about 15° and leaves the original route of Little Falls Skirting Canal. The feeder canal angling toward the river is likely the remains of the skirting canal that was used to bring water from the pool created by Historic Dam 1, 0.6 mile above Lock 5 at the head of Little Falls. The water passes through the narrow channel between High Island and the mainland. The water then flows through the channel formed by the mainland on one side and by a long concrete spillway on the other, beginning at the lower end of High Island to the upper inlet gate. Finally, the water passes into the feeder canal proper through the lower inlet gate and its confluence with the C&O Canal. Below Lock 5, construction of the C&O Canal virtually eliminated all traces of Little Falls Skirting Canal. Above the lock, the robbing of stones, as well as floods and the construction of the dam have obliterated the remains of older, historic structures.

Lock 5 was rebuilt after flood damage in both 1868 and 1878. The level of the coping was raised 6' above its original level, probably as an attempt to resist flood damage. A levee or guard wall is at this height and nearly perpendicular to the run of the lock. It extends to the berm bank on one side and 100' to the feeder inlet gate on the other. The concrete apron on the guard wall was apparently constructed as part of a 1938–42 restoration of the lower 22 miles by the Civilian Conservation Corps (CCC). Records indicate that the upper end of the lock was rebuilt for a drop gate in 1876 but restored to swing gates in 1939.

The lower 6' of Lock 5 was originally built of hammer-dressed stone from "a quarry less than 1 mi. distance" and the remainder of freestone from Aquia Creek. There are a number of stone masons' marks in the rebuilding. The guard wall and inlet gate abutments were rebuilt in concrete in the CCC restoration for flood resistance.

5.20 A service road leads to the river and the upper gate of the feeder canal. A path along the river goes to Dam 1. (Note: many of these types of paths become overgrown in the summer months and therefore difficult to find and/or navigate.) The swamp between the C&O Canal and the feeder canal provides excellent bird habitat. High Island (124' high) looms prominently between the feeder channel and the river. It is attractively wooded and has steep slopes with a level area on top. Sluices in the river on the far side were possibly for early bateaux boats.

LOCK 6 (Magazine Lock), BROOKMONT

5.40 (38.944737, -77.123348) Access: From the Capital Beltway (I-495) in Maryland take Exit 40, Cabin John Parkway/Glen Echo. Go 1.7 miles and merge onto the Clara Barton Pkwy. Follow the parkway inbound approximately 2.3 miles to parking on right. Access is also available on foot from Brookmont, which offers Montgomery County Ride On bus service. At the end of Valley Rd. (off Broad St.), you will find a footpath which leads across the parkway at grade, just upstream from the lockhouse.

The feeder canal (old Little Falls Skirting Canal) lies about 200 yards west of Lock 6. The lock is called the "Magazine Lock" after the U.S. Powder Magazine 0.3 mile upstream, where President Adams inaugurated C&O Canal construction on July 4, 1828.

As was the case with Lock 5, records indicate that Lock 6 was originally a typical lock with swing (miter) gates but was converted to one with a drop gate in the upper end. However, the lock only measures 90'8" between gate pockets, which contradicts the company records. The lock was reconfigured to the swing gate design in the 1938–42 restoration of the canal's lower 22 miles.

The stones are much worn, showing many replacements or partial rebuilding with whatever material was handy. The lock originally was built with

Canoe locking through Lock 6, ca. 1918.

28

Aquia Creek freestone with granite rubble backup stones common to the area. Probably the lock was built originally with wicket gates in the upper gate pockets to carry water around the upper gates and through culverts in the lock walls. The lower towpath wing wall shows many rope grooves as does the upper 18" of the exposed end of the wall. The lower wing walls had vertical aligning timbers fastened to the turns of the lock wall to line up the boats to minimize their bumping into the lock.

The lock has suffered repeated damage since the June 1972 flood. The towpath washout in 1972 uncovered a double row of wooden sheet piling at the head of Lock 6. Between Locks 6 and 7 much of the embankment was exposed to the river. For this reason a carefully laid and substantially built stone wall was originally built against the slope to its top.

The lockhouse is a one-and-a-half story whitewashed stone structure over a stone basement, 18' x 32'. The basement sidewalls were extended originally 6' on the south end to form a covered portion to the basement entrance, which supports a wooden porch for the first floor. The original lockhouse built ca. 1830–31 was destroyed in an 1847 flood and rebuilt in 1848. *Towpath Guide to the C&O Canal* author Thomas Hahn lived in this lockhouse 1972–75.

There are no toilets, picnic tables, or water sources at this lock. The lockhouse and surrounding area are closed off by a wooden fence. The lockhouse is available for overnight rentals via the Canal Trust's Canal Quarters program, 301-745-8888, www.canaltrust.org/quarters.

Lockhouse 6, 2012. *(Image courtesy Ed Kirkpatrick Photography)*

Rope burns at Lock 6, 2011. *(Image courtesy Steve Dean)*

Just opposite the footbridge over the canal the Lock 6 Trail makes a "C" route off the towpath for about 0.3 mile. This path gives great views of the feeder canal, where kayakers are often seen. Parts of the trail are directly along the stream bank—**USE CAUTION!** Just before turning inland to rejoin the towpath, take a short spur to a rocky ledge with great views of the river and of Little Falls Dam, about 0.15 mile upstream.

Forest cover along the canal is of two distinct types. The river bottom (south of the canal and in low, flat sections north of it) is predominantly sycamore and American elm with a considerable mix of black locust, box elder, and soft maple. On slopes north of the canal and on high dry rocky areas south of Widewater, the river bottom is a red-white-black oak mixture, predominantly white oak with other oaks, hickories, and Virginia pine intermixed. Tulip poplar is common in both areas.

Land in the area was patented May 16, 1726, as Magruder's and Beall's Honesty. There was also a six-man garrison built near Little Falls in 1692 under the command of Capt. Richard Brightwell.

FEEDER DAM 1 (Little Falls Dam)

5.64 Access: Lock 6 at mile 5.40.

This point was the scene of the original ground-breaking ceremonies on July 4, 1828. A path leads to the end of the old dam and the beginning of the feeder canal down to Inlet Lock 1 (likely this channel was originally part of the

Patowmack Company's Little Falls Skirting Canal). There were a number of cottages in this area on plots leased from the canal company, but all were destroyed in the floods of 1936 and 1943.

John Ballendine, an early developer of iron furnaces and mills, first attempted a bypass around the river rapids, ca. 1772. He called his land here "Amsterdam." George Washington indicated that Ballendine's bypass canal was never finished, but his effort may have included a partial dam at the head of the Little Falls to divert water into his channel. The same would have been true two decades later, when the Patowmack Company built its canal at Little Falls.

Between 1828 and 1830 the C&O Canal Company built Dam 1 at this location from the Maryland shore to Snake Island, but in 1831 let a new contractor complete the dam to the Virginia shore. As with all C&O dams (there were seven of them, although eight were originally planned), Dam 1 suffered severely from periodic floods, including 1832, 1836, 1868, and 1873. Today the old canal company dam is overshadowed by the new Little Falls Diversion Dam, which is about 1' higher and 100' upstream.

The Piedmont area begins at Little Falls, from which the Potomac Valley rises gently by a series of water-worn plateaus, principally of red sandstone, to the Blue Ridge Mountains west of the Monocacy Valley. The surface of the valley is characterized first by gently rolling country of rich farm lands, broken at points much farther ahead near the river by stretches of majestic cliffs.

5.74 Culvert #2, 6' span.

5.78 Little Falls Intake and Pump Station. Both works were constructed by the Army Corps of Engineers in 1959. The dam is a two-part masonry structure reaching from the Maryland shore to Snake Island and from the island to the Virginia shore, the latter distance being 1,500'. Although the dam is 14' high from the river bed, it impounds water at a level only 1' above the old dam. A 3' water main embedded in the upstream face of the new dam carries water to a Virginia pumping station. The pumping station on the Maryland side is a standby facility for pumping water directly from the Potomac to the Dalecarlia Water Treatment Plant on MacArthur Boulevard through a 4,500'-long, 10'-diameter tunnel. It is used in low-water periods when natural flow at Great Falls, Maryland, is insufficient for Washington's water supply.

Because of its deadly undertow, canoeists and kayakers MUST portage around the dam. DEATHS HAVE OCCURRED HERE; DO NOT ATTEMPT TO CANOE THIS DAM.

6.1x Large signs on both the Maryland and Virginia shorelines and floats in the river warn boaters to leave the river because of the dangerous dam ahead—the Little Falls Dam, mile 5.78.

6.4x Sycamore Island (38.95832, -77.131465) Access: From the Capital Beltway (I-495) in Maryland take Exit 40, Cabin John Parkway/Glen Echo. Go 1.7 miles and merge onto the Clara Barton Pkwy. Follow the parkway inbound approximately 1.2 miles to a parking area just past the pedestrian bridge over the parkway.

There is a parking lot with 20 spaces on MacArthur Boulevard at Walhonding Road (38.958303, -77.130849). A spiral footbridge crosses the parkway to access the canal. Paths from the two parking lots converge on a bluff where a gravel path leads downhill to a 1910 pedestrian bridge connecting to the towpath.

Just beyond the bridge over the canal are cables used to summon the caretaker on the island. The Sycamore Island Club has owned Sycamore Island (3.5 acres) and Ruppert Island (4.5 acres) upstream since 1885 (both are near the Maryland shore). Sycamore Island is used for club activities, while Ruppert Island is kept in a natural state. Sycamore Island is the finishing point for the annual Potomac Downriver Race for canoes and kayaks, sponsored each year by the Potomac Whitewater Racing Center (potomacwhitewater.org).

6.60 Upper end of Sycamore Island. Above are various islands, including Ruppert Island, the site of archaeological excavations by the Maryland Historic Trust that found artifacts dating back 15,000 years. The island is also known as "Indian Island."

LOCK 7, GLEN ECHO

7.00 (38.964611, -77.138363) Access: From the Capital Beltway (I-495) in Maryland take Exit 40, Cabin John Parkway/Glen Echo. Go 1.7 miles and merge onto the Clara Barton Pkwy. Follow the parkway inbound approximately 0.6 mile to a parking area. There is a footbridge at mid-lock to the lockhouse. The parkway closely parallels the canal to Cabin John Creek.

The lock is made of granite obtained from French's Quarry (0.8 mile away) except for the original coping, which is Aquia Creek freestone. There are few replacement stones in the lock walls, testifying to the quality of gray granite used. The original breast wall and all of the lock walls above the original gate quoins were removed and the lock walls re-laid to extend the lock and accommodate a drop gate in the upper end. It is 101'11" between gate pockets, a measurement that shows that the drop gate pockets are approximately 10' forward of the original swing gate pockets. The upper end of the drop gate pocket has no shoulders as the lock is made up by tapered log cribs that lined up boats entering the upper end of the lock and also prevented boats from damaging the lock walls. The original lock had masonry bypass culverts in the lock walls.

Room was left on the berm side of the locks in the lower section of the canal for a duplicate lock (to handle both upstream and downstream traffic simultaneously) should traffic warrant it. This practice was quickly abandoned, however.

The lockhouse sits on an island formed by the canal, lock, and bypass flume. It is a one-and-a-half story whitewashed stone structure over a full basement. The lockhouse was completed sometime before August 1, 1829, and was the first to be completed on the C&O Canal. An inspector on August 2, 1829, wrote a reference to its builder that read: "The Bearer James O'Brien (contractor) who has just finished Lock house No. 5 on Section 5 is an excellent stone mason, and has made one of the best if not the very best jobs of stone work on the line." In 1936 the lockhouse was somewhat carelessly rebuilt after flood damage had torn away portions of the structure. Dormer windows and plumbing were added at that time. The last locktender here was Charles Shaeffer, who began service in 1893 and was retained by the company until 1938.

On the bluffs above the lock on the opposite side of the parkway was the site of a Chautauqua that was part of a national movement. This particular Chautauqua had only one successful season, in 1891. Subsequently, a popular belief that the area was prone to malaria ended the endeavor. The Glen Echo Amusement Park occupied the site for many years, but closed after the 1968 season. It was acquired by the NPS, which removed some amusement structures and opened the park to the public in the summer of 1970. Since that time an extensive cultural, educational, and recreational program has been offered.

The large white frame house upstream from Glen Echo Park was the home of Clara Barton, founder and long-time head of the American Red Cross. In 1974 it became a National Historical Site under the NPS. It can be reached via

Drop lock mechanism at Lock 7 in 2011. (*Image courtesy Steve Dean*)

MacArthur Boulevard. It is currently open weekends for guided tours between 10 a.m. and 4 p.m., 301-320-1410, www.nps.gov/clba. Toward the river and through the woods is a side channel of the river, with Chautauqua Island beyond.

7.10 Concrete waste weir. At least one weir is on all but the shortest levels. Ahead the floodplain supports many fine tall elms and sycamores. This typical bottom land forest is a fine bird habitat. Ahead in the river is Cabin John Island, though changing river channels have destroyed its true island nature. In 1905 bluebells grew in wonderful profusion until boys in Glen Echo discovered they could be sold to visitors at the terminal of the Cabin John trolley line. In a couple of years the island was denuded, and the fields of bluebells never returned.

7.12 A modern concrete culvert carrying Glen Echo Run (old "Minnehaha" stream) replaced historic stone Culvert #5, described in 1831 as a "fine arched stone culvert," which was 112' long and had a 22' arch span and 5' rise.

7.50 A modern concrete box culvert carrying Cabin John Creek under the canal replaced Culvert #8 in the 1960s. A footbridge across the canal leads to a wide path that ascends about 0.3 mile and goes under the parkway to a parking area at the east end of the Cabin John Bridge on MacArthur Boulevard.

7.52 Cedar Island. Like Cabin John Island below, its island character is ill-defined and varies with the height of water in shallow river channels. The river itself is brown at flood time or olive green at others and is noisy among the rock islands that stretch to the Virginia shore. The floodplain in the spring is a green blanket splashed with myriads of wildflowers that all reach their blossoming peak at one time. Add a clear day with the white arms of the towering sycamores and the kaleidoscope of color is breathtaking.

8.12 The towpath comes directly onto the river bank, supported by a laid masonry wall. The high wooded island is Minnie Island.

The valley of the Cabin John Creek extends for two miles to the north. The once natural character of the valley has been dramatically altered by the Cabin John Parkway, which connects the Clara Barton Parkway with the Capital Beltway (I-495), and by various construction projects of the Washington Suburban Sanitary Commission, designed to reduce some of the pollution that entered Cabin John Creek and the Potomac in this area. Two sewer lines parallel the canal on the berm between Brookmont and Cabin John. The smaller one connects with a sewer down Cabin John Creek Valley and carries sewage to the Washington system in Georgetown. The larger one, built in the 1960s, is the Potomac Interceptor, which runs from Dulles International Airport to the Washington Treatment Plant at Blue Plains. The latter is 7' in diameter and is laid in the bed of the canal in some places. The vertical iron pipes noticed occasionally are ventilators of the old sewer, and the 2'–3' high masonry towers are ventilators of the Potomac Interceptor.

Cabin John Bridge

The bridge over the Cabin John Valley—the proper name of which is the Union Arch Bridge—is a beautiful structure carrying MacArthur Boulevard and a Corps of Engineers conduit supplying water for Washington from Great Falls. It is located 1,000' up Cabin John Creek, spanning both the creek and the four-lane Cabin John Parkway. Only the uppermost edge of the bridge can be seen from the towpath because of foliage and the Cabin John Parkway.

Construction began in 1857, and water was turned into the conduit December 5, 1863. The bridge itself was finished in 1864. The bridge is 450' long, with a 57.5' rise and a 220' span. At the time of its completion it was the longest single-arch masonry bridge in the world. The parapet walls are built of red Seneca sandstone, and the cut-stone arch is of granite from Quincy, Massachusetts, carried here via ocean vessels to Georgetown and then up the C&O Canal. The rubble arch and spandrels are of Seneca sandstone, and the abutments are of Port Deposit, Maryland, granite. The bridge has five spandrels at the west end and three at the east end to relieve the load. These spandrels are hidden inside the walled facade.

The first engineer of the bridge project and its principal designer was Montgomery C. Meigs (an Army Corps of Engineers officer who became Quartermaster General in the Civil War). He further used the canal by building a dam across Cabin John Run, with a lock to pass canal boats from the canal to the pool that extended up to and under the bridge. Meigs named the bridge the "Union Arch," a name that appears on the commemorative tablet on the bridge. William R. Hutton, a chief engineer on the C&O Canal, was the chief engineer of the Cabin John project when the water was turned on through the conduit inside the bridge in 1863. Two names that were originally to be included on commemorative stones were those of Meigs' assistant engineer, Alfred L. Rives, who had helped design the bridge, and Jefferson Davis, who was Secretary of War. Both men joined the Confederacy, and their names were therefore excluded from the final engraved stones.

The bridge was designated a National Historic Civil War Landmark January 30, 1973.

The Cabin John Bridge or "Union Arch" between 1880 and 1890. *(Library of Congress, Prints and Photographs Online Catalog)*

Lock Lengths And Extensions

The C&O Canal Company undertook two construction projects in the late-nineteenth century that aimed to alter the lengths of certain C&O locks.

There is a discrepancy between lock lengths as reported by experts such as Thomas Hahn and William Davies, and the C&O Canal Company records on the lengths of boats operating on the canal. A significant number of locks at the lower end of the canal have been measured at 90′–93.5′ long between gate pockets—i.e., the space for boats between the gates when closed. But the canal company's boat classification system and its lists of registered boats cite many boats as being 92′–95′ long. Additionally, to prevent boats from slamming against the gates when entering, or in the turbulence when water is filling or draining the lock, boats must be short enough to allow some clearance between each end and the proximate gate. This raises a curious question: How did a standard canal boat fit into some of these locks?

According to the C&O Canal Company records, a project to lengthen these locks to at least 100′ of usable lockage began in the winter of 1875–76. The upper end of several locks was rebuilt by removing the breast walls and all the walls upstream of the breast walls. These walls were then rebuilt to full depth, and new gate pockets for drop gates were constructed 10′ forward of the original gate pockets. This made the lock 100′–101′ between pockets instead of 90′–93′. For economic reasons, the wing wall extensions were built as stone-filled timber cribs rather than masonry. A drop gate pivoted at the bottom, so that when opened it lay flat on the bottom of the lock. An advantage was that the gate could be raised and lowered by one person working a cranking mechanism on one side of the lock. (See image of mechanism on page 33.)

As to which locks were actually extended and converted to drop gates, there are many discrepancies among the records of both the C&O Canal Company and the historians, and in the physical evidence. Today, only a few locks have drop gate mechanisms, as many were restored to swing (miter) gates in a 1938–42 canal restoration project.

In the winter of 1881–82, the company began another major program to extend the canal's locks, this time by 100′. Canal company president, Arthur Pue Gorman (who later became a powerful politician) had been promoting the idea of these lock extensions since June 1872. These locks were to allow the passage of two boats connected in such a way that they could be operated as one very long boat, thus saving canallers significant "locking through" time. It would also be possible to operate larger, more efficient boats that only required one additional mule to a pulling team. Until all locks were lengthened, such boats would need to be disconnected and locked through separately in the unaltered locks. The records seem to suggest that 14 locks were lengthened that winter. However, after the winter of 1882–83,

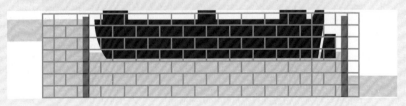

the company reported that only two more locks had been completed, and subsequently no further effort was made to lengthen locks for double boats. The costs of building the extensions and the mounting maintenance costs probably led to the abandonment of the extension project.

Locks extended on the upper ends were equipped with drop gates, and the extended walls built with stone-filled, timber cribs, with two layers of 2" planking. Locks extended at the lower end—as at Lock 25—had swing (miter) gates.

Upper extensions required that the breast wall and all walls above the breast wall be removed and the canal bed excavated an additional 8' for the 100' extensions before the stone-filled, timber cribs could be constructed. No such excavation of the canal or change of the original lock walls was necessary below a lock. Perhaps the explanation for an expensive upstream extension is that topography required it in certain places.

As was the case with the 1875–76 lock extension/drop gate project, the record is unclear on the number of locks that were doubled in length and which locks they were. A study of five canal experts who have reported on this subject (Harlan Unrau, William Davies, John Miele, Walter Sanderlin, and Thomas Hahn), reveals significant agreement on only 12 locks: 25 through 32, 37, 38, 43, and 60. Lock 43 is a good example of the difficulties that arise in trying to identify the lengthened locks with certainty, as most people today agree that Lock 43 reveals no signs of being lengthened, while Lock 44, the next lock up the canal (located in Williamsport), does appear to have been extended.

Where the stone from these extensions has been pirated for other purposes, leaving no windrow of stones, we are still able to determine which locks were extended downstream by the location of the mule rise, which in the case of the extended locks is 120' downstream (the overall length of the extended lock) from its normal position.

The lock illustration (opposite page) and historic image of a canal boat completely in the lock chamber of Lock 26 (above) both demonstrate the extremely tight fit of boats in the lift locks. *(Lock illustration courtesy of David T. Gilbert; historic image "Riley's Lock, No. 24, at Seneca, Md.," Thomas Hahn Chesapeake and Ohio Canal collection, Box 31, Special Collections Research Center, The George Washington University)*

LOCK 8, SEVEN LOCKS

8.33 (38.971559, -77.160636) Access: From the Capital Beltway (I-495) in Maryland take Exit 41, Clara Barton Pkwy. Go 0.8 mile and take the first possible exit for Carderock. Go 0.2 mile up the exit ramp; turn left to cross over the parkway; then left again, to get onto the parkway inbound. Go 1.9 miles to the parking area for Lock 8. A steep path leads 200' down to the lock. There is a canoe put-in/take-out on the river shore.

An alternate 0.45 mile route for hikers and bikers only is from MacArthur Blvd. to 79th St. to Riverside Ave. Go under the parkway. Turn left to dead end, right on old gated road, then follow path which leads to Lock 8 on left.

This lock is the first of a series known as "Seven Locks," which raises the canal 56' in a distance of 1.25 miles. The lock material is red sandstone, which was boated down the river 14.5 miles from the Seneca quarries. As an 1831 report put it, "It is the first with which we have met, which has the facing, or front range of its walls, made with the red sandstone of Seneca Creek . . . inferior, however, to granite."

The lock has had many repairs, and many original stones have been replaced with concrete, brick, and granite. Wooden timbers, serving as towrope rubbing boards, were bolted onto the water-side edge of some locks and aqueducts. They prevented the towrope from catching on rough spots and deformities on the coping stones and from creating rope burns or indentations on the edge of the stone. The lock was built with masonry bypass culverts in the lock walls around the upper gates, but this system was abandoned early on and a bypass flume constructed. Note four 1"-diameter blow holes, which lead down into the culvert openings to release air trapped in the culvert when water was let out of the lower lock. The lock has a masonry breast wall, with the downstream face flush with the downstream face of the miter sill of the upper lock gates, as did most, but not all, locks through Lock 27. The lock measures 140'8" overall length and 90'6" between lock gate pockets.

The mule rise here is 70' long and has a rise of 8'—the same as the lift of the lock. The canal is 100' wide just above the lock and would have served as a turning basin.

Construction of the lockhouses was undertaken within a few months of the official groundbreaking for the canal on July 4, 1828. On March 18, 1829, the canal company received a proposal from James O'Brien for erecting houses "Numbers 5 and 6." (Because there was not a house at every lock, the original lockhouse numbering did not match the lock number, No. 6 was the house at Lock 8, now Lockhouse 8.) The house was completed and ready for occupancy a year later. The first group of lockhouses to be completed apparently were assigned for occupancy and use late in the summer of 1830. A resolution adopted by the canal company stated that compensation for the locktenders "shall . . . in no case exceed $150 for a single lock, $200 where the same person keeps two locks, and $250 where three locks are kept by one keeper, per annum." One month later, Solomon Drew was appointed Keeper at Lock 8 at $100 per annum "and use of Lock house No. 6 on Section No. 7."

The house here is a typical 18' x 30' stone structure, with two rooms on each floor and a central fireplace on the first floor. Plaster was applied directly onto the masonry walls and ceiling lath. The exterior is random coursed stone, painted white. The house is attractively located 60' from the lock wall. The house is now occupied by the Potomac Conservancy and is open on Saturdays and Sundays 11 a.m. to 2 p.m. from May through October. River Center at Lock 8, 7906 Riverside Dr., Cabin John, MD 20818, 301-608-1188, www.potomac.org. A picnic table and portable toilet are here but no water source.

8.40 Culvert #9, 4' span.

8.57 Wades Island.

8.67 Culvert #10, 8' span.

LOCK 9, SEVEN LOCKS

8.70 Access: Lock 8 at mile 8.33 or Lock 10 at mile 8.79.

This lock and Locks 10 and 12 were equipped with drop gates. The lock was built of granite brought 1.25 miles by land from a quarry near Lock 7—except for the coping, which is Aquia Creek freestone, and a few feet of Seneca red sandstone. Many of the original lock stones have been replaced. The drop gate was installed 10' above the earlier swing-type gates so it is 101'8" between gate pockets instead of 90'–92' of the original. (Note: There is no record of when the conversion to a drop gate was completed.) The overall length of the lock is 141'5.5". The mechanisms for operating the drop gate are in working condition. The stone-filled wooden cribs now in place probably approximate those used during the operating period. Apparently the cribs had no standard dimensions, although they were generally 12' in length, 3'–4' wide on the upper end by 5'–7' wide on the lower end. Cribs here are post-1939 construction as are all cribs on the restored lower 22-mile portion of the canal. In addition to aligning boats and absorbing shock, they formed the upper end of the gate pocket. This lock also had vertical, heavy wooden timbers mounted at the lower end of the lock (on the lower wings) to align boats and absorb shock. Most of the locks on the restored (watered) canal were originally built with short gates on top of the breast wall at the head of the lock chamber.

The lower towpath wing wall has three iron cramps (staple-like devices for holding the coping stones together). One early-period cramp is .5" x 1.5" iron stock with turned-down ends, is "fully let" into stone (flush with the stone's

39

Early and mid-period iron "cramps" on the wing wall coping stones at Lock 9 (left) and a late-period cramp near the upper gate (right). *(Images Harpers Ferry Historical Association)*

surface), measures 13" overall, and was lead caulked. The other two are mid-period cramps, .5" x 2" iron stock with turned-down ends shaped into round stock; they are also "fully let" into stone and measure 13"–14" in overall length. Additionally, coping stones near the upper gate have a late-period cramp, which is 1" round iron with turned down ends, somewhat longer, and "half let" into stone (higher than the stone's surface). Indentations from now-gone cramps can be found on most locks along the canal.

LOCK 10, SEVEN LOCKS

8.79 (38.972631, -77.169278) Access: From the Capital Beltway (I-495) in Maryland take Exit 41, Clara Barton Pkwy. Go 0.8 mile and take the first possible exit, for Carderock. Go 0.2 mile up the exit ramp; turn left to cross over the parkway; then left again, to get onto the parkway inbound. Go 1.4 miles to the parking area for Lock 10. There is a picnic table and water fountain but no toilet. There is a canoe put-in/take-out on the river shore.

The lock was originally built of granite from a quarry near Lock 7 and from a quarry "four miles in the country. The transportation comes from land." Note several interesting stonemason's marks. The stones have stood up well with few exceptions. The lockhouse is about 100' below the lock, and the locktender here served both Locks 9 and 10. The house is a one-and-a-half story stone building over a full basement with dormer windows. The house was erected ca. 1830 by contractor J. W. Maynard. The first locktender was Thomas Burgess. Lockhouse 10 is available for overnight rentals through the Canal Trust's Canal Quarters program, 301-745-8888, www.canaltrust.org/quarters.

8.93 Culvert #12 (Rock Run) has a skewed arch—that is, it runs diagonally under the canal with its outflow end downstream of its inflow. It is 152' long, with a 12'-arch span and a 6' rise. This culvert is a fine example of an outstanding structure under the canal, and it is worth a careful climb down the stream bank to view it.

Lockhouse 10 in 2012. The lockhouse was extensively renovated in 2011–12 for use in the C&O Canal Trust Canal Quarters program. *(Image courtesy Ed Kirkpatrick Photography)*

Rock Run Culvert below Lock 11 is one of many beautiful canal structures the average canal visitor never sees. *(Image courtesy Steve Dean, 2011)*

House at Lock 11, 2011. Note the mile marker "9 miles to W. C." (Washington City) *(Image courtesy Steve Dean)*

8.96 A side path leads to Plummers Island, a 12-acre Potomac River island and home of the Washington Biologists' Field Club.

LOCK 11, SEVEN LOCKS

8.97 Access: Lock 10 at mile 8.79.

The lock is built of Seneca red sandstone and has interesting stonemason's marks. The lock has swing gates in both upper and lower pockets with no evidence of a drop gate. The one-and-a-half story, whitewashed stone lockhouse is on the towpath side of the canal, 42' from the lock's towpath wall and a few feet below the upper gate pocket. The last locktender in the post-operational period was Charles S. Stewart, who spent 51 years on the canal.

9.00 Old historic milepost marked "9 MILES TO W. C." (Washington City), probably gray sandstone.

LOCK 12, SEVEN LOCKS

9.29 Access: Lock 10 at mile 8.79.

Lock 12 is the first of three closely-spaced locks in the Seven Locks series. The lock is in a pretty setting with pleasant grassy areas in spite of its proximity to the Clara Barton Parkway and I-495 (the Capital Beltway). The lock was originally built of granite from a quarry near Lock 7 and transported by land 2.3 miles. There is also evidence that some or all of the original coping stones were dark red sandstone. Masons' marks are few. As is common in the locks below

Seneca, the towpath mule rise begins shortly before the lock and does not reach the level above the lock until about the lower gate pockets. The end of the lower towpath wing was thus exposed in historic times, and rope grooves are in evidence on the end of the wall 32" down from the top. Later substitutions of granite copings do not show rope grooves, proof they were installed later than 1924 (when the canal closed to navigation).

Lock 12 has swing gates in the lower gate pockets and a drop gate in the upper pocket. As with Locks 9 and 10, visible evidence indicates that these locks were built originally with all four swing gates. The lock measures 104'9.5" overall. Rock outcrops on the berm side that are exposed above and below locks—as is the case here—indicate that the lock was built on bedrock rather than on wood cribbing. The canal prism is 70' wide from Lock 12 to Lock 14.

9.30 Capital Beltway (I-495) bridges; upstream span goes directly over Lock 13.

LOCK 13, SEVEN LOCKS

9.37 Access: Lock 10 at mile 8.79. Lock 13 is located directly under I-495.

In his 1833 report to Congress, Capt. William McNeill of the Topographical Bureau noted that the lock wall facing stones are "granite from the country. . . transported by land 4 1/3 mi. with the exception of the coping and the hollow quoin which are from Seneca." The canal is a straight line from the head of Lock 12 to Lock 14. The original breast wall was removed in 1877 preparatory to rebuilding the upper pocket for a drop gate; but if this was done, the breast wall was later rebuilt at the head of the pocket, and regular swing-type (miter) gates were installed.

Of the canal locks below Seneca, this lock alone shows no evidence of having had masonry culverts around the upper gate pockets. It is also the shortest lock, being only 90'3" between gate pockets. Note that both sets of lock gates are long gates, with the breast wall at the upper end of the upper gate pocket. Stones in this lock are evenly spaced in height, with all 12 courses of stones being

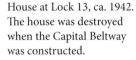

House at Lock 13, ca. 1942. The house was destroyed when the Capital Beltway was constructed.

12" thick. The upstream coping stone of the lower berm gate pocket is inscribed "W. H. Davis" (likely William John Hamilton Davis, who was initially a lock-tender at Lock 12 and then at this lock) with dates 14 Sept. 1923 through 1932 (one per year). On the same stone is a stylized rose with leaves and initials "S. D." (perhaps his brother Samuel Davis, who also worked for the canal company, sometimes as a locktender).

In 1830 work was completed on a stone lockhouse here for a locktender who would serve Locks 12, 13, and 14. It was destroyed when the Capital Beltway (I-495) was constructed. At some point during the operating period, wood-frame lockhouses were built at Locks 12 and 14. Both of those were demolished after 1939 due to their deteriorated condition.

LOCK 14, SEVEN LOCKS

9.47 Access: Lock 10 at mile 8.79; or the Carderock Recreation Area at mile 10.41. From Carderock walk downstream one mile on the towpath to Lock 14.

Lock 14 is the uppermost of the Seven Locks. Capt. McNeill reported that the lock is built of granite, "1/2 from the quarry in the country referred to, Lock # 10, the other 1/2 from a quarry 5 miles distant." According to historic records, Locks 14 and 15 were completely rebuilt between November 1871 and January 1872. All the locks were originally built 15' wide, but the width varied through the years as locks aged. As boats were 14'6" wide, locks sometimes had to be rebuilt when the walls tilted too far inward. A standard C&O Canal boat could not pass through many locks now.

Even though Lock 14 was sup-posed to have been rebuilt 1871–72, the masonry culverts around the upper lock

House at Lock 14, ca. 1938.

gates were retained, and all three culvert openings in both lock walls are open and operative. It is 93'4.5" between gate pockets.

A wooden lockhouse on the towpath side is now gone.

9.63 The extensive Naval Surface Warfare Center Carderock is visible across the canal and parkway to the east. The NSWC's expertise spans more than 40 disciplines, from electrical and mechanical engineering to computer engineering and phys-ics. The immense David Taylor Model Basin is one of the largest test facilities for the development of ship design in the world.

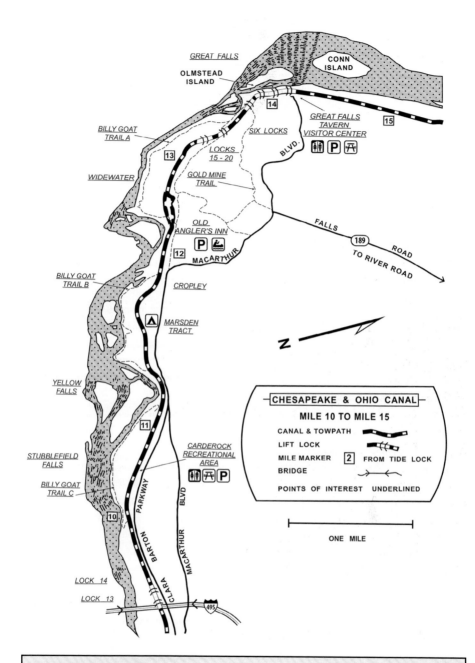

GREAT FALLS

OLMSTEAD
ISLAND

CONN
ISLAND

14

15

GREAT FALLS
TAVERN
VISITOR CENTER

BILLY GOAT
TRAIL A

SIX LOCKS

BLVD.

13

LOCKS
15 - 20

WIDEWATER

GOLD MINE
TRAIL

OLD
ANGLER'S INN

12

MACARTHUR

FALLS

189

ROAD

TO RIVER ROAD

BILLY GOAT
TRAIL B

CROPLEY

MARSDEN
TRACT

N

CHESAPEAKE & OHIO CANAL

MILE 10 TO MILE 15

CANAL & TOWPATH

LIFT LOCK

MILE MARKER   2   FROM TIDE LOCK

BRIDGE

POINTS OF INTEREST   UNDERLINED

ONE MILE

YELLOW
FALLS

11

CARDEROCK
RECREATIONAL
AREA

STUBBLEFIELD
FALLS

BILLY GOAT
TRAIL C

10

PARKWAY

BARTON

MACARTHUR   BLVD

CLARA

LOCK 14

LOCK 13

495

CAUTION! Copperheads are common in rocky (usually dry) areas, but also sometimes on the towpath itself. Rattlesnakes (Eastern timber) are very rare in the Potomac Valley. Non-venomous black rat snakes are even more common on the towpath and in adjacent trees. Also non-venomous, the northern water snake (which is sometimes mistaken for a copperhead or water moccasin) is common in swampy or watered areas of the canal.

Wildflowers

Over 1,500 species of vascular plants have been recorded in the C&O Canal National Historical Park, including over 260 non-native plant species, over 100 rare, threatened, or endangered species of plants in Maryland and the District of Columbia, and one federally endangered plant species. According to the National Park Service, the "number of rare

Bluebells on the towpath. *(Image courtesy Steve Dean)*

plants represents one of the highest concentrations of state-listed rare plants in the eastern U.S. Several species are globally rare, and some occur here because they are dependent upon special habitats and ecological conditions present along the Potomac River."

Some of the most common native wildflowers adding spring and summer color along the towpath include: spring beauty (*Claytonia virginica*), blue phlox (*Phlox divaricata*), Dutchman's breeches (*Dicentra cucullaria*), wild ginger (*Asarum canadense*), violets (*Viola papilionacea*), Jack-in-the-pulpit (*Arisaema triphyllum*), Mayapple (*Podophyllum peltatum*), bloodroot (*Sanguinaria canadensis*), and trout lily (*Erythronium americanum*).

Bluebells (*Mertensia virginica*) are quite common in the spring when hikers can find themselves strolling "bluebell alleys," especially around miles 97–105.

Other noted species: periwinkle (*Vinca minor*), gill-over-the-ground (*Glechoma hederacea*), cut-leaved toothwort or pepperroot (*Dentaria laciniata*), common mullein (*Verbascum thapsus*), coltsfoot (*Tussilago farfara*), birdfoot violet (*Viola pedata*), sessile trillium or toadshade (*Trillium sessile*), wild columbine (*Aquilegia canadensis*), Jefferson twinleaf (*Jeffersonia diphylla*), squirrel corn (*Dicentra canadensis*), redbud (*Cercis canadensis*), skunk cabbage (*Symplocarpus foetidus*), Star-of-Bethlehem (*Ornithogalum umbellatum*), garlic mustard (*Alliaria officinalis*), star chickweed (*Stellaria pubera*), red trillium or wakerobin (*Trillium erectum*), speedwell (*Veronica scutellata*), dwarf larkspur (*Delphinium tricorne*), dame's rocket (*Hesperis matronalis*), daisy fleabane (*Erigeron annuus*), dogwood (*Cornus florida*), celandine or wood poppy (*Stylophorum diphyllum*), grape hyacinth (*Muscari botryoides*), and spiderwort (*Tradescantia virginiana*).

The paw paw tree (*Asimina triloba*) thrives along the Potomac. It flowers in the spring and its fruit—called a cross between a banana and mango—can often be found in the early fall on the towpath.

Good sources for learning more about wildflowers along the canal are *Potomac Pathway: A Nature Guide to the C&O Canal* by Napier Shelton (Schiffer Publishing, 2011) and the C&O Canal Association's *Guide to Spring Wildflowers on the Towpath*, a document with photographs and notes based on a spring 2009 hike from Cumberland to Georgetown, found at www.candocanal.org/articles/flowers.pdf.

9.67 Concrete waste weir. The broad grassy area to left is the site of the lower of two CCC camps.

9.92 Carderock Pivot Bridge remains. This bridge was constructed in 1941 by the CCC for better access to its camps. Previously, access was by road from MacArthur Boulevard and passing under the canal through the Rock Run Culvert at mile 8.93. A pivot-type bridge was needed as the NPS was operating barges in the canal through the Carderock area to support the CCC work.

Billy Goat Trail Section C, 1.7 miles, starts here. Billy Goat Trail is a series of three blue-blazed side trails over the next five miles, with interesting views of the river. No bicycles are allowed on these trails, and dogs are not allowed on Section A, the most difficult.

10.02 Culvert #14, 4' span.

10.16 Stubblefield Falls, a succession of rapids in a narrow neck of the river, is visible in the winter. The wide pool ahead is a turning basin in the canal. It is a favorite haunt of turtles, which sit on logs protruding from the water and quietly slide off when disturbed, garnering them the "sliders" nickname.

10.34 A gated service road leads downhill to connect with the Carderock entrance road.

10.41 Carderock Recreational Area. (38.974560, -77.201968) Access: From the Capital Beltway (I-495) in Maryland take Exit 41, Clara Barton Pkwy. west toward Carderock. Take the Carderock exit off the parkway (at the Naval Surface Warfare Center). Turn left at the top of the exit and cross over the parkway. Follow the Carderock signs down the access road, passing through a modern road culvert under the canal. The recreation area extends to mile 10.95, with extensive picnicking facilities, toilets, and drinking water. Several short side trails in the next half mile lead to various parking areas at Carderock. A large covered pavilion with a fireplace can be reserved by calling the C&O Canal NHP permit office, at 301-767-3731; visit www.nps.gov/choh for current information.

10.42 Culvert #15, 11'9" span, 6' rise. Field pussytoes (*Antennaria neglecta*), pale violet (*Viola striata*), and wild ginger (*Asarum canadense*) have been noted below the road culvert.

10.96 Sign for the upper end of Billy Goat Trail Section C, and short path to the uppermost parking lot at Carderock.

11.10 The towpath continues directly on a river escarpment atop a high masonry wall. The towpath embankment on this level where it encroaches on the river is protected by a well-built slope wall of dry-laid masonry. Aside from the strength it provided, it was described in 1831 as the "most convenient and economical way to dispose of stone." Sheer rock walls and vistas up and down the turbulent river channel make this an extremely spectacular viewpoint. To canallers it was known as "Highwalls."

11.44 The broad path to the river is Section B of the Billy Goat Trail, leading 1.6 miles through varied, beautiful terrain: past old farms, up and down river cliffs, skirting pools and a pond, through open woods and magnificent patches of wildflowers. The loop ends after a sharp ascent from the south end of Sherwin Island to Cropley, Maryland.

11.52 Marsden Tract Group Campsite. (38.978697, -77.215888) A footbridge across the canal leads about 0.3 mile uphill to MacArthur Boulevard where there is a very small parking area (three cars maximum). Old roads to the left formerly led to farms on the plateau between the canal and river. One of these old roads, just beyond the footbridge, traverses old fields and former orchards before it passes through an area called the "Marsden Tract," on its way to the river and a connection with Billy Goat Trail. Group camping for organized scout and civic groups only is allowed by permit. Contact the C&O Canal NHP permit office at 301-767-3731. For more information visit www.nps.gov/choh/planyourvisit/camping.htm. The campsites have portable toilets; water is available in season from a water fountain on the berm side of the footbridge, but it may be turned off if water quality is poor.

Birdwatching

The C&O Canal is a superb location to study the spring and fall migrations of birds. Between 2007 and 2010 the National Park Service detected a range of 74 to 90 species of birds along the canal. (Some reports claim over 100.) Favorite spots on the lower canal include Carderock, Widewater, Pennyfield Lock, Violettes Lock, Seneca, and Sycamore Landing. The western part of the canal in Allegany County has particularly good areas for watching birdlife.

The original *Towpath Guide* included lists of sighted birds compiled 1966–69 by Peg Frankel, a lobbyist who helped the Nature Conservancy acquire sections of the C&O Canal prior to its designation as a National Park. According to a 2011 NPS resource brief, the 10 most common birds are (in order of most common): blue-gray gnatcatcher, unidentified chickadee, American goldfinch, northern cardinal, eastern tufted titmouse, red-eyed vireo, acadian flycatcher, Carolina wren, common grackle, and white-breasted nuthatch.

Birds considered as "watchlist" species include: cerulean warbler, Kentucky warbler, prairie warbler, prothonotary warbler, wood thrush, and worm-eating warbler. Also of conservation concern and considered "stewardship" species: acadian flycatcher, brown thrasher, Carolina wren, eastern towhee, indigo bunting, Louisiana waterthrush, pine warbler, red-bellied woodpecker, red-shouldered hawk, white-eyed vireo, yellow-throated vireo, and yellow-throated warbler.

See www.nps.gov/choh/upload/C-O-Canal-Bird-Checklist2.pdf for a downloadable checklist.

11.75 Previous site of Potomac Granite Mill and wharf on berm. The two-story mill operated in the early 1900s, cutting building stone from pits in the vicinity.

11.76 Culvert #17, 8' span, 5' rise, carries a stream from a flat wooded area; constructed in 1828–30 of granite gneiss.

12.26 Culvert #18, 8' span, constructed in 1830.

12.27 Path to canoe launching site in river. The upper end of Billy Goat Trail, Section B, comes in here.

CROPLEY

12.28 (38.981897, -77.226205) Access: From the Capital Beltway (I-495) in Maryland take Exit 41, Clara Barton Pkwy. west toward Carderock. Once on the parkway go approximately 1.5 miles and turn left at a t-intersection onto MacArthur Blvd. Continue 1.1 miles and turn left into the large parking lot opposite Old Angler's Inn. (Do NOT park in the inn's parking lot.) Walk downhill to a lower parking lot and cross a footbridge over the canal to reach the towpath. There is an overflow parking lot on the left, about 0.1 mile farther along MacArthur Blvd.

The Old Angler's Inn is a popular restaurant in the area. (301-365-2425, www.oldanglersinn.com) It has a certain notoriety, however, as on a wet, cold day in May 1961 on a C&O Canal Association hike, author Tom Hahn, Senator Paul Douglas, Justice William O. Douglas, Secretary of the Interior Stewart Udall, and several other hikers were ordered into one particular area of the restaurant or told to leave altogether by the then-owner, either because they were wet and muddy, or because they were consuming their sack lunches inside while ordering nothing but beverages.

The "Berma" Road (considered a corruption of Berm Road), 1.4 miles long, accessed from either the lower or upper parking lot, is a pleasant alternative to the towpath between Cropley and the guard gate above Lock 16. The road runs on top of the conduit carrying water from the Potomac River at Great Falls to Washington, D.C. It is shaded and rock bluffs offer a variety of interesting rock formations. Among the rock debris of a quarry (or mine) are iron rails that probably led to the canal. The Berma Road offers great views of Widewater and the towpath. Cross back to the towpath at the guard gate bridge at mile 13.74 if you use the road.

12.36 The concrete wall on the berm side of the canal is likely a remnant of a loading dock of the Potomac Granite Company, as a rock crusher was located near here.

12.38 A towpath wall blocked off Culvert #18 in the early 1900s. Several gold mines were in operation after the Civil War on the hillside above the canal in this area. The Maryland Mine operated until ca. 1940.

12.47 Fine view of Sherwin Island in the Potomac. (Also known as Cupid's Bower.)

12.51 Interesting rock folds just ahead and at mile 12.60. Synclines and anticlines can be seen in rocks throughout the Great Falls area where the canal, roads, quarries, and former mining operations have exposed many hidden formations.

12.60 This section of the towpath has been a trouble spot for years. The towpath here and at Widewater ahead is restored, having been an area of major breaks from Hurricane Agnes in June 1972, the flood of 1996, and most recently, Hurricane Hanna in the fall of 2008.

WIDEWATER

12.62 Access: Old Angler's Inn at mile 12.28.

Widewater provides one of the most attractive scenes along the canal. With its scenic coves and tiny rock islands it offers excellent boating. It is about 400' wide x 0.75 mile long, with a maximum depth of about 65'. An old high river channel on the north side of Bear Island was used here instead of constructing the canal in the cliffs. Stone walls sporadically support the towpath to the concrete bridge at mile 13.00. Several benches in this section provide excellent resting spots with views of Widewater.

12.69 Billy Goat Trail Section A, 1.7 miles, begins here. This section is a rugged and challenging hike with some rock-scrambling required. Dogs and bicycles are not allowed.

> CAUTION! Section A of the Billy Goat Trail covers extremely difficult and dangerous terrain. It is not for small children or inexperienced hikers. Hikers should be properly outfitted, including appropriate footwear.

13.00 Waste weir and concrete bridge, built 1939, over waste weir flume. The towpath in the Widewater area was known as "Log Wall" by old canallers because of the log cribs supporting it. The cribs washed out in the 1924 flood.

13.20 Side trail, an emergency cut-off trail leading to Billy Goat Trail Section A.

13.37 The towpath crosses a rock causeway across an old dammed-off channel of river on the first of two wooden bridges. The 100'-long, 15'-high causeway and guard wall were built about 1850. The towpath ahead is on a boardwalk over bedrock. Moss and lichen, prickly pear cactus, Virginia pear, red cedar, white and green ash, and stag sumac were abundant on the lake shore in years past.

LOCK 15, SIX LOCKS

13.45 Access: Lock 20 at Great Falls Tavern (mile 14.30) or from Old Angler's Inn (mile 12.28) via the towpath. End of Widewater. Lock 15 is the first of a series of locks known as "Six Locks," located in a one-mile stretch.

The lock is located in an old river channel that begins at the foot of Lock 18 and continues down through Widewater, an area much subjected to floods high enough to overtop the towpath above the guard gate. Large, stone-filled, wooden cribs on the berm side of the lock were replaced 1938–42 by a concrete wall with a 30' spillway, 1' below the top of the lock. The cribs were simulated below the dam on each side of the spillway to preserve the historic appearance.

Historic records show this lock was completely rebuilt November 1871–January 1872, and its appearance shows evidence of even more rebuilding. Much of the upper extension wall and wings were replaced with concrete in the 1938–42 CCC restoration, and part was plastered over with a special mixture of sand and cement to simulate the red sandstone of the original stones. The wooden floors of the gate pockets were also replaced with concrete during that period. All the locks in the Six Locks series were originally built of red sandstone boated down the river from Seneca.

This lock was badly damaged in the 1972 flood, as was Lock 16. The lock was built with masonry culverts around the upper gate pockets, and the masonry culverts in the berm lock wall may still be operable, while those on the towpath side have been stoned up. The NPS rebuilt Lock 15 in 1976.

Two lockhouses have existed at Lock 15. The first was built of stone on the towpath side of the lock, opposite the center of the lock. It was demolished in an 1889 flood. About ten years later a frame lockhouse was built on the berm, but it was destroyed by a fire within a few years. (It was still standing in 1900, as was the lock shanty—a weather shelter to protect the locktender while waiting for boats.)

A canal boat enters Lock 15, ca. 1900.

LOCK 16, SIX LOCKS

13.63 Access: Lock 20 at Great Falls Tavern (mile 14.30) or from Old Angler's Inn (mile 12.28) via the towpath or Berma Road.

As was Lock 15, this lock was built on the west bank of the old river channel. The bypass flume is 40'–60' wide. The lower berm wing wall extended to the face of the spillway, which is constructed of stone-filled wooden cribs as in Lock 15. These were replaced 1938–42 as described for Lock 15. This lock is 91' between gate pockets. The NPS rebuilt Lock 16 in 1976. The lock was originally faced with cut Seneca red sandstone.

Note inscriptions in the coping stone at mid-lock on the towpath side that read "J. W. Fisher, Jr." and "W. Spong." Fisher was a canal superintendent for the Georgetown district. Willard (known as Willie) Spong was the son of boat captain Samuel Spong from Sharpsburg, Maryland. In Georgetown on September 12, 1916, 11-year-old Willie—along with his younger sister Sarah, age 6, and his older brother John, age 13—died as a result of an accident aboard his father's boat. On the upper berm lock wall coping is a canal boat carving.

The lockhouse here was erected in 1837 probably from improved specifications adopted in 1836, rather than the original lockhouse specifications adopted in 1828. There are two rooms on each floor in this two-and-a-half story stone house (18' x 30'1"), with fireplaces at each end of the building. In a ca. 1900 photo there was a small porch at the front doorway.

House at Lock 16 in the early 1900s.

The Spong Family Tragedy

Canalling was often a family business. The father was boat captain, and his family was the crew. Usually, the mother cooked, cleaned, and helped steer the boat, while the children tended the mules. During the canalling season, their boat was their home, and the tight 12' x 12' cabin functioned as living quarters.

Samuel Spong of Sharpsburg, Maryland, captained Boat No. 74 with his family beside him on the long trips from Cumberland to Georgetown. On September 10, 1916, the Spongs reached Georgetown with their typical load of coal. Captain Spong locked out of the canal through the tide lock and tied up for the night alongside a seawall of the Capitol Traction Company power plant, where the freight was to be unloaded the next day. At that spot a steam pipe came straight out of the power plant's wall, and an elbow joint turned the pipe down into the river.

Early the next morning Captain Spong and his oldest son Thomas were on the boat getting ready to unload. Spong's wife, Nina, was also awake, but three other children— Willie, age 11, Sarah, age 6, and John, age 13—were asleep in the cabin. Without warning, an eruption of steam from the power plant came with such force that it blew the elbow joint off the pipe and shot into the cabin. Nina Spong rushed in to save her children but was herself badly scalded. All three children died that day.

A full story on the tragedy by Susan Fauntleroy, Park Ranger, C&O Canal National Historical Park, can be found at: www.nps.gov/choh/historyculture/thespongchildren.htm.

Three of the Spong family children died as the result of a tragic accident on the canal.

GUARD GATE, GUARD WALL, AND WINCH HOUSE

13.74 Access: Lock 20 at Great Falls Tavern (mile 14.30) or from Old Angler's Inn (mile 12.28) via the towpath or Berma Road.

In the area from Lock 18 down through Widewater (1.5 miles) the canal was built in an old river channel. In the highest floods, the river would overtop the towpath and flow through the channel into the Widewater area. To prevent flood waters from reaching the vulnerable Widewater area, in 1852 the canal company constructed a stone and earth guard wall, 15' high x 500' wide, stretching from the hillside on the berm to the river. The 13'-long guard gate was constructed to allow the canal to pass through the guard wall in normal conditions. However, during extreme floods heavy planks would be dropped down between the gate abutments to block the water both in the prism and that overtopping it, and force the excess water to flow along the guard wall and back into today's river channel. The structure on top of the gate is a winch house, which holds the planks and the mechanisms for lowering them into place. The current winch house was built around 2010; the original one was destroyed by the 1889 flood. Alongside the winch house is a footbridge providing access between the towpath and Berma Road.

13.83 Just above the guard gate is the upper trailhead of Billy Goat Trail Section A. This popular hiker's route, laid out by the YMCA Red Triangle Club between 1918 and 1920, is a spectacular alternate route to the towpath. The trail is very rugged (allow at least three hours), and hikers should be properly outfitted. In a short distance, the trail becomes rocky, with steep climbs and descents. The land on the river side of the towpath is Bear Island. Wildlife, wildflowers, and geologic formations along the trail are outstanding. The view is so exceptional that it must be experienced to be believed. Winds whipping up and down Mather Gorge (named for Stephen T. Mather, first NPS director) provide natural air-conditioning for the summer hiker.

13.85 The towpath comes onto the top of a heavy slope wall known as Mary's Wall. It is 900' long and in places as high as 70', with a sheer drop to an arm of the river in a deep curving gorge—a spectacular view. In the original construction, rows of plank piling were driven deep inside high walls such as this. A major wall stabilization project was completed in 2011–12.

13.88 Catfish Hole in the river and several fine viewpoints are reached by trails leading to the river. The cliffs across the channel are on Rock Island, which can be reached on foot at low river stages. Extreme care must be exercised. This area offers fine views across the wild, rocky terrain of the Potomac below the falls to the Virginia shore.

13.91 A structure with blow-off valves for releasing excess water in the Washington Aqueduct is visible on the berm hillside during the winter months. Beyond is a rocky promontory affording a magnificent view, reached by trail from the berm side of Lock 19.

LOCK 17, SIX LOCKS

13.99 Access: Lock 20 at Great Falls Tavern (mile 14.30). (Note: Lock 17 is just upstream from NPS milepost 14.)

Lock 17 has 90'10" between lock gate pockets. The canal between Locks 17 and 18 widens into a spacious pool 300' long x 100' wide. This lock was known to boatmen as the "Crooked Lock." Watch for bald eagles which nest on Conn and Olmstead Islands.

14.05 The Olmstead Island Bridges lead across river channels to the Great Falls Vista, one of the most spectacular sites along the towpath. The trail-bridge system here and an earlier one near Lock 20 washed out in major floods. The current series of bridges is designed with removable railings to prevent flood debris collecting against them and adding stress to the structures. While it is anticipated that these bridges may well survive major floods, the difficulty in building sustainable structures such as these testifies to the frailty of man in attempting to overcome the overwhelming power of natural forces. The current trail is fenced to prevent damage to the fragile island habitat. The numerous fish ladders in the river were built 1885–92, but were not successful in causing shad, striped bass, and white perch (which historically had been reported in the pools below the falls) to migrate above the falls, as had been hoped. Despite thousands of visitors each year, an abundant wildlife population calls the falls area home.

14.08 A short wing dam 100' above the lock diverted water into a feeder ditch along the rock-walled outer side of the towpath to a now-bricked in culvert under the towpath 16' below Lock 18. This structure would have provided the canal below Lock 18 with additional water when necessary. The feeder dam was damaged by an 1837 flood, and the system seems to have been abandoned subsequently.

LOCK 18, SIX LOCKS

14.09 Access: Lock 20 at Great Falls Tavern (mile 14.30).

The lock rests on solid rock and was built originally of Seneca red sandstone with a backing of rubble granite. Locks 18, 19, and 20 are located just below the break of the Great Falls of the Potomac. An old river channel once divided near the foot of this lock, with one channel being used for the canal below and the other represented by the river's current channels. Historically, the towpath was often washed out here, turning the canal into a river channel once again. This necessitated the building of the guard wall and guard gate at mile 13.74. Lock 18 is 91'2.5" between gate pockets. Again, as with most of the locks

Lock 18 in the early 1900s. The lockhouse burned ca. 1930.

from Georgetown to Seneca, this lock was built with masonry bypass channels around the upper gates. The bypass flume is 10' wide with low, dry-laid, battered native stone walls. The flume discharges over a stone wall. Bypass flumes vary in design as locktenders had considerable leeway in the manner in which they maintained flumes.

Ruins of a one-and-a-half story stone lockhouse are 6' east of the bypass flume. The house measured 18' x 30'2" and was built of native stone with some Seneca red sandstone. The lockhouse was one of original stone lockhouses on the canal, completed in 1830 and built according to 1828 specifications. It remained in good condition until it burned in 1930. A lock shanty previously existed on the berm side of the lock at the upper end. Uphill from Lock 18 is the turnaround loop historically used by trolleys of the former Washington & Great Falls Railway & Power Company. The company opened its rail line from Wisconsin Avenue at Bradley Lane in 1913. Operations ceased in 1921. On the hillside are old Civil War gun emplacements and the ruins of the Maryland Gold Mine. The spectacular anthills of the Allegheny mound ant have been seen along the hillside trails. Note: They will bite if their mound is disturbed.

LOCK 19, SIX LOCKS
14.17 Access: Lock 20 at Great Falls Tavern (mile 14.30).

The lock was built of Seneca red sandstone, probably on bedrock. Some of the present coping stones are possibly taken from older structures, as one

56

stone is inscribed "May 24, 1817." (To see it one must stand on the berm side and look across the lock.) The lock is 90'11" between gate pockets and 139' in overall length. The lock has a 9' lift (1' higher than normal), and the towpath has a rather sharp mule rise. Deep rope grooves are along the lower towpath wing copings and the top of the exposed end of the wing wall.

The only structure known to have existed at Lock 19 was a board and batten shanty seen in ca. 1900 photos. Originally it was intended that the locktender in House #12 (the present Crommelin House or Great Falls Tavern Visitor Center) would tend both Locks 19 and 20. That there never was an original stone lockhouse here is supported by the lockhouse numbering system—House #12 being at Lock 20 and House #11 at Lock 18. Sometime after ca. 1875, the first frame dwelling north of Lock 19 was used as a residence by a locktender.

Around 1900, the lower end of the bypass flume was crossed by a narrow board-decked log footbridge with log railings. Modern wooden bridges across the lock and bypass flume now lead to a berm road. Just across these bridges the Lock 19 Loop Trail begins, indicated by a concrete marker. Slightly farther upstream and just below Great Falls Tavern, the Gold Mine Trail is indicated by another concrete marker.

> The 800-acre Great Falls National Park offers spectacular views of the Potomac from the Virginia shore. Access: From the Capital Beltway (I-495) take Exit 44 west, Rt. 193, Old Georgetown Pike. Go 4.5 miles to a 4-way junction with a sign for the park and turn right. Go 1.0 mile to the park entrance station. This is an NPS fee area, 9200 Old Dominion Dr., McLean, VA, 22102, 703-285-2965, www.nps.gov/grfa/. To view Great Falls from the Maryland shore, see Lock 20 at mile 14.3.
>
> This is the site of George Washington's Patowmack Company canal to bypass the Great Falls, built 1755–1802. Remains of a head gate (upstream from the visitor center), the prism of the canal, and remains of five locks (at the downstream end of the mile-long canal route) can be seen along the line of the trail that follows the canal.

LOCK 20 (Tavern Lock), SIX LOCKS

14.30 (39.001748, -77.246836) Access: From the Capital Beltway (I-495), take Exit 41, Clara Barton Pkwy. westbound and continue 1.8 miles to a T-intersection where the parkway ends. Turn left onto MacArthur Blvd. and go 2.3 miles to a 3-way junction at the entrance to Great Falls. Turn left and go 1.2 miles downhill to the entrance station. This is an NPS fee area.

Lock 20 is the uppermost of the Six Locks. One of the most popular locks on the canal, it is directly in front of Great Falls Tavern Visitor Center, near the head of the Great Falls of the Potomac. The visitor center is open Wednesday–Sunday, 9 a.m. to 4:30 p.m. (closed Thanksgiving, Christmas, and New Year's

Day). Exhibits, concessions, restrooms, and water are available. The Charles Fenton Mercer, a replica of a canal packet (passenger) boat, operates between April and October (not operable in low water). The approximately one hour mule-pulled boat trip departs from the dock on the canal berm just below the tavern and locks through Lock 20 on its way upstream and on return. Historical narration and entertainment is provided during the trip. C&O Canal NHP Great Falls Tavern Visitor Center, 11710 MacArthur Blvd., Potomac, MD 20854, 301-767-3714, www.nps.gov/choh.

There are numerous short trails in the Great Falls area, both upstream and downstream from the tavern. Trail leaflets are available in the visitor center. The most detailed map of these trails is the Potomac Appalachian Trail Club Map D, December 2011 edition, available for sale in the visitor center or at www.patc.net.

The lock was originally built of Seneca red sandstone but has been extensively repaired with limestone, granite, concrete, and brick. A pipe bypass lies under the brick patio in front of the tavern. Originally this was an open trough-type bypass flume with a bridge over it for pedestrians. The lock is 91' between the lock gate pockets and 142'2" in overall length.

Once visible in the river were the remains of a triangular stone-filled wooden crib. This was a support or pier for an old semi-suspension bridge to viewpoints for the falls. The timbers for the crib were said to be timber supports from the Maryland Gold Mine on the hillside near the intersection of MacArthur Boulevard and Falls Road. The original bridge was erected ca. 1880 to Conn Island from a point abutting the towpath at the southern end

Great Falls Tavern at Lock 20.

of Lock 20. The bridge was destroyed in the 1936 flood and another built and subsequently lost in a succeeding flood. Access to the Maryland viewpoint was not available until the network of bridges and trails below Lock 18 was developed many years later.

In 1869 Howard Garrett built a feed store on the towpath side of the canal near the northern end of Lock 20. The building was replaced by a larger structure in 1879 and razed in 1910. Two small buildings—a mule stable and a feed house or barn, built ca. 1900 and razed ca. 1913—stood 350' north of Lock 20 on the towpath. In 1879 the canal company had a telephone line installed from Georgetown to Cumberland, a distance of 184 miles (plus 16 miles of branch lines to houses or officers of the canal company and to major shippers). It had 48 telephone instruments, and for a brief time was the longest commercial telephone line in the world. One instrument of this private industrial telephone system was installed in Garrett's store ca. 1879. A small clapboard lock shanty stood at the northeast corner of Lock 20 until ca. 1939.

Great Falls Tavern (Crommelin House)

Undoubtedly one of the most outstanding habitable structures on the canal, this building has experienced a long and colorful career as a locktender's house, a tavern, a hotel, and even as a private club. It is now an NPS Visitor Center for the C&O Canal National Historical Park and offers exhibits, interpretive programs, and guided walks suitable to the season.

The lockhouse (historically #12) as originally built was placed under contract in 1828 and was probably finished in 1829. The two-story north and south wings were added by late 1831. Plastering with "a composition of Sand, common lime if necessary, and Shepherdstown cement" for the exterior of the building and erection of "a porch in front of the stone center of the house" were authorized in 1831. Slatted shutters (Venetian blinds) were added in 1832, and the structure was painted in September 1832—the date when the enlarged structure seems to have been completed.

An 1831 report of Colonels John Abert and James Kearney of Topographic Engineers stated: "At this lock we found an excellent hotel kept by Mr. Fenlon. The house is built upon the ground of the company, and with company's funds, and is a necessary and great accommodation to those who visit this interesting work." W. W. Fenlon was the locktender of both Locks 19 and 20 in addition to being a tavern keeper and seems to have had some kind of supervisory responsibility for the rest of the Six Locks as well.

Soon after its completion, this structure was named "Crommelin House," after the Dutch banking family that made loans to the federal government that allowed the federal district cities (Washington, Georgetown, and Alexandria) to fulfill their commitments to purchase approximately $1.5 million in C&O Canal Company stock. During the second and third quarters of the 19th century, the house at Great Falls served as a hotel or tavern and lockhouse and sometimes as both. Beginning in August 1848 until after the Civil War, the canal company ruled that the locktender at Great Falls could not sell intoxicating liquors. In September 1849 the canal company ruled that Crommelin House should be used as a lockhouse for the locktender of Locks 19 and 20, perhaps de-emphasizing the role of the structure as a tavern. In June 1851 the canal company allowed the "Ball Room" (north wing of the first floor) to be rented as a grocery store. In January 1858 Henry Busey, tender of Locks 19 and 20, was allowed to re-establish a hotel or "ordinary" at Crommelin House for the accommodation of visitors to Great Falls. Beginning in 1853, the construction of the line of the Washington Aqueduct affected life at Great Falls considerably, and by 1861, Crommelin House had been damaged by the construction.

In 1830 two hundred dollars were allotted specifically for a kitchen in the house. In 1876 a separate frame kitchen was erected near the east end of the south wing by Howard A. Garrett, who leased what was then known as the Great Falls House. Around 1929 William A. Case replaced the kitchen built by Garrett with another frame kitchen (now gone) in the same location.

Fences, walks, and porches have undergone many changes during the existence of the Great Falls Tavern. There have been various buildings in the tavern area through the years. A carpenter and repair shop existed in various forms to the north, from the beginning of the canal era to ca. 1939. Several other frame structures were associated with construction of the Washington Aqueduct between 1852 and 1863 and were then razed between 1874 and 1880. The existing brick and stone residence on the hill above the tavern belonging to the Washington Aqueduct was begun in 1874 and completed in 1877. The stone gatehouse of the Washington  Aqueduct opposite the northeast corner of the tavern was begun in 1853 and completed in 1877. Most famous (or perhaps infamous) of the buildings associated with the construction of the Washington Aqueduct was a large one-and-a-half story frame structure north of the tavern and near the present traffic circle that was originally used as a barracks for laborers on the aqueduct. From the end of the Civil War to 1878 it was occupied and used by Richard Jackson, who maintained a notorious saloon and café there. Jackson's establishment was conveniently located just outside canal company property, where the sale of intoxicating liquors was strictly prohibited, so Jackson fell heir to a lucrative canal patronage.

Howard Garrett built three houses on the berm bank south of the tavern between 1883 and 1884. The first was a frame house, the second a log cabin used as a lockhouse for the Lock 20 locktender. The third was a frame house used as a lockhouse for the Lock 19 locktender. Other buildings stood in the area at various times but, like these, are now all gone.

14.33 A masonry overfall or spillway (now covered over) built 1882–83, 70' long, 12' wide, extended from the upper towpath wing wall of Lock 20 to the lower wall of the waste weir just ahead. Photos of later operating years of the canal show the overfall in use with water 1' below the top of the coping stones of Lock 20— the normal operating level of water in the canal. While tow animals walked through water, the mule driver walked along an elevated board on the river side of the overfall.

14.34 Stone and concrete waste weir. Just upstream of the weir is an observation platform overlooking the river. The platform is atop the Army Corps of Engineers Washington Aqueduct Intake. Beyond is the crest of the Great Falls water supply dam, built 1864–67 and 1884–86, 2,800' long. It was raised from 7.5' to 10' in 1896.

14.36 Just upstream from the observation platform the blue-blazed River Trail begins and goes along the riverside for 1.0 mile, returning to the towpath at mile 15.23.

Bald eagles have nested successfully on Conn Island since 1986. No longer classified as endangered, the bird's population has steadily increased both nationwide and along the Potomac River. In addition to the Conn Island site, Napier Shelton's guidebook *Potomac Pathway: A Nature Guide to the C&O Canal* (Schiffer Publishing, 2011), notes eagles' nests at miles 1.5, 6.2, 18.2, 21.7, 29, Whites Ferry, and near Harpers Ferry.

Visitors can view the Conn Island nest from the Washington Aqueduct platform (see mile 14.34) or the blue-blazed River Trail (see mile 14.36) accessed from the Great Falls Visitor Center. For more information visit www.nps.gov/choh/naturescience/baldeagles.htm.

14.50 On June 12, 1861, a company of District of Columbia Volunteers, part of Col. Charles P. Stone's Rockville Expedition, was posted along the canal to guard the fords and ferry crossings in the vicinity of Great Falls. They were the first Union troops to guard this site.

15.23 Upstream end of the blue-blazed River Trail.

15.26 Culvert #21 (Cool Spring Branch), 8' span. Further upstream on Cool Spring Branch is a shaft of the Ford Gold Mine, one of several opened in the hills on the berm following the Civil War. Gold was known in the vicinity prior to this, but the years 1867–1916 saw the greatest activity here. An extensive network of trails threads through the area of gold mine shafts and adits (entries). The Ford Mine Trail leading from the upper end of the parking lot is a good starting point. Gold mine shafts are dangerous and should not be entered.

15.63 The flat area on the berm is the location of the old Sandy Landing, reached by taking Sandy Landing Road from River Road.

15.85 Culvert #22, 8' span, with a Seneca red sandstone arch that carries a stream from a ravine with fine, mature woods. Note the unusual variety of vines and

heights they attain. During summer months, trumpet vines can be seen bloom-
ing 40'–50' up in the trees. A path leads 200' to the riverbank opposite the lower
end of Bealls Island (formerly Trammel Island) with numerous small islands
downstream.

15.98 Intake of Rockville Water Plant.

16.30 Attractive sheer rocks on the berm.

16.43 More rock-walled cliffs on the berm. The towpath is directly on the riverbank.
Lock Island begins in the river.

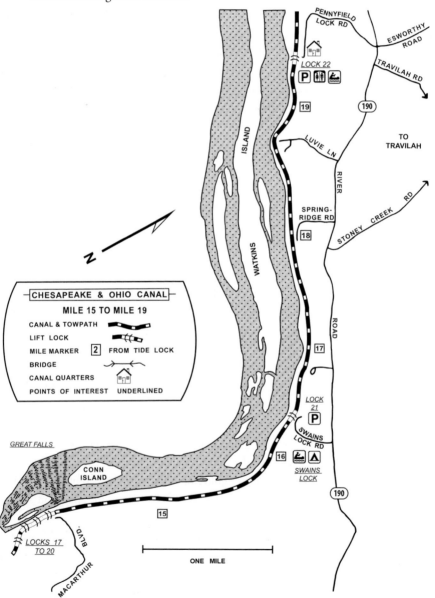

LOCK 21 (Swains Lock)

16.64 (39.031634, -77.243531) Access: From the Capital Beltway (I-495), take Exit 39, Rt. 190, River Rd. west. Go 3.5 miles into the town center of Potomac, Maryland, and continue for 2.2 miles to a left turn onto Swains Lock Rd. This is a well-signed but obscure turn, easy to miss. Go 0.3 mile downhill to the parking lot.

The lock (formerly known as "Oak Spring Lock") is built of Seneca red sandstone, boated down 6.3 miles from Seneca. The original facing stones were pebble finished with a 2"-wide ax-finished border. It is 90'7" between gate pockets. The lock was built with masonry culverts around the upper lock gates. The stump of a lower snubbing post (there were two originally) is 7.5' away from the inner face of the towpath wall and 14'4" above the upper end of the lower gate pocket. Note the rope grooves on the lower towpath wing wall.

The original stone, one-and-a-half story lockhouse (historically #13, now Lockhouse 21) has fireplaces on the upstream end on both floors. The upstream end of the house was at some time removed (probably because of a major flood) and extended 14'6" in length. A concrete, covered bypass flume is between the lock and the house.

There is a bridge across the lock to the lockhouse that was long occupied by the Swain family. This family was associated with the canal from the construction era to the early twenty-first century.

Jesse Swain was the locktender here when the canal closed in 1924. His uncle, John Swain, was a locktender downstream at Seven Locks. A grandfather, born ca. 1817, worked on some of the original canal construction jobs. Swain's house was flooded in each of the classic floods: 1889, 1936 (when the Harpers Ferry and Shepherdstown bridges went out), 1942, and 1972.

The stream in the ravine on the berm above the lock formerly flowed under the canal through a culvert. Historic records show two additional small culverts on this level which are no longer in evidence. Oak Spring is on the berm just over the bridge across the ravine, now with a wooden cover. Culvert #23 just above the lock washed out in 1831.

> Horseback riding is permitted upstream from Lock 21 to Offut Street in Cumberland (mile 181.8.). Note: horses are not permitted in the Paw Paw Tunnel (mile 155.2), but can be ridden over it on the Tunnel Hill Trail. See: www.nps.gov/choh/planyourvisit/horsebackriding.htm.

16.64 Swains Lock Hiker–Biker Campsite. Swains Lock is the first of 31 hiker–biker campgrounds located along the towpath at irregular intervals ranging from 3–13 miles. There is a put-in/take-out on the river shore and day-use area with picnic tables and grills; the upstream end has five overnight campsites.

Camping is allowed in designated areas only. These primitive hiker-biker camps, usually intentionally located away from public road access, consist of a leveled area, fireplace, water pump, picnic table, and portable toilet. They are available on a first-come, first-served basis. Towpath users should not count on the water pumps along the canal to work or have potable water. Bring water purification tablets. See page xvi or www.nps.gov/choh/planyourvisit/camping.htm for camping regulations.

16.67 Concrete waste weir, 6' span, has date of 1906—the earliest known date of use of modern concrete on the canal. This is the site of Culvert #23, which washed out in 1831.

17.36 Beginning of the Washington Suburban Sanitation Commission Filtration Plant, which ends at mile 17.54. The modern stone-faced building ahead was built in 1968.

17.60 Cross the gas pipeline of Transcontinental Gas Pipe Line Corporation. The pipeline is part of a 10,200-mile system, extending from South Texas to New York City.

17.74 Culvert #25 (Watts Branch), 115' long, 20' span, 10' rise above spring line, arch of Seneca gray sandstone. This winding stream, with its numerous branches, drains an extensive and varied terrain five miles back from the canal. Much of the valley is now developed, and there are few trails. Opposite is Watkins Island, which includes several smaller islands around its perimeter.

17.78 Cross pipeline of Columbia Gas Transmission, which operates a 12,000-mile network.

17.98 Beginning of a mile-long stretch of beautiful cliffs with occasional houses on the crest. Along the greater part of the distance between Swains and Pennyfield Locks, the embankment on the river side of the towpath is sustained by a beautiful and well-built sloping stone wall of dry masonry.

18.86 The canal makes a sharp bend around a 70' cliff attractively decorated with cedars and pines.

19.48 The picturesque rocky berm makes a nice approach to Pennyfield Lock ahead.

LOCK 22 (Pennyfield Lock)

19.63 (39.054972, -77.290334) Access: From the Capital Beltway (I-495), take Exit 39, Rt. 190, River Rd. west. Go 3.5 miles into the town center of Potomac, Maryland, and continue another 5.4 miles, to a left turn onto Pennyfield Lock Rd.; then go 0.8 mile downhill to an extensive parking area, to both the left and right. To reach the towpath, turn left and walk through the gated road to a vehicular bridge over the canal. There are two portable toilets at the downstream end of the parking lot and two more on the berm side of the lock. A backless bench on the berm side looks downstream onto the lock.

The lock walls are built of Seneca red sandstone boated 3.5 miles down river from Seneca. At some point in the past, planks were bolted onto the coping stones on the towpath side and later were replaced with cement, raising the lock wall on that side about 8". Below inlets, the canal carried its maximum water supply that would be reduced downstream by seepage, evaporation, and the canal's current (thus necessitating the dams with their inlets periodically along the canal). This lock is the first below the inlet from Dam 2 (2.28 miles upstream), and apparently at times the flow would be sufficient to overflow the top of the lock wall creating slippery and muddy conditions on the towpath. Locks with this problem were sometimes fitted with towpath-side planking to keep overflow onto the towpath from occurring.

The lock was built with masonry culverts around the upper gates inside the lock walls. A wicket stem opening was sleeved through the concrete used in elevating the lock. This meant that the culvert in the towpath wall here was used after concrete came into general use on the canal in 1906. Where masonry culverts in the lock walls were still operable, they probably were used in conjunction with the four cast-iron wicket gates located in the bottom of the lock gates to speed the filling of the lock, and thus the time it took to lock through.

The lockhouse on the river side of the towpath is a one-and-a-half story stone house over a full basement, built of roughly coursed, greenish-gray shale except for the cut Seneca red sandstone window,

Lockhouse 22, 2014. This lockhouse is available for overnight rentals via the C&O Canal Trust Canal Quarters program. (*Image Harpers Ferry Historical Association*)

door sills, and lintels. The 18'2" x 32'2" lockhouse was seriously damaged by fire in 1935. Locktender George Pennyfield operated a warehouse here in the late nineteenth century that was washed away in the 1889 flood. This lockhouse is available for overnight rentals via the Canal Trust's Canal Quarters program, 301-745-8888, www.canaltrust.org/quarters/.

This area of the river was a favorite base for President Grover Cleveland's bass fishing expeditions. He often stayed at a white frame house (demolished in 2009) adjacent to the Pennyfield's house. Local legend has it that "Ma" Pennyfield—who cooked for the president when he was staying in the adjacent house—once called up the stairs to ask, "Mr. President, do you want your eels skunned or unskunned?"

An old quarry is located on the hill just below the lock; a Civil War outpost (said to be a signaling station) is on the hill above the lock. A put-in/take-out point exists on the river shore.

19.67 Waste weir. A 100'-long mooring basin is above the lock.

19.95 Former site of granary and landing area.

19.96 Former site of John L. DuFief's mooring basin and dock.

20.01 Culvert #30 (Muddy Branch), 16' span, 8' rise. Note: NPS milepost 20 is approximately a half mile upstream from this culvert. The sandstone arch was badly damaged in the 1972 flood. The culvert was rebuilt in 1979. Muddy Branch Ford was utilized by famed Confederate Partisan Ranger John Singleton Mosby

The Pennyfield waste weir in 2012. Waste weirs were used to drain the canal in winter and when the level needed repair. Some waste weirs were probably originally made of wood, others of stone. Concrete began to appear on the canal ca. 1906. The weirs were often built near a lock so as to provide easy access to the locktender. *(Image courtesy Steve Dean)*

on June 10, 1863, which was the first time his band of raiders crossed the Potomac. They routed a small squad of Union cavalry guarding the river near Seneca, destroyed their camp, and took a team of mules from a canal boat. The size of the culvert under the canal was large enough that the raiders could pass beneath the waterway rather than find a means to cross over it.

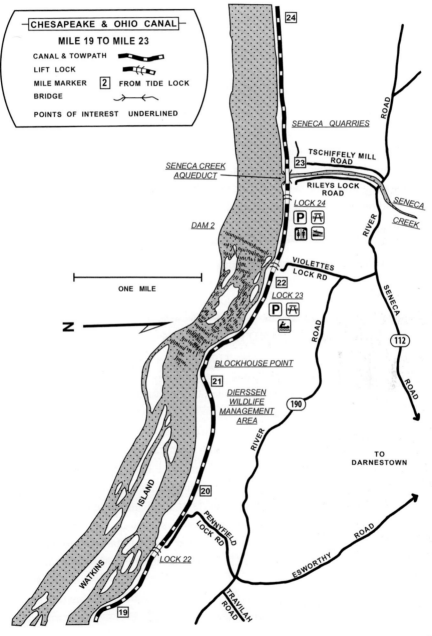

20.08 The levee on the river side marks the beginning of the first pond of Maryland's Dierssen Wildlife Management Area, serving primarily as a waterfowl sanctuary. Two ponds here are watered from the canal. The sanctuary ends at mile 20.90. (See: dnr.maryland.gov/wildlife/Publiclands/central/dierssen.asp.)

20.82 A large gas pipeline swath goes uphill and downhill from the canal/towpath.

21.02 Blockhouse Point Conservation Park features excellent views of the canal and the Potomac River. Named for the Civil War fort built by the Union army to protect the river, the 630-acre park offers natural and cultural history and over seven miles of hiking trails. 14750 River Rd. Darnestown, MD 20854, www.montgomeryparks.org/.

Opposite milestone 21 are the lovely cedar-topped cliffs depicted in Justice Douglas's book, *My Wilderness: East to Katahdin* (Doubleday, 1961). In 1968 a section of this dramatic cliff fell into the canal during the blasting for a sewer.

21.07 The towpath comes directly onto the riverbank. Rapids in the river here are popular with canoeists. Much of the embankment on this level is protected from the river by a well-laid stone wall constructed on a broad footing.

21.12 Sheer cliffs on the berm reach 150'.

21.55 End of the passage around Blockhouse Point. Here the cliffs recede, giving way to a broad, flat area on the berm.

22.02 Historic milestone, "22 MILES to W. C." (Washington City). Note: NPS milepost 22 is approximately a half mile upstream from this milestone.

22.04 Former site of Culvert #33, 6' span, which washed out in 1868 and was not rebuilt. The stream was diverted into the canal.

LOCK 23 (Violettes Lock) AND INLET LOCK 2

22.12 (39.067226, -77.328483) Access: From the Capital Beltway (I-495), take Exit 39, Rt. 190, River Rd. west. Go 3.5 miles into the town center of Potomac, Maryland, and continue for 8.2 miles, to a left turn onto Violettes Lock Rd.; go downhill 0.6 mile to a parking lot.

Anticipating that a community would develop at this location, the canal company named the site Rushville for Richard Rush, the one-time Secretary of the Treasury whose success in arranging Dutch loans for Washington, Georgetown, and Alexandria indirectly helped the canal company in one of its frequent financial crises. The prospects of Rushville becoming a viable commercial town soon faded with the westward expansion of the canal. This is now a favorite fishing and canoe launching area. A put-in/take-out for canoeing in the river is available here. There is one picnic table but no water source.

This stretch of the canal to Georgetown was re-watered during the CCC restoration project 1938–42. However, desirable water levels are often not sustained due to time and flood damage.

Alfred ("Alf" or "Ap") Violet or Violette was the last locktender here during the operating period, but his wife Kate Violette was employed as locktender in 1938 during the receivership period. It is not clear what duties locktenders had once navigation ceased in 1924, but there was likely some responsibility for oversight of canal structures and the lockhouse.

A frame lockhouse (historically #15) was constructed on the berm side of Lock 23 in 1830, but the record for it is less clear than for other houses in the early construction period. The lockhouse apparently burned in 1930, but 1939 Park Service records show a log lockhouse on a stone foundation at this location.

Violettes Lock and the inlet lock have adjoining wing walls and are very similar in construction. Violettes Lock runs N68°W in line with the canal, while the inlet lock runs N85°W, a difference of 17°. As the inlet lock is between the towpath and Lock 23, a mule crossover bridge was located over the inlet lock at the lower end. A modern vehicular bridge now crosses the inlet lock and Lock 23. Both locks are built of Seneca red sandstone, but Lock 23 is smoothly cut and evenly coursed, whereas the inlet lock is roughly cut and coursed. Both types of stones interlock at the middle of the connecting wall at their lower ends. Lock 23 was built with masonry bypass culverts around the upper lock gates; three culvert openings are visible in the bottom of each lock wall. The lock has no bypass flume, although one is shown on old maps.

Alfred and Kate Violette, the final locktenders and concessionaires at Lock 23.

This inlet lock fed water into the canal for the 17.10 miles of canal lying between Dam 2 and Lock 5, where the inlet from Dam 1 enters the canal. Historically, the inlet here was known as the "Seneca Feeder." It also served as a river lock, letting boats in and out of slackwater above Dam 2. The inlet lock was in very active use when this was briefly the only watered section of the canal (from late 1830 to the fall of 1833, when the canal opened from Dam 3—the Government Dam—above Harpers Ferry). Most of the later C&O Canal freight boats could not use this lock, since it is only 88'5" between gate pockets, though the 15' width was retained. However, boats that could operate in the river were generally smaller than the standard freighters that came to dominate the canal after it opened to Cumberland in 1850. New inlet lock gates were installed in 1988.

The numbering of this inlet lock can be confusing, as it was known as Lock 24 in 1831, when this was the upper limit of the canal. Later it became known as Inlet Lock No. 2, and the lift lock at Seneca upstream became Lock 24. Sometime after the original construction, the top of the inlet lock was elevated 39" on the upper end, probably at the same time the top of the wall of Lock 23 was also raised. Both of the locks served as guard locks to protect the canal below from high water, as they both pass through the low guard wall at this location. Lock 23 was rebuilt by the NPS 1978–79.

A portion of the Patowmack Company navigation, the Seneca Cut, a 1,320-yard channel or "skirting canal," is on the Virginia side of the river at the far end of the feeder dam. The channel is known to canoeists as the "Seneca Break" or "Washington Cut." One can make a roughly four-mile round trip using the inlet from Dam 2 to get to the river above the remnants of the dam, crossing the river there, then traversing the "Seneca Breaks" to below the rapids, and finally crossing the river again to the Maryland shore and returning to Lock 23 on the canal. The challenging run through the "Breaks" is about 1.5 miles long.

FEEDER DAM 2

22.15 The 2,500' arched stone dam (Old Seneca Dam) was originally built to raise the level of the river behind it 4'. The contract for the dam was awarded in 1828, the first year of canal construction. The dam was originally built of stone-filled wooden cribs and snaked across the river, taking advantage of small islands and rock outcrops. Much of the original dam is now reduced to scattered rubble. Some sections, such as the lower end, were rebuilt with stone capped with concrete. One stone of a later rebuilding has the date "1902." The dam, even in its current deteriorated condition, impounds a five-mile slackwater lake, 5' deep, which supports heavy recreational use of the river. Indications are that the guard dike here was elevated 3.5'–4.5' at the same time the upper ends of Inlet

Lock 2 and Lock 23 were elevated 3'4". The dike begins at the high point of land on the towpath side of the canal near the ruins of an old house and continues upstream to the head of the locks. Across the locks it continues up the berm to the turning basin at Lock 24 (at Seneca), gradually increasing to a height of 5' or more. Under the canal company it was extensively rebuilt in 1867 and 1877. The upper end of the dike was obliterated by the enlargement of a parking lot near the former lockhouse. Canoeists should be wary of the unmarked dam.

22.34 Modern concrete waste weir built in 1971. Changes in the runoff patterns of Seneca Creek and a golf course on the berm between Locks 23 and 24 dictated the need for the construction of a waste weir to dispose of storm water. At the time of the construction, a beautiful cross-section of the towpath and a portion of the canal bed liner were exposed, presenting a fine opportunity to study the original towpath and canal prism construction here. Indications are that the location of the new waste weir was the site of a historic informal overflow or "mule drink," as the towpath was 2' lower in elevation for 100' and armored with stone chips and one-man stone.

LOCK 24 (Rileys Lock) AND SENECA AQUEDUCT

22.82 (39.069167, -77.340877) Access: From the Capital Beltway (I-495), take Exit 39, Rt. 190, River Rd. west. Go 3.5 miles into the town center of Potomac, Maryland, and continue for 9.1 miles to a T-intersection. Turn left, still on River Rd.; go 0.7 mile; and just before the bridge over Seneca Creek, turn left onto Rileys Lock Rd., and go 0.8 mile to the parking area at Lock 24, Seneca Creek. Portable toilets and a water fountain are available, but the fountain is frequently turned off. There are picnic tables along the river near the boat ramp and across the aqueduct near the river.

Tschiffely Mill Road on the opposite (west) side of Seneca Creek leads to quarries and the remains of the Seneca Stonecutting Mill. The local flood in September 1971 and the flood from Hurricane Agnes in June 1972 badly damaged the Seneca Creek area downstream from River Road.

The structure here is unique for the C&O Canal in that it is a combination lift lock and aqueduct. The lock on the lower end of the aqueduct lifted the canal boats 8.5' to the level of the aqueduct that spans Seneca Creek. Both the lock and the aqueduct were built of Seneca red sandstone. The lock measures 90'4" between gate pockets. Immediately upstream of the upper gate pockets the canal bed is floored with large stones and the canal becomes the three-arch Seneca Creek Aqueduct. Several upper courses of facing stones are the same for both the lock and aqueduct, and other courses interlock. The aqueduct is 126' between the upstream and downstream wing walls. Its two piers are 7' wide. There are substantial abutments anchoring the aqueduct on either side of

Seneca Creek. Three shallow arches rest on the piers and abutments, which are 40' on center. The arches span 33' at the spring line (where the curve begins), and have a 7.5' rise from the spring line to the keystone. The upper berm wing wall of the aqueduct has a concrete waste weir 12' wide x 8.5' high that released excess water from the canal into Seneca Creek. The aqueduct was rebuilt in the winter of 1873–74.

An extremely heavy but relatively localized rain on September 11, 1971, raised the level of Seneca Creek about 8' above the slackwater level of the Potomac River, which was not significantly affected by the local storm. Seneca Creek, however, became a raging torrent with houses, boats, trees, and other debris torn loose upstream and collecting against the aqueduct with great force. The debris blocked the east and middle arches, after which the west arch took the brunt of the heavy objects battering the structure. Eventually that arch collapsed, leaving only five upper courses of stone in the upstream parapet. The stabilization that followed has prevented further flood damage, including the flood following Hurricane Agnes in June 1972.

Note the spur fences on the river side of the towpath wings, with each picket surmounted by a tall, round arrowhead. Note also the ornamental stone cap on the lower towpath wing fence on the downstream face in which "1889 June 2" is cut over a horizontal line indicating the flood's high-water mark that year.

Water taxi at Lock 24 (Rileys Lock), ca. 1920.

A very well restored lockhouse, one-and-a-half stories over a full basement, is on the berm side of Lock 24. The last locktender here in the post-operating period was Mrs. John C. Riley. Local troops of the Girl Scouts of America provide interpretation on many weekends.

The Darby Mill and a warehouse were below the lock on a wide basin opposite the towpath, and a country store was across the lock on the river side of the towpath. The Trump National Golf Club is visible across the Potomac River.

In canal operating days, the canal from below Lock 35 downstream to Lock 23 was watered from the Dam 3 inlet 1.5 miles above Harpers Ferry. On August 27, 1828, the Virginia Free Press printed a bid request from contractors for the construction of the canal from Rushville (Violettes Lock) to Harpers Ferry. However, construction above Point of Rocks was stalled until a legal battle with the B&O was resolved in January 1832. Progress was noted in a letter dated November 1, 1833, from C&O Superintendent of Repairs Charles B. Fisk (one of the canal company's young engineers), reporting from Rushville: "The water from the feeder above Harpers Ferry is now within one mile of this place. . . . Boats will be able to leave Harpers Ferry in three days." On November 14 he reported by letter to Washington that boats with a two-foot draft could

Canal boat crossing the Seneca Aqueduct. Note the waste weir spilling excess water from the canal into Seneca Creek.

navigate the canal and suggested draining the canal and making repairs after Christmas. (The canal normally closed in late November or early December and would reopen in March—using the winter closure to make substantial repairs, including reconstruction of structures that required it.)

On June 12, 1862, 90-day volunteers from the District of Columbia, part of Col. Charles P. Stone's Rockville Expedition, took positions at this location to guard the river crossing, Dam 2, and the Seneca Aqueduct. They were the first Union troops to protect this section of the border.

22.88 The road across the canal goes to several points of interest: at 0.2 mile from the towpath the road forks, with the right fork leading to Tschiffely Road and the old Tschiffely Mill site 0.8 miles away at River Road. The left fork (which is partially blocked near the fork by a large boulder) leads around the edge of a swamp, formed by the silting in of a former boat basin in the canal. This is a popular area for bird watching, especially during warbler migration in the spring. On the far side of the swamp are the ruins of the Seneca Stonecutting

Several mills have been located at the site of Tschiffely Mill near the west end of the River Road bridge over Seneca Creek. Earlier mills were the Mitford Mill and (Ulton) Darbys Mill, the latter of which was acquired by W. B. Tschiffely ca. 1900. One of the early mills burned during the Civil War and was rebuilt from the timbers of the Duffief Mill, which had been located on Muddy Branch. The Tschiffely Mill operated until 1931. Water for the mill was impounded one-half mile up Seneca Creek, and carried by a flume to the head race, creating a fall of 13'. The mill was destroyed sometime after 1956. Worthington Tschiffely (son of W. B.) once said that during the migration of eels from Seneca Creek to the river, they would get into the head race in such numbers that they would interfere with the operation of the mill.

Mill, which is outside the C&O Canal NHP boundaries. Farther along the road, the hillside to the right has many old quarry openings.

22.93 The boat basin was the scene of an accident when the passenger packet *Anna Wilson*, picking up steam after passing through Rileys Lock, collided with a downstream freight boat loaded with watermelons. The steamboat sank without serious injuries to the passengers, but local people eagerly collected the watermelons floating in the basin.

23.03 End of the swamp. Quarries ahead were worked from 1774. By 1900 quarry operations had stopped because the quality of the stone had deteriorated.

Seneca Stonecutting Mill

The stonecutting mill was the center of one of the industries associated with the canal. It operated from 1837 to the early 1900s. Red (and some gray) sandstone milled here was used in many of the structures of the C&O Canal, and before that, for the Patowmack Company Canal at Great Falls, Virginia, as well as for many public buildings in Washington. Stone was boated down the river until the canal opened, after which it was transported via the canal. The stone cut in the mill was quarried elsewhere, as at Goose Creek in Virginia, Marble Quarry (above Whites Ferry), Cedar Point Quarry (near Violettes Lock), and other quarries in the immediate vicinity. Prior to the construction of the mill, masons cut stones in the quarries or at the sites to which the unfinished stones were shipped.

A water turbine, powered by canal water diverted into a mill race, rotated a shaft running through the center of the building. Belts attached to overhead pulleys transferred water power from the shaft to milling and polishing machines. Gondolas pulled by mules and pushed by men carried large stone blocks along narrow-gauge rails to the mill. Remains of the strap iron rails can be traced from a nearby quarry. The stone blocks were shaped by hammers and stone chisels before being cut by 6' x 8" toothless saws of tempered steel. An overhead pipe dripped water on the saws to keep them cool. A former workman at the mill reported that if a saw cut an inch in one hour in a three-foot square block, that was progress! By 1910 the better-quality stone from the quarries had been quarried and cut, resulting in the demise of Seneca's stone industry.

Claude W. Owen, in *History of Potomac*, *"Seneca, Once a Commercial Center" (Potomac Almanac, 1970)*, said,

When I was quite young I saw the quarry and mill in operation. They had no modern tools for quarrying. Of course no electricity for drilling the stone. I have seen a colored man sit on a large block of stone, sometimes as large as a six foot cube, with three powerfully built colored men armed with heavy sledge hammers striking in rhythm a drill the seated man held in his hands. The slightest miscalculation by either of the three meant a badly broken leg, but it never seems to have happened. The mill was powered by a large wheel propelled by the water overflow from the basin. After passing the mill wheel, the water traveled down hill to Seneca Creek, less than a hundred yards away and on to the river.

23.10 Beginning of the extensive loading wharfs and retaining walls of the quarry operations. Over the years a number of companies worked the quarries, including the U.S. government and Georgetown College.

23.33 Culvert #35 (Bull Run), 8' span. Culverts #35 to #71 were built in 1831. Across the canal bed are the foundations of an old mill on the left side of the ravine and an old quarry on the right. Quarry openings continue on the berm side of the canal for some distance. The first extensive quarrying took place in the 1780s, when the Patowmack Canal at Great Falls was under construction, and some quarrying may even have been done in the revolutionary period. Remains of stone masonry walls along the berm testify to old loading areas. The sheer

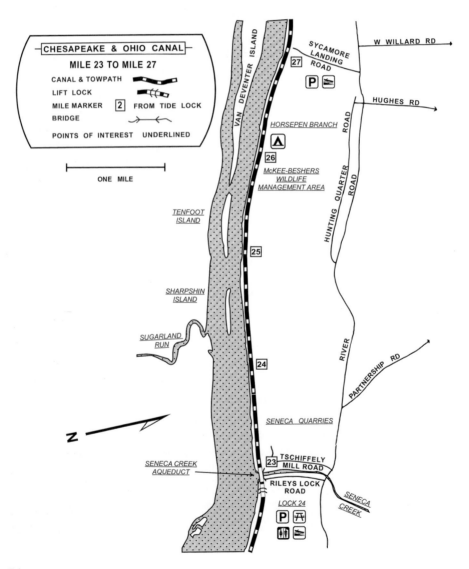

cliffs ahead are of red sandstone (Triassic), the source of stone for the Seneca Stonecutting Mill.

The level from Lock 24 to Lock 25 was known by boatmen as the "Eight Mile Level."

23.43 There is a spring on the berm side, but the canal prism here is marshy and overgrown.

23.7x Masonry walls on the berm side.

23.81 The hill on the berm side recedes as the river flat continues upstream for six miles, extending inland as much as one mile due to a southward shift of the Potomac in recent geological time. The flat is marked by numerous swampy areas where wood ducks, pileated woodpeckers, and prothonotary warblers nest. The far edge of the flat is followed by River Road.

Historically, the Seneca region played an important role in early canal company dreams, when anticipation of significant canal trade and the available water supply at Seneca Creek encouraged settlement of the area. From late 1830 until fall of 1833, the Seneca area was the head of canal navigation and enjoyed a temporary boom. However, Seneca's dreams faded as canal construction pushed up the river. In 1839, when expectation for a canal extension to Baltimore was at its height, one of the proposed routes was from Seneca to Baltimore. This "Maryland Canal" or "cross cut" canal was never built, and hopes for Seneca's development into a significant river and canal town disappeared. Seneca became a thriving little village, however, and remained famous largely because just upstream from it was the area where red Seneca sandstone was quarried, cut, and shipped via the canal for use in many of the C&O Canal structures and numerous buildings in and around Washington, including the Smithsonian Castle and Luther Place Memorial Church at Thomas Circle.

23.92 Culvert #37 (Beaver Dam Creek), 10' span. The culvert was rebuilt in 1843 and again in 1863.

Here there is a nice view of the widewater lake created by Dam 2 below Seneca. Across the Potomac River the Trump National Golf Course and the Algonkian Regional Park and Golf Course are visible for a considerable distance along this stretch of the towpath. There is a boat ramp at Algonkian Park from which watercraft are launched.

24.34–24.64 Wooded Sharpshin Island. The name aptly describes this little sliver of land in mid-Potomac. The topography of the Potomac islands changes with floods, which extend the islands downstream. A comparison of recent topographic maps with those of 80 years ago reveals considerable changes in some of the islands.

24.96–25.63 Wooded Tenfoot Island, larger than its name implies, is probably named for its elevation. The island was purchased by the Potomac Conservancy in 2001.

According to local legend a moonshine still was operated on the island during Prohibition, with the smell of fermenting mash permeating the air on both shores. Concrete ramps allowed unloading raw materials and loading the distilled product. The still was never raided, and moonshiner Earl Blatt retired to live happily ever after.

25.63–27.65 Van Deventer Island (known earlier as Gassaways Island).

25.91 McKee-Beshers Wildlife Management Area begins here. McKee-Beshers WMA has 2,000 acres of woodlands, fields, wooded bottom land, and managed wetland impoundments (green-tree reservoirs). Hunting is permitted in season. (www.dnr.state.md.us/wildlife/publiclands/central/mckeebeshers.asp)

> Though hunting in not permitted in the C&O Canal National Historical Park, be advised that the NPS has designated hunter access areas. Hunters with guns and game are allowed to cross and traverse the towpath in some places.

26.10 Horsepen Branch Hiker–Biker Campsite. The nearest road access is Sycamore Landing at mile 27.21.

26.77 Culvert #38 (Horsepen Branch), 10' span. The line of the canal from Georgetown to Cumberland was divided into three divisions of approximately 120 sections each (for a total of 368 sections). A separate contract was made for the excavation of each section, the average section being one-half mile long. Culverts were similarly identified with the numbers of the sections on which they were built, this particular one being on Section 43. Up to Harpers Ferry the canal was 60' wide at the top and 42' at the bottom, making for longer culverts than on the 50' wide canal above Harpers Ferry.

CAUTION: Opposite Culvert #38 is a very large hole in the canal prism, which is cordoned off by a fence. For safety reasons, do NOT enter the fenced-off area.

26.94 Brightwells Hunting Quarters is a 1,086-acre tract with a four-mile river frontage patented in 1695 by Richard Brightwell. The original stone boundary marker was destroyed during the building of the canal; a replacement stone is said to have been later sunk in the canal bed.

27.21 Sycamore Landing (39.074731, -77.420193) Access: From the Capital Beltway (I-495), take Exit 39, Rt. 190, River Rd. west. Go 3.5 miles into the town center of Potomac, Maryland, and continue for 9.1 miles to a T-intersection. Turn left, still on River Rd. Continue 4.8 miles and turn left on Sycamore Landing Rd. Follow 0.8 mile to parking area. There is a dirt boat ramp for small boats. This parking area provides easy access to trails in the McKee-Beshers WMA—a favored spot for bird observers.

27.65–29.86 Selden Island.

28.46 Culvert #39, 4' span. The culvert was repaired in 1985.

29.35 Culvert #41, 4' span. Culvert #40 is missing in the culvert numbering series. This indicates two streams may have been diverted into one culvert, or one stream bed may have ceased to carry water, allowing a culvert to be eliminated. This was a fairly common practice used to save money in culvert construction.

29.86 Culvert #42, (Chisel Branch and Cabin Branch), 12' span.

30.5x Chisel Branch Hiker–Biker Campsite. The nearest access is at Lock 25 (Edwards Ferry) at mile 30.84.

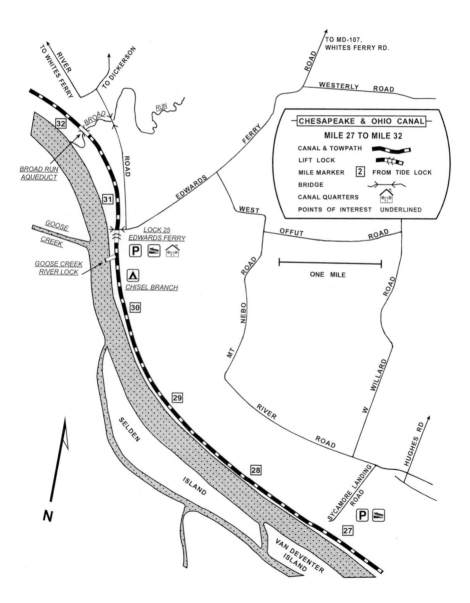

Montgomery County is entirely in the Piedmont Physiographic Province. The river is generally swift-flowing. One hundred and thirty-six islands are located in the river in this county, 101 of them being smaller than five acres. Primary shoreline woody vegetation includes sycamore, maple, willow, elm, cottonwood, white ash, green ash, hickory, walnut, paw paw, and pin oak. Principal submerged shallow water aquatic vegetation includes water willow, lizard's tail, and spatterdock.

The numerous undeveloped islands in this region and the contiguous band of relatively undisturbed shoreline woodland between the canal and the river provide large amounts of excellent habitat for numerous fur-bearing species, songbirds, waterfowl, predatory birds, and reptiles. Fur-bearers found along the river and canal include fox squirrel, gray squirrel, mink, raccoon, otter, deer, fox, opossum, and muskrat. The principal sport fish found in the Potomac in this stretch are sucker, perch, carp, catfish, smallmouth bass, and sunfish.

GOOSE CREEK RIVER LOCK

30.64 Access: 0.2 mile downstream from Lock 25 (Edwards Ferry). Immediately downstream from a wooden bridge over a creek, take an evident footpath for about 60 yards to the lock.

The lock admitted boats from the Potomac River and from Goose Creek on the opposite Virginia shore. The Goose Creek and Little River Navigation (incorporated by Virginia on March 15, 1832) was a canalization of Goose Creek and Little River. (A canalization uses the stream for navigation except at rapids, where short canals are built around obstructions.) The canals and locks of the Goose Creek and Little River Navigation are largely obliterated, though there is a guard lock and a two-lock combine near the Potomac River on the south side of Goose Creek on the Virginia side of the river. You can find other locks along Goose Creek—typically around mill dams. Documentary evidence indicates that only one official boat ever passed through the navigation system on the Virginia side, but it is believed that the system was used informally from time to time.

Three river locks—this staircase lock opposite Goose Creek, the one opposite the Shenandoah River at Harpers Ferry, and the one opposite Shepherdstown—were built in an effort to respond to stipulations by the Virginia Legislature in 1833 to provide access to the canal for boats from Virginia.

The locks here were completed between 1837 and 1838. There are indications that they were built to the specifications of 1837 (the first set of specifications being those of 1828, and the second set those of 1830). The coping stones are Aquia freestone; other stones are roughly-cut, roughly-faced, and roughly-coursed Seneca sandstone. The Goose Creek River Lock is a two-lift lock combine with a total lift (depending on the river level) of 15.5', joined by a middle set of gates. (A combine is a set of two or more locks without intervening basins or levels and sharing a gate.) Each lock is 90' between the gates.

The Goose Creek River Lock (shown here in January 2009) provided access from the C&O Canal to the Goose Creek and Little River Navigation on the Virginia side of the river. *(Image courtesy Steve Dean)*

The upper lock appears to have an 8' lift with the lift of the lower lock depending on the river level, but normally 7.5'. There is a four-gate waste weir at the upper end of the upper lock, having been put there after the lock was abandoned (otherwise boats could not have passed through the lock). There was a raised mule bridge over the inlet connecting the river locks with the C&O Canal. The canal prism is wide enough to allow boats to make the turn into or out of the inlet to the lock, but there is also a basin just above the river lock to facilitate that maneuver.

LOCK 25, EDWARDS FERRY

30.84 (39.103463, -77.472933) Access: From Poolesville go west on MD-107/Whites Ferry Rd. 2.2 miles and turn left onto Edwards Ferry Rd. Go 4.3 miles to a T-intersection; turn left and go 0.2 mile, crossing over the canal to the Edwards Ferry parking lot. Facilities include a boat ramp, one permanent chemical toilet, and one portable toilet. There is no drinking water available. The lockhouse is available for overnight rentals via the Canal Trust's Canal Quarters program, 301-745-8888, www.canaltrust.org/quarters.

The site is named for the Edwards Ferry that operated on the Potomac 1791–1836. *Martin's Gazetteer of Virginia* (The Society, 1835) lists an Edwards Ferry post office on each side of the Potomac. The river slackwater here is three-eighths of a mile wide.

The lock was completed in 1830. Bolts in the coping stones indicate that the lock was raised 6" by bolting timbers on top. This was probably due to a silting problem, necessitating a greater depth of water in the lock. There is also evidence of timbers having been bolted at the lower end of the lock walls to minimize damage to the lock should boats hit it.

Lock 25 was the first lock to be extended in length to allow two connected boats to lock through at a time, in one direction. (See page 36.) The lock extension was made of Seneca rubble and stone-filled wooden cribs. Little remains of the extension and its lower lock gates except for the windrow (pile of stones) which filled the cribs.

The lockhouse on the towpath side at the upper end of the lock is of brick, one-and-a-half stories over a full basement, 18'8" x 31'6"—a bit larger than the 18' x 30' standard. The bypass flume and the area above are grassy and attractively landscaped. There is evidence of a boat basin about 150' square dug into the berm bank just above the lock. This was probably the base for a canal company scow that provided access across the canal to Edwards Ferry. The scow was replaced with a bridge early in the historic operating period. In 1839 the bridge that pivoted on the berm side of the lock was decayed to the point of being unfit for use. The bridge was vital because travelers on an important country road connecting Maryland and Virginia crossed at Edwards Ferry. The bridge was later replaced with a "small horse bridge," but wagons were compelled to make a six-mile detour to cross the canal at Conrads Ferry (now Whites Ferry). No additional difficulty was experienced with the Edwards Ferry bridge until 1850, when stronger abutments had to be constructed.

Lockhouse 25 in 2012 restored as a Canal Quarters property. *(Image courtesy Steve Dean)*

Union troops commanded by Col. Charles P. Stone took possession of the Maryland side of Edwards Ferry on June 14, 1861, just days after Confederate forces had crossed near here and let the water out of the canal. These were the first Union troops placed at this location, which was an early crossing point for Maryland Confederate volunteers and supplies bound for Virginia.

The Civil War was hard on the Edwards Ferry pivot bridge. In late June 1863, Union General Hooker ordered engineers to build two pontoon bridges across the river at Edwards Ferry, so that his army (marching north through Virginia) could confront the Confederates who had already crossed into Maryland via the Shenandoah Valley to the west. Crews also built two bridges over Lock 25, which, along with the pivot bridge, allowed the Union army to cross the canal. Temporary supply depots were established along the canal to service the army as it passed into Maryland. So many men crossed over the swing bridge that it became disabled and was no longer able to turn on its pivot. Following his July 1864 raid on Washington, Lieutenant General Jubal Early crossed his infantry and artillery back into Virginia at Whites Ford and his cavalry at Edwards Ferry.

The ruins adjacent to the lockhouse are of a canal country store last operated by Gene Jarboe's sons, Sam and John. Gene Jarboe drowned in the canal while loading cattle. The store closed in 1906. The NPS extensively re-stabilized these ruins between 2008 and 2010. Records indicate that a warehouse and/or store existed on the berm side of the lock throughout most of the canal's operating years. Former locktenders John Walters and Charlie Poole ran a store in a wood-frame house on the berm side after Jarboe's store closed.

30.89 Waste Weir and Culvert #43 are separated by a few feet of stone masonry retaining wall. This 6' culvert (in 1976 protected from further damage by an earthen dam across the canal bed) was built on a wooden foundation.

The stretch beyond here is peaceful and offers attractive secluded woods and a nice walk along the old fences next to the towpath. The hike to Broad Run Trunk (about two miles round-trip) makes a nice Sunday afternoon walk.

BROAD RUN TRUNK (Wooden Aqueduct)
31.94 Access: From Lock 25 at mile 30.84.

The setting is very attractive with Broad Run flowing clear. This wooden aqueduct is one of the more interesting features of the canal. The structure was originally a double culvert built of twin 16' arches and listed as Culvert #44—the only two-span culvert on the canal. In 1846 a flood washed out the culvert, and a wooden trunk was hurriedly thrown across the span to carry the canal across Broad Run. The temporary structure was replaced by another wooden trunk in the winter of 1856. In its later configuration it was a wooden trunk about 8'5" high and 30'2" long over red sandstone abutments. Although it was not classified as an aqueduct, it served as one. Today the trunk carrying the canal prism is gone, and a bridge carries the towpath over Broad Run.

31.95 A 1,106-acre tract beginning 100 yards above the mouth of Broad Run was patented on April 26, 1721, to Daniel Dulaney, a wealthy colonial lawyer and land developer from Ireland.

32.04 The towpath passes a turf farm.

32.43 Site of lost Culvert #45, 10' span, on Abrahams Branch. Culvert traces are now completely gone except for the outflow ditch from the towpath to the river. The creek now enters directly into the canal bed carrying much debris. Many of the "lost culverts" apparently were abandoned because of the tremendous amounts of silt carried into them. One thing we must appreciate in the operation and maintenance of historic canals is that hydraulic control features must be added or deleted (whether or not the canal is watered) as the surrounding drainage patterns change.

32.65 High-voltage power lines.

32.7x Underground natural gas pipelines operated by Dominion Transmission, Inc., which supplies the Dickerson power plant, and Columbia Gas Transmission Corporation.

32.93 Culvert #46, 3' span. There are notable wildflowers the next three miles. This is also a good area for observing owls (including the barred owl), raccoons, deer,

Broad Run Trunk (aqueduct) was originally a twinned-culvert, the only one like it on the canal, or perhaps anywhere. *(Library of Congress, Prints and Photographs Division, HABS, Reproduction Number HABS MD, 16-MARB.V.1--1)*

groundhogs, rabbits, squirrels, moles, and flying squirrels. The turf farms ahead (an extensive industry in the area) attract shore birds during fall migration.

The canal ahead returns to parallel the river. Note: NPS milepost 33 is 1.37 miles upstream from milepost 32—one of the longest "miles" on the towpath.

33.27–35.1x Harrison Island—paralleling the canal for approximately two miles—is perhaps the largest island in the Potomac. Heater Island below Point of Rocks (mile 46.85) was closely related to Harrison Island during Native American occupation. Though both islands are on the Maryland tax rolls, both were generally reached from the Virginia shore.

The Piscataway (Canoy) tribe fled to Harrison and Heater Islands in the 1690s. The main fort at the upper end of Heater Island was described by Vandercastle and Harrison, representatives of the Governor of Maryland, as being 50–60 yards square and containing 18 "cabins," with nine additional cabins outside the stockade. A smallpox epidemic in 1705 decimated the colony. The Tuscarora Indians arrived from the Carolinas in 1711, occupying the Canoy Islands (Harrison and Heater) until 1713, when they continued northward leaving behind a legacy of a few place names along the Potomac.

33.27 The October 21, 1861, Battle of Balls Bluff on the Virginia shore opposite Harrison Island was one of the earliest Civil War battles, with the Confederates routing Union forces on the bluff overlooking the Potomac on the Virginia side of the river. Col. Edward Baker, who had command of the Union force on the bluff, personally oversaw the transfer of a large packet boat from the canal to the river, and other smaller boats were transferred from the canal to the river as well. In the last stages of the battle, the Union force retreated down the heights in disarray. Many drowned when smaller boats became overcrowded and capsized during the evacuation. Canal legend has it that this area is haunted by the spirits of departed soldiers, and canal boatmen avoided overnight stops at this point of the canal.

33.68 Culvert #46 1/2, 2' span, box culvert (an uncommon rectangular as opposed to arched design). Note: if a culvert needed to be added to the existing system, "1/2" was added to the nearest culvert number downstream. Changes in runoff through the years sometimes created a need to add or delete culverts.

34.01 Culvert #47, 6' span. The towpath arch stones each have designs cut into their face.

34.28 Culvert #47 1/2, 3' span. The wooden floor is in place. This is the beginning of a notable wildflower area.

34.43 Turtle Run Hiker–Biker Campsite. Road access at Whites Ferry at mile 35.50.

34.50 Culvert #48, 4' span, skewed 20° to the canal run. (Culverts are normally perpendicular to the towpath.)

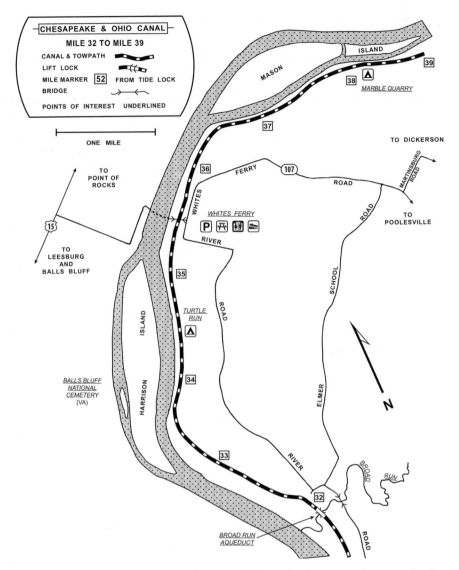

CHESAPEAKE & OHIO CANAL

MILE 32 TO MILE 39

CANAL & TOWPATH
LIFT LOCK
MILE MARKER 52 FROM TIDE LOCK
BRIDGE
POINTS OF INTEREST UNDERLINED

ONE MILE

TO POINT OF ROCKS

TO LEESBURG AND BALLS BLUFF

15

MASON ISLAND

39

38 MARBLE QUARRY

37

36 FERRY 107 ROAD

WHITES FERRY

TO DICKERSON

MARTINSBURG ROAD

TO POOLESVILLE

WHITES

RIVER

35

TURTLE RUN

ISLAND

34

HARRISON

BALLS BLUFF NATIONAL CEMETERY (VA)

ROAD

SCHOOL

ROAD

ELMER

33

RIVER

BROAD RUN

32

BROAD RUN AQUEDUCT

ROAD

N

34.82 Culvert #49, 10' span. This culvert was believed to have served as a road culvert to Conrads (Whites) Ferry about one mile above, although it could be used only when the river level was low. The ornate stonework of the arches is unique on the canal.

34.90 Harrison Island fish trap extends from the upper part of the island to the Maryland shore. A Mr. Nelson reported Native Americans repairing the fish trap in 1724. Fish traps were sometimes used as sluices by the Patowmack Company in its improvement of river navigation, although they would sometimes require widening or other improvement to effectively funnel water into a deeper channel for boats.

86

35.03 Culvert #50, 4' span. Generations of farm trash have collected at the upstream end.

35.47 Culvert #51, 9' span. This culvert is unique and worth stopping to study for those interested in canal structures. The culvert consisted of stone arches under the towpath and berm banks, with wood apparently used for both the top of the culvert and the floor of the canal prism above it. The wood separating the canal and culvert is no longer present, leaving the culvert open and the structure confusing as it now appears.

35.49 Pass under an old iron, wood-planked road bridge on red sandstone. Until after the Civil War, access to Conrads Ferry was via a culvert. A year before the war ended, General Superintendent Spates estimated it would cost $700 to construct a wooden bridge to replace the culvert (probably Culvert #49), which was "very much filled up so that carriages and wagons could not pass through it." Such a bridge was built in 1855 or 1856, but soon proved unsatisfactory because the grade was so steep that it was impossible for heavily-laden wagons to ascend. In 1871 this situation was corrected by extending the approaches, which required adding trestles under the bridge. However, that resulted in a narrow 20'-wide space for the passage of boats. The old bridge originally had an 11.5' clearance (the minimum clearance for bridges was 12'), and that defect was corrected at the same time. By 1876 a new bridge was needed and the current iron bridge was built and opened to traffic in June of that year. The new bridge eliminated the piers that were an impediment to navigation, and instead used the present-day abutments. This bridge is a classic example of the iron bridge technology of the mid-1870s.

WHITES FERRY

35.50 (39.154861, -77.518206) Access: From Poolesville follow MD-107/Whites Ferry Rd. 6.2 miles west. Turn right into the parking lot. From Edwards Ferry (Lock 25) follow River Rd. 5.1 miles and turn left into Whites Ferry parking lot. There are two portable toilets and a boat ramp (fee). Whites Ferry Store is open mid-April through October. The ferry to Virginia operates daily 5 a.m. to 11 p.m., weather permitting. 24801 Whites Ferry Rd., Dickerson, MD 20842, 301-349-5200.

Whites Ferry has been in operation close to 150 years. Originally known as Conrads Ferry, it became Whites Ferry after the Civil War, when Lt. Col. E. V. White of Virginia purchased it. He named the ferry boat after his commander, Gen. Jubal A. Early. This is the last regular ferry operation on the Potomac, where there were once about 100.

35.53 Stabilized granary ruins on the berm. Canal boats tied up to iron rings fixed in the granary wall. Chutes from the granary loaded grain directly into canal

The 1876 road bridge and granary (background) at Whites Ferry. Only the foundation of the granary remains.

boats. The 34' x 138' wooden building (which burned in the 1960s) was two stories high on a red sandstone foundation.

35.67 Culvert #52, 4' span. Twenty feet upstream is a twentieth century steel pipe culvert with concrete rubble in-wings and spandrels.

35.79 Culvert #53, 4' span. Osage orange (*Maclura pomifera*) hedge grows on the river side of the towpath. The canal bed is generally sparsely watered. Moss, algae, chickweed (*Stellaria media*), and watercress (*Nasturtium officinale*) form a green cover when there is water.

36.42–38.15 Lower Mason Island—one of the largest in the Potomac. Just above here is a fine stand of Virginia cowslip (*Mertensia virginica*), or bluebell, which blooms in the latter half of April. Bluebells are among the loveliest and showiest flowers on the floodplains, their principal habitat.

36.56 Culvert #54, 6' span, rebuilt in 1973.

36.93 Culvert #56, 6' span, was replaced in 1914 by the C&O Canal Transportation Company, which operated the canal after 1896 in the receivership period. A 3' diameter pipe now carries the stream from the adjacent berm fields.

37.67 The cliff on the berm is the first seen in some miles. These high red cliffs of Triassic sandstone constrict the course of the canal where the Potomac is now only a stone's throw away.

38.15–38.86 Upper Mason Island. A narrow channel separates this from Lower Mason Island. Upper Mason Island is also known as Oxley's (or Ox) Island.

38.17 Culvert #60, 4' span.

38.2x Marble Quarry Hiker–Biker Campsite. Nearest access is from Dickerson Conservation Park at mile 39.63. The marble quarry to the east is noted for its "Potomac marble" conglomerate used for the columns in Statuary Hall in the U.S. Capitol. Although beautiful, with varied and richly-colored inclusion, the stone was hard to work and resulted in columns with drums of irregular lengths.

38.35 Fine cliff on the berm, with a heavy growth of polypody fern (*Polypodium virginianum*) and saxifrage (*Saxifraga virginiensis*).

38.72 Culvert #63, 8′ span, carries a stream from a wooded ravine. This and the two preceding culverts give access to a large, unbroken, hilly forest on the berm for further exploration. There were six Native American fish traps in the river from here to Brunswick.

38.xx The river here is the site of Whites Ford, which crossed over the upper tip of Mason Island, and which was the favorite crossing of the Potomac by Confederate armies. Among others, Gen. Robert E. Lee's forces began their first invasion of the North when they crossed here September 4–7, 1862; Gen. J. E. B. Stuart's cavalry crossed October 12, 1862; and Gen. Jubal Early crossed on July 14, 1864, following his raid on Washington.

39.17 Waste Weir. Site of lost culvert #64.

LOCK 26 (Woods Lock)

39.37 Access: Dickerson Conservation Park at mile 39.63.

The lock is built of red (and some gray) sandstone boated 17 miles from the Seneca quarries. The lockhouse, which was wood frame over a red sandstone rubble wall basement, burned in 1969. The lock has been filled in to prevent its collapse. It has also been known as Fitchs Lock. A magnificent silver maple tree stands next to the lockhouse ruins.

Lock 26 is in a peaceful, rural setting. The lockhouse burned in 1969, but the foundations have been stabilized.

The lock was probably completed in 1831, apparently to the 1828 lock specifications in its lower portion, for the three culvert openings are visible in the lower course of stone in each lock wall. However, the upper portion of the lock seems to have been built according to the specifications of 1830, with the upper gate pockets in front of the breast wall rather than on top of it. Locks 26 and 27 seem to be the only locks known to have been built to the specifications of both 1828 and 1830. Lock 26 was extended on the lower end by stone-filled wooden cribs in 1881–82.

39.49 This abandoned waste weir is a good example of an old masonry and wood waste weir that was no longer needed at some point in the operating period. It may be an original. Most, if not all, were replaced with concrete after 1906. The barely visible riprap and lowering of the towpath of about 1' here gives some indication that the abandoned waste weir may have been used as an informal overflow after being covered up.

39.63 Dickerson Conservation Park and the Potomac Warm Water Fishing Area. (39.194685, -77.469402) Access: From Dickerson, take MD-28/Dickerson Rd. south 1.2 miles. Take slight right onto Martinsburg Rd. Go 0.5 mile and turn left to stay on Martinsburg Rd. Follow 2.0 miles then take dirt road 0.3 mile to a parking lot.

Culvert #65, 12' span, located just below the parking lot for Dickerson Conservation Park and the Potomac Warm Water Fishing Area. This culvert is unique as it is both "skewed" (at a diagonal to the canal rather than perpendicular as with most culverts) and "rifled" (the stonework in the barrel is laid out diagonally rather than in level courses). It has a spring stone at the inflow with "1832" cut in the face. The path on the other side of the pedestrian bridge leads to a fishing hole in the Potomac. The canal bed is watered above, with bass propagating nicely.

40.04 Culvert #66, 6' span. The culvert is located at the lower end of the Dickerson Generating Station—a site of past controversy over fly ash dumped in the canal through the years, expansion of the plant, and the location of a sewage treatment plant. The fly ash was removed in 1974, and the canal was watered and landscaped up to Lock 27. The generating station has both coal-fired steam generators and gas-fueled combustion turbines.

40.3x A road from the generating station crosses the canal. The channel that carries cooling water from the power plant has been modified to serve as a whitewater training course. The original modifications were made in 1991 for use by canoe and kayak paddlers training for the 1992 Olympic Games. The course is not open to the public. For more information, contact the Potomac Whitewater Racing Center, potomacwhitewater.org.

41.34 Culvert #68, 6' span, restored in 1974.

The "skewed" and "rifled" construction of Culvert #65 (shown here in 2011) makes it unique to all other culverts on the canal. *(Image courtesy Steve Dean)*

LOCK 27, SPINKS FERRY

41.46 Access: From Monocacy Aqueduct at mile 42.19.

Referred to as "Campbells Lock" (sometimes corrupted to "Camels Lock") in old records. The lock was built of Seneca red sandstone in 1831 that was "boated down 5 miles from a quarry near the river below the Point of Rocks, with the exception of the coping which is from Lee's Quarry near Seneca." Other stone came from ledges 2.5 miles north of the lock. An old road grade parallels the canal on the berm. No traces exist of the pivot bridge that once crossed the lock, providing access to Spinks Ferry. The lock was probably completed in 1831. Like Lock 26, work done prior to 1830 included laying culverts in sidewalls (Lock 27 is the uppermost so built) under 1828 specifications, with the breast wall above the upper gate pockets under 1830 specifications. The lock was stabilized by the NPS in 1985.

This lock was extended a lock's length on the upper end in 1881–82. The lock extends 128' above the upper end of the upper gate pocket. Little of the extension's wooden cribs and planking remains above ground, except for the windrow of stones with which they were filled. The cribs and planking are most likely intact a few inches below soil level. The remains of a cast iron wicket gate (of the extension's lock gate) appear about 98' above the upper gate pocket.

The stone lockhouse is one-and-a-half stories over a full stone basement with end chimneys. The level above (to Lock 28) was known as "Eight Mile Level" though it is actually 7.47 miles long.

41.52 Typical three-opening waste weir.

41.59 Possible location of Spinks Ferry on the Potomac; the ferry probably operated before the canal was built and may have ceased operating in the 1830s.

41.80 The historical significance of the foundations and parts of walls of the building on the river side of the towpath are unknown.

41.97 Culvert #69 (Little Monocacy), 20' span, completed in 1832. This stream drains the area around Dickerson and the south side of Sugarloaf Mountain. Hurricane Agnes badly damaged this already weakened structure in 1972, but it was rebuilt 1974–75. The berm bank carried a road from Lock 27 to the Monocacy Basin. During the Civil War, the Confederates invading Maryland in early September 1862 destroyed the Little Monocacy Culvert, which was the most extensive damage inflicted to the canal during the campaign. It was not repaired until October 13, 1862, which delayed Union Gen. McClellan's use of the canal as a supply line to Harpers Ferry.

42.10 Monocacy Basin, 500' long x 100' wide, with stabilized granary ruins on the berm bank, near the parking lot for the aqueduct. Otho W. Trundle built the granary in 1865. Frederick O. Sellman was a farmer and merchant who boated and loaded wheat at the granary. Behind the granary was another building that housed a store and the Mouth of Monocacy Post Office, established by the mid-1850s, with Sellman as the postmaster.

42.1x Parking lot and picnic area for the Monocacy Aqueduct. (See 42.19 for access.)

42.17 Cross the unmarked Montgomery–Frederick County line.

Lock 27, Spinks Ferry.

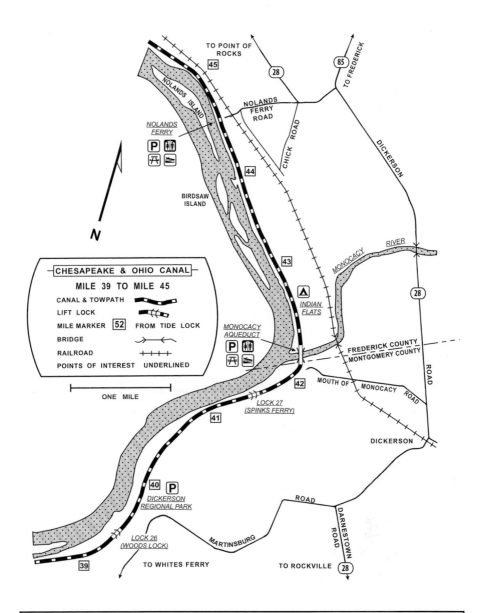

CHESAPEAKE & OHIO CANAL

MILE 39 TO MILE 45

CANAL & TOWPATH
LIFT LOCK
MILE MARKER [52] FROM TIDE LOCK
BRIDGE
RAILROAD
POINTS OF INTEREST UNDERLINED

ONE MILE

TO POINT OF ROCKS
[45]
[28]
[85] TO FREDERICK
NOLANDS FERRY ROAD
NOLANDS ISLAND
NOLANDS FERRY
CHICK ROAD
DICKERSON
[44]
BIRDSAW ISLAND
MONOCACY RIVER
[43]
INDIAN FLATS
MONOCACY AQUEDUCT
FREDERICK COUNTY
MONTGOMERY COUNTY
[28]
[42] MOUTH OF MONOCACY ROAD
LOCK 27 (SPINKS FERRY)
[41]
ROAD
DICKERSON
[40] DICKERSON REGIONAL PARK
ROAD
LOCK 26 (WOODS LOCK)
MARTINSBURG
DARNESTOWN ROAD
[39]
TO WHITES FERRY
TO ROCKVILLE [28]

One of the colorful characters along the canal was "Squirrelly" Lambert, a squatter on Park Service property, who with his chickens, goats, and mounds of trash avoided eviction from the 1940s until his death in 1967. According to canal lore, Lambert was arrested and hauled into court in Frederick, Maryland, where he was convicted of selling intoxicating beverages at the Monocacy Aqueduct. After fining him $500 for habitual bootlegging, the judge asked Lambert if he had anything to say to the court. Lambert replied, "Yes, Sir! I'm going to have to raise the price of my liquor to pay this fine!"

MONOCACY AQUEDUCT

42.19 (39.222563, -77.449987) Access: From Dickerson take MD-28/Dickerson Rd. 0.3 mile north of the railroad overpass. Turn left on the Mouth of Monocacy Rd. and go 1.2 miles to the fork. Take the left fork 0.1 mile to the parking lot. There are toilets, a picnic area, and boat ramps, but no water. A path from the picnic area goes under the (downstream) arch of the aqueduct. Supplies and prepared food are available at the Dickerson Market, 22145 Dickerson Rd., Dickerson, MD 20842, 301-349-5789.

The Monocacy Aqueduct, 516' long with seven 54' arches, is the largest of the canal's 11 stone aqueducts. It is often called not only one of the two finest features of the C&O Canal (the other being the Paw Paw Tunnel), but one of the finest canal structures in the United States. Construction of the aqueduct began in March 1829 and was finished in April 1833. In 1972 it suffered damages from Hurricane Agnes, losing much coping stone and railing. It underwent extensive repair work 1975–77 and an NPS stabilization project 1975–79. Another major stabilization was completed in 2005.

Initially, stone from Nelson's quarries four miles away at the base of Sugarloaf Mountain was used, but it was found to be of insufficient strength. The first three partially-constructed piers had to be torn down. Subsequently, closer quarries on the Johnson farm were found to provide good stone. The stone was transported to the construction site via a rude tramway and wagon. Sugarloaf Mountain can be seen in the distance upriver from the aqueduct.

In 1831 the Superintendent of Masonry reported the following workforce was needed at the aqueduct:

> 60 men quarrying at the white quarry: 100 men cutting the white stone, 13 four-horse teams transporting the white stone; 33 masons, including tenders, drivers, etc.; two four-horse teams hauling cement; 1 boat and 5 men transporting sand; 10 men procuring backing [stone]; 10 carpenters; 235 total number of men.

Note the interesting dedication plaque at the mid-point of the aqueduct.

The towpath was on the river side of the canal. There was a towrope riding timber on the canal side of the towpath to keep the towrope from catching in the stonework. Wooden rubbing rails were bolted horizontally on the inner walls of the trough (canal) to minimize the shock of boats bumping the walls. There are remains of a fine charcoal-wrought iron fence, and at the ends of the aqueduct are grooves in the iron worn by the towropes. The main posts of the fence were capped with hollow, cast-iron decorative tops set on the spikes of the posts, with sheet lead to wedge in the tops. In the stabilization completed

The Monocacy Aqueduct as it appeared in the early 1900s. The aqueduct is considered by many to be the most beautiful structure on the canal.

in 2005, fencing that is removable at times of flood was used along much of the aqueduct, so that debris overtopping the aqueduct does not catch on it. A section of the old fencing bent by just such debris was left as testimony to the power and height of Monocacy floods.

Downstream of the aqueduct toward the Potomac River on the near side of the Monocacy was the first settlement on that river, established in 1708 by Swiss prospector Louis Michel.

42.3x A systematic exploration of the river terrace for historic and prehistoric artifacts and traces of human development above the aqueduct was carried out by Catholic University in 1966–67. The exploration site is described as "A Woodland Site in Piedmont Maryland." Recorded settlement in the area began 1740, at which time Charles Carroll of Carrollton began development of Carrollton Manor, a 17,000-acre tract on which this site is located. Pottery fragments found here were from the pottery series Marcey Stone, Stoney Creek, Albemarle, and Chickahominy. Stone artifacts included projectile points, a knife, choppers, and un-worked flakes. Indications were that quartz (readily available in the form of river cobbles) was the most popular artifact. Samples of artifacts indicate that the site was occupied from Early Woodland times through Late Woodland. Based on artifact analysis, the historic period of occupation was from 1715 to 1865. The heaviest period of occupation was probably around 1825.

42.40 Indian Flats Hiker–Biker Campsite. Access: The Monocacy Aqueduct parking lot at mile 42.19. The berm dike (the berm canal wall) here is nicely shaped and narrow (2'–3' at the top).

42.44 Culvert #70 (Little Tuscarora Creek), 6' span, carries the stream from a flat wooded area. The culvert was replaced with a concrete structure on the towpath side and the berm side is repaired to near its original appearance. The canal bed is usually dry and carpeted with wildflowers most of the distance to Nolands Ferry.

42.58 Remains of the original "Macadam" towpath, particularly the 4' along the canal side where the mule would have walked. "Macadamized" historically means that the towpath was covered first with a 6" layer of 2" stone, then a 4" layer of 1" stone, and finally a layer of fine gravel that was replaced periodically. Macadamizing some parts of the towpath that were particularly prone to becoming muddy when wet was an experiment during the heyday of the canal in the 1870s. However, it was tried only in the Monocacy division and was discontinued, likely due to the expense.

42.90 There are three Native American fish weirs (rock dams) visible at low water in the Potomac within a three-quarter mile stretch, one near NPS milepost 43.

44.04 Culvert #71 (Tuscarora Creek), 16' span, carries the stream from a wooded depression between cultivated fields.

44.08 Upper end of Birdsaw Island.

44.25–45.45 Nolands Island.

44.40 Beginning of Nolands Ferry Area.

On September 4–5, 1862, during the Maryland Campaign of 1862, Confederate Brig. Gen. D. H. Hill's forces tore out the banks of the canal, damaged Lock 27 and would have broken the Monocacy Aqueduct but were unable "for the want of powder and tools." When Confederate Gen. Robert E. Lee sent three separate forces to surround and capture Harpers Ferry, the force commanded by Brig. Gen. John Walker was first ordered to make another attempt to damage the Monocacy Aqueduct. Walker failed too, writing that the structure was too well constructed for the crowbars and dull drills with which he had been provided. In October 1862 the canal company discharged Thomas Walter, locktender at Lock 27, for collaboration with the Confederates during the invasion of Maryland. A petition from his neighbors claimed that he had actually tried to talk the Confederates out of doing more damage to the canal, but the company refused to reinstate him.

Hauling Ford crossed the river here and passed under the Monocacy Aqueduct. This ford was also used by the Confederates on their invasion of Maryland in early September 1862.

NOLANDS FERRY

44.58 (39.249948, -77.482726) Access: From Dickerson take MD-28/Dickerson Rd. north 3.7 miles. Turn left onto MD-28/Tuscarora Rd. Go 0.4 mile and turn left onto Nolands Ferry Rd. Go 0.8 mile to parking lot. There are portable toilets, a picnic area, and a boat ramp.

Here was one of the most ancient crossings of the Potomac, the Monocacy Trail, a variation of the "Warriors Path." The Treaty of Lancaster of 1744, with the Six Nations, provided for Native Americans to travel unmolested from the Susquehanna River southward through Maryland to the Carolinas on the "Indians Road." This traffic tended to keep the Monocacy Trail maintained. When 3,000 Hessians (mercenaries hired by the British from many German states), captured at the Battle of Saratoga and paroled on their honor, were ordered to march south to Charlottesville, Virginia, they followed the "Indians Path." The discouraged army crossed at Nolands Ferry on Christmas Day 1778 in a snow storm with ice floating in the river, and continued to Leesburg for the night. "Mad" Anthony Wayne, with a detachment to join Lafayette before Yorktown, also crossed here in 1781.

The Noland (or Newland) family operated the ferry as early as 1758. Produce from the Shenandoah Valley was shipped across the Potomac by ferry as the shortest route to Baltimore. A thriving community of stores, blacksmith, wagon shop, tailor, shoemaker, and taverns was established around the ferry. Highway robbers waylaid farmers and teamsters en route to market. Captain Harper, the notorious Robin Hood of Loudoun County, Virginia, generous to the poor and gallant only to young and beautiful maidens, reportedly made his largest hauls on the ferry approaches. The nickname "Rogues Road" spread, and travelers avoided the crossing.

Construction of the canal interfered with traffic across the river. A Buckeystown, Maryland, merchant and flour miller wrote two letters in November 1833 to the canal company complaining that canal construction had cut him off from his customers in Virginia. He demanded that a bridge be constructed across the canal. The canal company's 1848 Annual Report noted that the boat previously used as a ferry across the canal was unfit for further use, and that a substantial bridge (the abutments for which can be seen upriver from the ferry crossing) had been erected over the canal. However, the bridge was too late to assist in the resurrection of Nolands Ferry. With the erection of the Point of Rocks Bridge across the Potomac, Nolands Ferry became an almost forgotten place.

An 1848 wooden bridge over the canal was built by Lewis Wernwag and was replaced by a skew, Pratt truss iron bridge in 1870. In turn, it was replaced by a steel Pratt truss bridge in 1913, which was carried away in the 1936 flood.

Shirley Jackson, self-appointed guide at Harpers Ferry who died in 1950 at age 68, and who claimed that his father had been the valet of Gen. George McClellan, told of treasure buried in the vicinity of Nolands Ferry or the Monocacy Aqueduct. The key to finding the treasure is to follow the ghost of the person hiding it: either a robber who operated at Nolands Ferry, or one of Mosby's men sharing in the loot of the robbery of the payroll train upriver. According to local lore, the ghost is seen on moonless nights crossing the Monocacy Aqueduct carrying a lighted lantern.

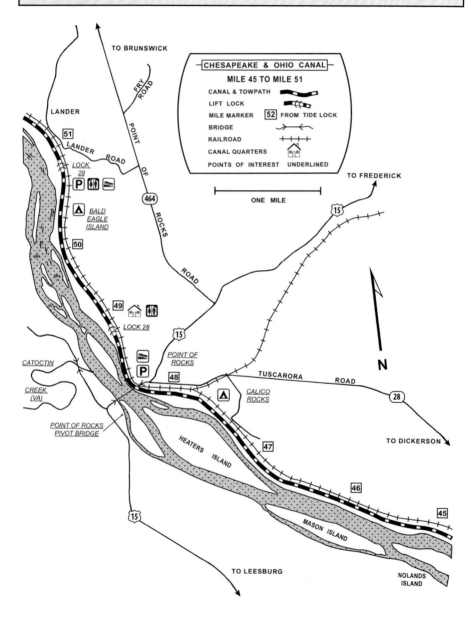

44.76 The large, interesting stone building on the riverside houses the Frederick County Water Treatment Plant. It is a fine example of how a modern service building can blend well with an historic site.

45.10 The 1,200'-long Tuscarora Feeder was built in 1833. The inlet of this historic auxiliary feeder has been covered with soil. Few people know of the existence of the feeder from Tuscarora Creek or have viewed it. It is filled with large trees, but still about 5' deep. The dikes rise about 3' above the level of the surrounding fields. It is about 33' from the top of one dike to the other.

The feeder would have served to add additional water to the canal if the intake from Dam 3, a mile above Harpers Ferry, proved inadequate to maintain the new 40-mile section down to Dam 2 that opened to navigation in the spring of 1834. There are no records indicating if or when the feeder was used; but once the next section of the canal opened between Dam 4 and Dam 3 in June 1835, the Tuscarora Feeder was less likely to have been needed. At that point the Dam 4 inlet would have become the primary inlet, and the Dam 3 feeder would have served as a supplemental source.

The Upper Potomac River In Frederick County

The Potomac River flows through 16 miles of Frederick County, Maryland. Here, the river flows from the Blue Ridge Mountain Physiographic Province to the western division of the Piedmont Province. The river is predominantly moderate to swift-flowing. There are no slackwater regions. Some whitewater occurs in the vicinity of Knoxville.

The high ridges of South Mountain in Maryland and the Blue Ridge Mountains in Virginia rise up from the banks of the river in the vicinity of Weverton and Knoxville. The Catoctin Mountains abut the river, forming spectacular cliffs at Point of Rocks, Maryland. The major tributary river of the Potomac in Frederick County is Catoctin Creek. It joins the Potomac near Lander, Maryland.

Forty-one islands are located in the Potomac River in Frederick County, most of them in the lower half of the river. Twenty-six of the islands are smaller than five acres. The primary shoreline woody vegetation includes maple, sycamore, willow, white ash, green ash, and river birch. The principal submerged aquatic vegetation includes wild celery, water star grass, and various pond weeds. Emergent shallow water vegetation includes water willow and lizard's tail.

Numerous fur-bearing species, songbirds, waterfowl, predatory birds, and reptiles reside along the immediate shoreline of the Potomac River in Frederick County. The stretch of river between Catoctin Creek and the Monocacy River offers well-protected wildlife habitat because of the numerous undeveloped islands in the area.

Principal fur-bearers include beaver, fox squirrel, gray squirrel, mink, raccoon, otter, deer, muskrat, fox, and opossum. The principal sport fish found in this stretch are sucker, carp, catfish, small mouth bass, and sunfish.

45.45 Ahead is a beautiful stretch of the canal with frequent views of the river, and, as one nears Point of Rocks, the Catoctin Mountains.

46.55 An old wooden flume once in the canal bed was the remains of a former fish propagation area of the Kanawha Club. Similar structures divided the canal bed into a series of pools.

46.80 Beginning of "Calico rocks," a limestone conglomerate also called "Potomac marble." This conglomerate is composed of coarse and fine pebbles in a matrix of fine gray to red limestone containing grains of quartz. The first use of this stone may have been in the pillars of the U.S. Capitol Rotunda. Red sandstone from quarries abundant in this area was shipped by railroad and canal. A wharf was on the berm near here. Do not cross the railroad tracks.

46.85–48.25 Heater Island is now a Maryland Wildlife Management Area that was once inhabited by members of the Conoy tribe and was later farmed by the Nelson family.

47.10 Across the canal and railroad is private Camp Kanawha, concealed behind the picturesque formation of calico rocks. (THIS IS NOT A LEGAL PUBLIC CROSSING.)

47.20 Houses of the settlement of Rock Hall were known ca. 1847 as "Woodland." Ahead is a fine upriver view of the Catoctin Mountains, with Furnace Mountain across the river.

47.57 Kanawha Spring. A large circular dam or dike was built around the spring in the 1950s by the NPS.

The pivot bridge at Point of Rocks was replaced with a permanent bridge in 1845. It is shown here in 2013. *(Image courtesy Ed Kirkpatrick Photography)*

47.65 Calico Rocks Hiker–Biker Campsite. The nearest access is from Point of Rocks at mile 48.20. Cross unmarked town line of Point of Rocks.

47.75 Culvert #72 completed 1832, 16' span, drains the lower eastern slope of Catoctin Mountain. The outflow of the culvert under the railroad tracks feeds into the inflow of the canal culvert. The railroad culvert has sidewalls of stone with an arch of patterned brick, well worth seeing. The canal culvert was rebuilt in 1869.

47.79 Washington Junction and the picturesque Point of Rocks Railroad Station, on the National Register of Historic Places. Here the B&O Railroad's Metropolitan Branch to Washington, D.C., breaks off from the mainline to Baltimore. This branch opened in 1873 and provided alternative shipping to Washington. However, it terminated on the eastern side of the city as did the railroad's Washington Branch from Baltimore. This left the C&O Canal as the best method of shipping to the industries and wharfs in Georgetown or along the Potomac River. Maryland Area Regional Commuter (MARC) trains stop at the station.

48.01 Culvert #73, completed 1831, 6' span, carries the stream flowing in between the fields.

48.16 Culvert #74, completed 1831, 4' span, carries a small stream coming from the center of town.

POINT OF ROCKS

48.20 (39.273218, -77.540045) Access: Take US-15 to MD-28 at the west end of Point of Rocks. Turn right onto Commerce St.; follow and turn right at the railroad crossing.

The road crosses a bridge over the canal that replicates the appearance of the historic pivot bridge at this site and continues to the boat ramp and parking area. The area was known as Johnson's Point. Point of Rocks is the first of nine "Canal Towns" along the canal. Visit www.canaltowns.org for more information.

A pivot bridge was built here 1833–34 by Lewis Wernwag, and was rebuilt as a permanent bridge in 1844. However, that bridge was so low it created problems for many boats and so was rebuilt again in 1852 with a 17' clearance. The other known pivot bridges of this type were at Ft. Frederick and below the Antietam Aqueduct. This bridge was used by vehicles to get to the bridge over the Potomac that washed out in 1936. Of the 20 Potomac floods from 1896 to 1942, six covered the towpath in this area. The 1936 flood was 17' above the towpath, covering it for 54 hours—the worst flood here on record.

On June 9, 1861, Confederate troops burned the turnpike bridge that spanned the river here. This was another early prominent crossing point for Maryland Confederate volunteers and supplies heading to Virginia. A ford also existed at this location and was used by, among others, Confederate Brig.

Gen. John Walker on his way to participate in the Battle of Harpers Ferry in September 1862.

48.38 Pass under the US-15 bridge over the Potomac. Other bridges (destroyed by floods) have crossed here in the past. The canal prism is constricted by rocks from the railroad here (where the CSX Railroad actually owns land in the canal prism and several places ahead).

48.40 Point of Rocks Railroad Tunnel. The 788' tunnel opened in 1868 and was rebuilt in 1909. This is the location of the Lower Point of Rocks Narrows—the first of the four narrow areas that were the focus of the C&O Canal and B&O Railroad legal battle 1828–32. The original passage along the river was created by blasting away part of the bluff and using it to create a base on which the railroad and canal were constructed under the compromise of 1833. A single track ran along the edge of the bluff until the double-tracked tunnel opened in 1868. In 1961 the former ledge along the canal was widened for one track by using part of the former canal prism and the other track was moved to the center of the tunnel to allow for the higher cars now in use. Improvement of this tunnel (Point of Rocks Tunnel) and the next (Catoctin Tunnel) will likely be accomplished in the near future to allow intermodal (double-stacked) trains to pass through them.

48.44 Wooded Patton Island.

48.55 Upstream portal of Point of Rocks Tunnel. The steep mountainside continues. A large stone wall (railroad) is in the canal bed. There are many attractive river views along here.

48.90 Waste Weir with 1917 date in the concrete.

The charming Baltimore & Ohio Railway Station at Point of Rocks is now on the National Register of Historic Places.

Canal Town, Point Of Rocks

The Canal Towns Partnership is a collaboration of nine historic communities between Point of Rocks and Cumberland that offer services and amenities to visitors along the canal. Visit www.canaltowns.org to learn about points of interest, services, lodging, and food sources in these towns.

Point of Rocks is important in canal history because of its position at the point where the Potomac cut through Catoctin Mountain—the first of the Appalachian ridges. Above Point of Rocks were two of four narrows at the foot of cliffs between here and Harpers Ferry that were wide enough for either the canal or railroad, but not both. This situation led to a major legal confrontation between the Baltimore & Ohio Railroad and the C&O Canal in 1828, with a ruling in favor of the canal by the Maryland Court of Appeals in 1832. In 1833, under pressure from the Maryland legislature, the two companies agreed to a compromise plan for getting both works through the narrows. The B&O built the double-track Point of Rocks Tunnel through the Catoctin Ridge just after the Civil War. However, when the B&O deeded canal lands in 1938 to the federal government, it retained sufficient canal land to construct tracks around the tunnel. That was done in the 1960s, dramatically narrowing the prism of the canal. At that time the double-track in the tunnel was replaced by a single track in the center of the tunnel, thereby allowing passage of higher freight cars.

After its days as a thriving transportation village, Point of Rocks became a quaint country town boasting a peaceful setting between the river and the mountains. Point of Rocks continued to suffer from the ravages of the river. After flooding in the 1990s, the Federal Emergency Management Agency implemented a program to purchase and demolish structures in the low-lying older part of town. Today nearby housing developments have given the town a more suburban character. Point of Rocks is one of the busiest stations on the MARC Brunswick Line. The station has over 500 parking spaces.

LOCK 28 (Point of Rocks Lock or Mountain Lock)

48.93 Access from the pivot bridge at mile 48.20.

One-seventh of the stone was brought 46 miles on the B&O Railroad (at six cents per ton per mile) from the granite quarries of the Patapsco to Point of Rocks, and thence by wagon nearly one mile to the lock. The remaining stone was transported in wagons from a quarry of hard flint stone in Virginia, four miles away. This lock, completed in 1833 and also known as Dents Lock, has only a 6' lift. Except for Lock 13, Lock 28 is the most downstream of the locks built entirely to the specifications of 1830, without bypass culverts in the lock walls and with the placement of the breast wall at the upper end of the upper gate pocket. Lock 28 may have been extended on the lower end. At times a feed store or warehouse was located nearby.

The lock is 90'9" between the gate pockets. The bypass flume, which helped to control the proper operating level of the canal (2' below towpath level,

1' below the top of the lock coping), seems to have been a shallow ditch paralleling the lock and terminating in a box culvert. Generally, when there is a bypass flume covered over, it indicates a roadway passed over the lock. There is a report of a pivot bridge here during the Civil War, and there are well-defined road traces leading from the lock to the river and from the covered section of the flume into the woods.

The lockhouse sits back off the towpath 34' from the lock, oriented perpendicularly to the run of the lock. The one-and-a-half story brick house measures 18' x 30'3"—nearly standard size—over a full stone basement. The original chimney in the center of the house has been removed. The lockhouse is available for overnight rentals via the Canal Trust's Canal Quarters program, 301-745-8888, www.canaltrust.org/quarters. A portable toilet and picnic table are available.

48.96 Waste weir.

49.29 Culvert #75 (McGills Branch), 8' span. Built in 1833 (as were all the culverts through Culvert #94), it carries a stream from a deep wooded ravine.

49.66 Culvert #76 (Slip Bottom Branch), 4' span.

49.70 Informal overflow. This overflow is about 54' long, a relatively short one. Culvert #77 was planned here but not constructed. Instead, water was let into the canal, and the excess water would drain off the overflow.

Lockhouse 28, ca. 2013. *(Image courtesy Ed Kirkpatrick Photography)*

49.88 A stone wall encroaches into the canal (legally so). The smoky overhanging cliff ahead is impressive.

49.99 The railroad enters the Catoctin Tunnel of the B&O Railroad (now CSX), built just after the Civil War. The canal bed ahead is filled with stone from the railroad construction. Also ahead is a fine overhanging rock. This tunnel represents the Upper Point of Rocks Narrows (also known as Williams Point), the second of the four areas that provoked the legal battle between the canal and railroad. As with the Lower Point of Rocks Narrows, originally the single track ran along the base of a bluff, with the double-track tunnel opening in 1868 and the old ledge widened in 1961 for one track, while the other track was moved to the center of the tunnel. This tunnel is also proposed for improvement to allow passage of the intermodal trains.

50.11 The railroad emerges from the tunnel.

50.31 Bald Eagle Island Hiker–Biker Campsite. Nearest access is at Lock 29 (Lander) at mile 50.80.

50.67 Culvert #78, 12' span, carries Poplar Branch from the wooded valley beyond the railroad.

LOCK 29 (Catoctin Lock), LANDER

50.89 (39.306507, -77.558006) Access: From Point of Rocks take US-15 north 1.0 mile to MD-464; turn left toward Brunswick and continue 2.8 miles to Lander Rd.; turn left toward the river and go 1.5 miles to Lander (also known as Old Catoctin Station). Cross the railroad tracks, turn left, and follow the berm side of the canal to the lock, about 0.2 mile. A boat ramp, parking area, and portable toilets are located at the river, reached by the road crossing over the lock.

Lock 29 was another lock once extended by stone-filled timber cribs on the upper end; the remains are about as good as we find, and the position of the wooden lock sill is still apparent. This lock, Lock 28, and all locks through Lock 44 above were built according to the lock specifications of 1830. There are indications here that the bypass flume and the lock were always bridged, even though no pivot bridge traces remain. The turns of the lower wing walls bear bolt holes and bolts, as is common, indicating that they once held vertical fender timbers to keep boats from bumping the lock walls.

The lockhouse is on the berm at mid-lock, 20' back from the bypass flume. It is brick, one-and-a-half stories over a full basement with a center chimney. A boat basin extended about 100' below the lock. Locktender L. H. "Bugs" Cross lived in the house until 1962. William H. Fulton was an earlier tender. There was a possible boat basin above the lock. The local community has furnished the lockhouse and provides interpretation at times on weekends in the summer.

51.06 Waste weir, late period, concrete applied over the original stone walls.

Lock 29 (Catoctin Lock) at Lander, 2011. *(Image courtesy Steve Dean)*

51.09 Culvert #79 (Sugartree Branch) 10' span, carries the stream from the valley along Lander Road.

CATOCTIN CREEK AQUEDUCT
51.53 Access: From Lander at mile 50.89.

This 130' aqueduct is considered by many as the most beautiful on the canal. The sharp bend in the canal on the upstream side gave rise to the term "Crooked Aqueduct." A local flood on October 31, 1973, caused the center and upstream arch of the aqueduct to collapse. A temporary steel-frame bridge carried the towpath across the Catoctin Creek until 2011. Due largely to the efforts of Lander resident George Lewis, the Catoctin Aqueduct Restoration Fund (CAR) was established, and in 2006 the C&O Canal NHP entered into a formal funding agreement with CAR. Under the 2009 American Recovery and Reinvestment Act (ARRA), the C&O Canal NHP awarded a $3.93 million contract to Corman Construction of Annapolis Junction, Maryland. The new reinforced-concrete structure integrated stones recovered from the original arches. The restored aqueduct was dedicated and opened on October 15, 2011.

The CSX Railroad crosses Catoctin Creek just above the aqueduct on a handsome two-arch bridge, making a pair of fine structures. Canallers called Catoctin Creek "Jug Creek."

51.88 There is a buried culvert here; now served by a metal pipe.

52.27 Culvert #81, 4' span, drains a small stream from the ravine on the berm.

52.51 Culvert #82 (Little Catoctin Creek), 16' span, was restored in 1925, but was washed out again by a flash flood in 1987. All but the towpath part of the culvert is now exposed. A small bridge carries the towpath across the creek. The Brunswick rail yard begins.

53.17 Culvert #83, 4' span.

Right: The weakened Catoctin Aqueduct (known also as "Crooked Aqueduct") prior to the 1973 collapse. Below: The restored Catoctin Aqueduct one month after it was reopened in October 2011. *(Image courtesy Steve Dean)*

53.21 Informal overflow. The towpath is well rip-rapped here to resist water erosion from the overflow. It is 59' long, has a well-defined channel to the river, and the towpath is about 1' lower here—all good signs of an earlier overflow.

53.51 Unmarked boundary line of the town of Brunswick.

53.59 Culvert #84, 10' span, possibly a road culvert, carries Tobacco House Branch.

53.97 Culvert #85, 4' span.

54.0x The Brunswick Family Campground is located between the towpath and the river. It is owned by the city but managed by the River and Trail Outfitters. The towpath here is also used as an access road for the camp. Watch for fast moving

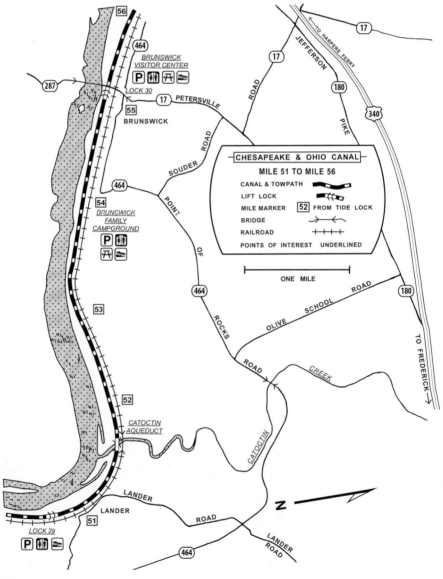

vehicle traffic. Well water, toilets, a boat ramp, boat rentals, and picnic grounds are available. 40 Canal Towpath Rd., Brunswick, MD 21716, 301-695-5177, www.potomacrivercampground.com.

54.56 Water Pollution Control Facility for Brunswick.

54.57 Culvert #86, 6' span.

54.69 A brick B&O Railroad roundhouse once located here provided limited locomotive service from open pits on the unenclosed side, away from the towpath. The first railroad station in Brunswick was built in 1834—one of the earliest railroad stations in the country. The current station serves commuter trains into Washington.

54.81 Culvert #87, 8' span, carries the stream from the center of Brunswick.

54.95 Waste Weir. This is the site of former flour and feed mill buildings. The first mill at this site was built in 1845. In 1890 the mill had a daily capacity of 85 barrels of flour and purchased canal water to power the mill wheel. One of the mill buildings is said to have been used for Union army courts-martial during the Civil War and was used later for several murder trials. The mill was abandoned as a commercial enterprise in 1962 and burned in 1972.

LOCK 30, BRUNSWICK

55.00 (39.311220, -77.630749) Access: From US-340 take the MD-17/Burkittsville Rd. exit toward Brunswick. Continue on MD-17 south through three roundabouts, approximately 1.0 mile. Turn right onto Petersville Rd. Go 0.9 mile to the next traffic circle and take the fourth right onto Petersville Rd. (Sign A). Take slight right onto South Maple Ave. Continue straight through traffic light to the MARC Train parking area. After crossing the second set of railroad tracks take an immediate right and follow the road to a large parking area along the river. There are restrooms, picnic tables, grills, and a boat ramp.

The Brunswick Heritage Museum/C&O Canal NHP Visitor Center is located at 40 West Potomac St., 301-834-7100, www.brunswickmuseum.org, www.nps.gov/choh/planyourvisit/brunswickvisitorcenter.htm. Hours of operation change seasonally.

Brunswick (formerly Berlin) is the second of nine "Canal Towns" along the canal. Visit www.canaltowns.org for more information. The quaint town has restaurants, specialty shops, and antique stores.

Lock 30 was extended on the upper end to allow two boats to lock through at a time in one direction (see page 36). The timber cribbing for the drop gate of the extension is still visible here.

Louis Wernwag built the first pivot bridge across the canal at Berlin (now Brunswick), for which he was paid $401. The bridge was rebuilt in 1841 and again in the 1870s. The pivot was probably on the berm side of the lock. In 1836 the canal company purchased a house near the lock to serve as a lockhouse, rather than building one.

55.03 Pass under the bridge carrying MD-17. The first wooden bridge was built here by the Loudoun and Berlin Bridge Company about 1859 and was burned by Confederates on June 9, 1861. The Union Army of the Potomac built pontoon bridges here to cross back into Virginia in October 1862 following the Battle of Antietam and in July 1863 following the Battle of Gettysburg. An iron toll bridge was built in 1893 and remained until the 1936 flood. The current bridge was constructed in the early 1950s.

55.45 Culvert #88, 8' span.

Lock 30 at Brunswick in the early 1900s. Note the pivot bridge in the open position (right), the locktender's shanty, and the extension of the lock upstream, so as to lock through two boats in one direction at the same time.

Canal Town, Brunswick

Brunswick is one of the largest towns on the canal, with a 2010 population of 5,870. The town is located on a portion of a 1753 royal land grant made to "Hawkins Merry-Peep-O-Day." The town was laid out and named Berlin in 1780, though locally it was called "Eeltown." Ferry operations across the river began sometime prior to 1822. Ten years later the post office was established under the name of Barry.

During the Civil War the bustling canal town's population increased to 500 but dwindled to 200 by 1890. The town was officially named Brunswick in 1890, the year when the B&O Railroad built its eastern switchyard center and repair shops. At this time Brunswick became the busiest railroad town along the Potomac until the B&O shifted many of its activities elsewhere. Emphasis gradually turned from the railroad to the canal, river, and the area's recreation potential. Today this Washington-commuter, Main Street community celebrates its historical significance and attracts many visitors to the area.

Visit www.canaltowns.org to learn about points of interest, services, lodging, and food sources in the Canal Towns.

A day in May finds a plentiful supply of birds calling: the intricate song of the indigo bunting, the tinkling of wood warblers, the busy calls of vireos, the rattle of cow birds, and the clarion call of the wood thrush. At 2:30 p.m. on a sunny day a barred owl lights on the horizontal limb of an oak, peering indistinctly about through his wide eye rings and from time to time exercises his wings without flying. A young rabbit hops leisurely down the towpath. –Grant Conway, Potomac Appalachian Trail Club

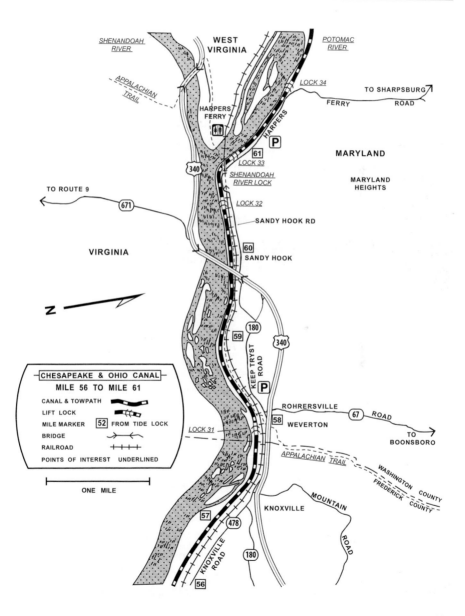

CHESAPEAKE & OHIO CANAL
MILE 56 TO MILE 61

CANAL & TOWPATH
LIFT LOCK
MILE MARKER   52 FROM TIDE LOCK
BRIDGE
RAILROAD
POINTS OF INTEREST   UNDERLINED

ONE MILE

56.01 Culvert #89, 8' span. Red sandstone ringstones.

56.17 The marshalling hump for switching cars on the railroad is no longer active. Rail fans would gather along the road above the track to watch. The black color of the canal bank is due to soot from over a century of use by coal-burning switch engines.

56.45 Culvert #90, 6' span.

57.01 Culvert #91 (Knoxville Branch), 12' span. Although the area shows much improvement since the 1930s, there is still significant debris along the railroad visible from the towpath. Though no documentation has been found, the general area between the railroad tracks and the canal and river was reportedly one of the largest "hobo jungles" in the Mid-Atlantic states between World Wars I and II.

57.06 Knoxville. Site of Knoxville Basin ahead.

57.37 Culvert #92, 6' span; the stream drains the east slope of the tip of South Mountain.

57.39 In addition to a view of the rapids and small tree-covered islands is a nice panorama of the northern end of Virginia's Short Hill, the southern end of Maryland's South Mountain, and the river gap between. A fisherman's path at the edge of the river provides a diversion from walking on the towpath from about mile 56.34 to the mouth of Israel Creek.

57.85 Cross unmarked Frederick–Washington County line. The old road (now a path) on the river side leads across a ford in Israel Creek to the Potomac River and ruins of the intakes for the power system of the Weverton Mills.

57.8x Weverton Ruins. Access: From Lock 31 at 58.01. Extensive stone walls 20'–30' high sit on the river's edge just above the remains of a stone-filled log dam in the Potomac. The 3.5'-high dam, following a ledge of rocks angling upriver, was completed in 1847 by Charles B. Fisk, chief engineer of the Canal Company at that time. The dam was built for Caspar Wever's manufacturing company in exchange for land associated with a waste weir and channel that the canal company found was necessary at the upstream end of Lock 31. These stone walls are about all that remains of the ruins of Weverton, ca. 1834–77. These walls are part of three river intake sluices or headgates, designed to take water to the Weverton Mills. The tailrace paralleled the canal for some distance and was troublesome to the canal in times of high water. The canal company purchased the land and destroyed the dam in 1877.

LOCK 31, WEVERTON

58.01 (39.329916, -77.681966) Access: From US-340 in Maryland turn left onto Keep Tryst Rd. (opposite Valley Rd.). Continue on Keep Tryst Rd. about 1.0 mile. The road descends down a hill to the railroad track, where there is a triangular parking area and a trail across the railroad tracks and canal to the towpath. (Keep Tryst Rd. makes a very sharp turn at this parking area and ascends to eastbound US-340.) The lockhouse was damaged by fire in 1989.

The lock was completed in 1833. In the mid-1830s a pivot bridge was built at the lock, primarily for access by the Weverton Manufacturing Company. No trace of the bridge is now visible. This bridge caused difficulties between the canal company and the Frederick and Harpers Ferry Turnpike Company, the latter complaining that persons traveling between Weverton and Harpers Ferry were taking advantage of the bridge to use the towpath, thus avoiding the road and its toll. In an effort to curb this traffic, it was ordered that the pivot bridge over Lock 31 be turned and locked when not in use. In 1850, Weverton industrialist George Rothery sought and obtained permission to erect a footbridge over the canal below the lock to shorten the distance his workers had to walk between the factories and boarding houses. The bridge was to have been 17' above the canal (the accepted standard), but there is no record as to whether or not the bridge was built.

The lock is unique in that a sawmill race goes under the upper part of the lock. A mill was obviously in use when the canal was built, and the canal crossed the tailrace. A culvert was built to carry waste water from the mill wheel. Apparently the mill took water from Israel Creek and provided a head of about 15'. Most of the headrace was obliterated in construction of old and new US-340. As water from Israel Creek was insufficient to operate the mill in the dry season, an arched intake from the canal was provided for the mill to augment its water supply by buying canal water. The 6' span culvert under the lock, which provided for the tailrace from the mill, was undoubtedly built by the contractor of this lock and the cost included in its footings. This lock was the most expensive of the first 32, except for the tide lock, costing nearly $4,000 more than the average.

Lock 31 is believed to have been built on a wood timber foundation. The tilting of the lock walls toward each other over the years caused the canal company to cut back the face of the local ashlar (finished stone) to maintain sufficient width for the passage of boats. The stone face was cut back until the towpath wall ashlar was so weakened that it was replaced with concrete. When the upper towpath gate pocket was replaced with concrete, a wooden gate bumper block 4" x 6" was placed in the concrete to prevent damage to the cast-iron wicket gates (and the lock itself) when the wicket gates were accidentally left open. This is common on the canal. When the stone ashlar was removed from the towpath wall, the stones were stored in two piles on the river side of the towpath. Their placement indicates that they were removed with a crane in two phases.

The canal is quite wide below the lock for about a half mile; the remains of several stone docks are visible in the wide berm dike. A 42'-long, dry-laid stone wall on the berm above the lock serves as a berm dike retaining wall and was probably used for a loading dock.

Lock 31 was an extended lock, as were locks 25 through 32. This one was extended on the lower end. The towpath rise is quite abrupt here and begins just below the lower end of the lock extension. The rise seems to be more abrupt from here on than the normal 150' gradual rise at the locks downstream. A stone-filled, wood timber crib in front of the berm wing wall was once used to help line up boats for entering the lock and to prevent them from bumping the upper wing walls. They are more common on the berm, as the towpath itself serves as a sturdy base for the upper towpath wing wall. As with most locks, there are stop plank slots in the upper extension walls (the portion of the lock wall just above the upper gate pocket) about 2' above the upper gate pocket. Planks in these slots held back water above the lock during repairs. The fact that they were not formed in the concrete walls indicates their lack of importance in the late operating period.

58.06 Waste weir. Typical concrete over original stone walls.

58.07 The Appalachian Trail (www.appalachiantrail.org) joins the towpath from here to Harpers Ferry. For a spectacular view of the Potomac River, follow the Appalachian Trail north across US-340 (on a footpath underpass) up to Weverton Cliff, the southern tip of South Mountain. (CAUTION: this is a steep climb over rocky terrain with a series of switchbacks.)

58.08 Informal overflow.

58.19 Culvert #93 (Israel Creek), 20' span, drains the beautiful Pleasant Valley between South Mountain and Elk Ridge. About 60' above the inflow of the culvert is the beautiful railroad bridge over the creek. A "tragedy" occurred here in 1916 when the Savage Distillery burned, destroying 650 barrels of whiskey. Alcohol spilling into Israel Creek burned all the way to the Potomac. Prior to its burning, however, the distillery was listed in the National Institutes of Health Bulletin as a source of Potomac pollution due to some of its spent mash spilling onto the ground and washing into the river.

58.72–58.99 Millers Narrows. This was the third of the four narrows at the heart of the C&O Canal and B&O Railroad legal battle, 1828–32. At this location, as at the one above it, space had to be provided for the Frederick–Harpers Ferry Toll Road as well as the canal and railroad.

58.91 The towpath is directly on the riverbank, walled in many places, with a fine high cliff on the berm. Sandy Hook Bridge and the Harpers Ferry Water Gap are ahead—an outstanding river view.

An Industrial Ghost Town

The story of Weverton centers on its founder, Caspar W. Wever (1786–1861), an engineer with an ambitious dream. After working for the federal government on the National Road and as superintendent of construction on the B&O Railroad, Wever aspired to be his own boss. Reconnoitering land for the railroad, he estimated a 15′ drop in the Potomac in the 2.5 miles downstream from Harpers Ferry, which if harnessed would create enough waterpower to turn 300,000 to 600,000 spindles—equal to or greater than the massive textile mills at Lowell, Massachusetts—and turn the wheels for other industries he would attract.

He purchased land at the foot of Pleasant Valley for factory, home, and town sites, and chartered the Weverton Manufacturing Company. Wever's business misfortunes included his first conflict with the C&O Canal Company in 1832, when his land was condemned for the canal right-of-way. After winning damages from the canal company, Wever then obtained an injunction to stop construction of the canal on his property until he was paid in full.

Because his lease charges were so high, most of Wever's stone-walled, two-storied factory buildings lay idle. Wever had also made a serious miscalculation—the river fall did not provide enough head (i.e., pressure) to produce efficient power. A proposed bill for establishing a National Foundry at Weverton failed, further dampening Wever's plans. Prior to the Civil War, a mysterious utopian experiment in communal working and living was established at Weverton. The commune operated the Weverton Cotton Mills for only a few months before war erupted and the Union army took over the buildings for barracks. In the 1860 census—a year prior to his death—the aspiring industrialist Caspar Wever designated himself a "farmer."

After an 1877 flood further damaged Weverton's surviving buildings, the canal company acquired the property and demolished the dam which was diverting floodwater and destroying portions of the towpath embankment. The mid-nineteenth century town—once an ambitious dream—eventually disappeared with scarcely a trace.

59.09 Sizable cave on the berm 20′ above the railroad. Harpers Ferry is in view as the canal follows the bend of the river.

59.50 Probable abandoned culvert, now covered; the present metal pipe was placed in the canal several years ago to water the canal prism for fishing pools. Possibly Culvert #94, 6′ span, built in 1833.

59.58 Pass under Sandy Hook Bridge, carrying US-340. Hostelling International–Harpers Ferry is a short distance back up the road on the berm. 19123 Sandy Hook Rd., Knoxville, MD 21758, 301-834-7652, www.hiusa.org/harpersferry. River and Trail Outfitters has bikes and canoes for rent, provides river float trips, and has hiking and river guides. 604 Valley Rd., Knoxville, MD 21758, 301-695-5177, www.rivertrail.com.

SANDY HOOK

59.60 The Village of Sandy Hook with its row of old houses facing the railroad and the canal was once a busy town. Before the railroad was centered in Brunswick,

Sandy Hook had repair shops and a station between the tracks and the canal. Across the street from the Sandy Hook Station was the post office, known earlier as "Keep Tryst." Because of its proximity to Harpers Ferry, Sandy Hook served as the headquarters for a number of Union generals during the Civil War. The Frederick–Harpers Ferry Toll Road (chartered 1805) passed through here. Today the Harpers Ferry Road leads to Sharpsburg through delightful, rolling countryside. Several paths cross the wet canal bottom to the village, but use caution crossing the tracks as there are frequent trains.

According to legend, Sandy Hook was named for a quicksand deposit at the edge of the river which took the lives of a teamster and his horses. Present-day canoeists taking out at Sandy Hook report mud but no quicksand. There is still danger on the river, however, and the stretch between Dam 3 and Sandy Hook is recommended only for expert canoeists.

59.71 A large plastic pipe culvert runs under the towpath. The berm is in poor condition here.

59.83 A stone foundation on the berm marks a railroad ruin. Just beyond are several large red sandstone blocks said to have been dumped off a disabled railroad car. Another foundation (concrete) beyond the berm again indicates the presence of the railroad.

59.91 The "Long Wall," built to resist flood damage to the canal, extended from this point to the head of Lock 33, a distance of 0.82 mile. Built on the river side of the towpath opposite the mouth of the Shenandoah River, the face of the wall rose from the bedrock of the river to as much as 12' above towpath level.

The Frederick And Harpers Ferry Turnpike

The state of Maryland authorized The Frederick and Harpers Ferry Turnpike Company to construct a toll road between the two towns. The western terminus of the road connected with the Wager toll bridge over the Potomac River at Harpers Ferry. In Maryland, the road followed the edge of the river east to a point downstream from the present-day US-340 bridge, where it ascended a hill, then known as "the hill above Millers Narrows." As was usual, whenever the construction of the canal interrupted or displaced a road, the canal company was forced to build a substitute road at its own expense.

The turnpike company charged a variety of tolls for wagons, carts, and horses; for droves of cattle, pigs, sheep or turkeys; and for riders on horseback. They even charged a toll for pedestrians. The turnpike company plagued the canal company with complaints that pedestrians were allowed to use the towpath to avoid paying tolls. The C&O did strictly forbid the use of the towpath for wagons, carts, and horses for other than company use but found it difficult to limit pedestrian use. At one stage the complaints were so strong that the canal company ordered the pivot bridges over the canal from Point of Rocks to Harpers Ferry to be locked in the open position to minimize use of the towpath by pedestrians. This was more of a nuisance than a solution, as pedestrians simply used the closest culvert under the canal.

On the canal side, the towpath was rip-rapped with one-man stone throughout much of this distance, though little remains in view due to floods.

60.16 Elk Ridge (or Maryland Heights) on the berm overlooks Harpers Ferry. The area below the confluence of the Potomac and Shenandoah Rivers was called the "Bull Ring" because of the circling turbulence at flood stage when the Shenandoah's flow exceeded that of the Potomac. Many Native American campsites have been excavated in the vicinity of Harpers Ferry. Native American tribes reportedly shared the fishing grounds during the spring run of yellow suckers.

60.20 Just below Lock 32 are the fragmentary remains of what may be the only extant section of the Patowmack Company sluice canal around the rapids at this location. Elsewhere, the construction of the C&O Canal destroyed all traces of the bypass channel that protected boats in the river from the rapids above and below the mouth of the Shenandoah. A rock outcrop about 20' out in the river may mark the river side of the channel.

LOCK 32, SANDY HOOK

60.23 Access: From Lock 33 at mile 60.70.

Lock 32 is a short distance below the mouth of the Shenandoah River and in the gap between the Blue Ridge in Virginia and its extension, Elk Ridge, in Maryland. The canal, railroad, and Harpers Ferry Road are crowded between the river and the cliffs. Of all the locks on the canal, Lock 32 is the most subject to flood damage, particularly from Shenandoah floods. When flooded, the

Harper's Weekly "Hood Pencil Drawing 1833" depicting the approach to Harpers Ferry.

Shenandoah overrides the Potomac, dashes against the Maryland shore, turns and runs down the canal scouring everything in its path. The construction of the canal bed at Lock 32 causes floodwaters to wreak havoc on the lock walls. Currently, the NPS attempts to maintain the ruins but not to rebuild the lock.

The lock was completed in 1833. Lock 32 bears evidence of much rebuilding and the effects of floods in recent decades. It is 89'8" between gate pockets. The towpath was elevated behind the now-gone Long Wall, so there is no towpath rise at this lock. Lock 32 is the uppermost of a series of eight extended locks, continuous from Lock 25. Little remains of the stone-filled timber cribs except for a shallow windrow of rubble rocks. Much of the canal bed above the lock has been scoured to bedrock by floods. Adjacent to the berm side of the bypass flume are high stone walls that are the remains of a canal carpenter shop, last run by Greenwald Keyser. The long rapids in the river are called "White Horse."

60.25 The C&O Canal NHP lands run through Harpers Ferry National Historical Park property, which includes four thousand acres of battlefields, nearly 20 miles of hiking, museums, and the restored historic Lower Town. Directly across the Potomac is Loudoun Heights, the northern end of the Blue Ridge Mountains at the Virginia–West Virginia border. Harpers Ferry NHP hiking trails lead to spectacular views on both Loudoun Heights and Maryland Heights the southern end of Elk Ridge on the Maryland side.

> Flooding in this area is caused primarily by the steep gradient of the Potomac River, the narrow gorge below Harpers Ferry, and the confluence of the Potomac and Shenandoah Rivers. Records from 1889 until recently show that river water reached the towpath every two years and rose 5' above the towpath every five years. Floods reached 21' above the towpath in the 1889 and the 1936 floods. Great damage was also done in the floods of 1843, 1852, 1877, and 1890, as well as more recent ones, including 1996.

60.34 The high, old dry wall on the berm side supports the railroad grade. This is the last of the four sections between Point of Rocks and Harpers Ferry where the canal and railroad shared the narrow right-of-way. At one time the B&O was to have built a high board fence between the canal and the railroad at the narrows to prevent unduly frightening the tow animals. The fence was never built, and it was found that the locomotives did not "spook" the mules as had been feared. The first "iron horse" to reach the Maryland shore opposite Harpers Ferry was the "Arabian" on December 9, 1834.

60.51 The original towpath has been completely obliterated by floods. The towpath now is maintained at a level near that of the canal bed in operating days. During one repair from a flood, stones were taken from the Shenandoah River Lock just ahead and used to build a continuation of the river wall across the lock.

SHENANDOAH RIVER LOCK

60.62 Access: From Lock 33 above.

Completed in 1833, this was the first river lock to be constructed. A "mule tracking bridge" that the B&O Railroad built alongside the first Potomac bridge allowed boats to be towed between the river lock and the then-Virginia shore at Harpers Ferry. Initially, the canal company had planned for Harpers Ferry to be a major transshipment point for products to and from the Shenandoah Valley via boats using skirting canals along the Shenandoah and the Winchester & Potomac Railroad. However, in May 1841 the railroad tore down the tracking bridge and was not forced to replace it until the following year. Ultimately, however, the canal company could not reach an agreement with the landowners—the Wager family—to build a wharf at or near the Point (where the two rivers meet) in Harpers Ferry. The W&P Railroad also cut into the once heavy traffic down the Shenandoah River, thus the river lock was rarely used.

Modern approach to Harpers Ferry, 2009. *(Image courtesy Steve Dean)*

Little now remains of the lock above ground. A portion of the lock lies under the towpath, which continued on grade after the abandonment, although while in use, there was a mule crossover bridge high enough to allow boats to enter or leave the lock. The lock was originally 15' wide, but by the time of the Civil War it had narrowed, due to the tendency of the lock walls to slump inwards. As large freighters were not passed through the lock because of the failure to establish a wharf across the river, it was used only by smaller boats able to operate in the river. The narrowing likely was not a problem and therefore was not corrected.

The 1889 flood greatly damaged the Long Wall and essentially destroyed the river lock. When subsequent repairs were made, much of the river lock was taken down and the stones used elsewhere. When the Long Wall was repaired, it was built across the top of the old river lock.

60.66 Old bridge piers leading across the river to Harpers Ferry are the remains of the B&O's 1837 bridge that carried both the railroad and the turnpike across the Potomac.

60.67 Pass under two railroad bridges. The first is the 1894 bridge now used by the CSX Winchester branch, and the second is the 1931 bridge for the CSX main line. Both bridges lead into the tunnel. Pedestrians and bicyclists can use the first bridge to cross the Potomac River into Harpers Ferry. At press time, the NPS has plans to replace the current spiral staircase for easier bicycle access.

LOCK 33, HARPERS FERRY

60.70 (39.329395, -77.731919) Access: Minimal parking is available along the Sandy Hook/Harpers Ferry Rd. The best access is from the Harpers Ferry NHP Visitor

The Bridges Of Harpers Ferry

The C&O Canal's victory in the legal battles around Point of Rocks forced the B&O Railroad to switch to the Virginia (now West Virginia) side of the Potomac to build its line to Cumberland. Thus the railroad began a decades-long struggle to construct an efficient route through Harpers Ferry.

In 1837 the B&O opened its first bridge across the river to Harpers Ferry. The bridge carried both the railroad and the turnpike across the Potomac. The bridge was designed and built by B&O Engineer Benjamin Latrobe, Jr. and Lewis Wernwag, a famous builder of wooden bridges who was residing in Harpers Ferry at the time. A wooden bridge was built on the masonry piers; those piers remain in the river today. Shortly after the opening in 1837, defects were discovered that required expensive repairs. The bridge was both modified and rebuilt in subsequent years—especially during the Civil War, when it was rebuilt as a result of floods or destruction nine times in four years.

In 1894 the B&O opened its second bridge. At the same time they built a double-track tunnel to replace the single-track line that ran along the base of Maryland Heights. The new construction eased the railroad's curvature. The 1837 bridge became a single-lane highway bridge.

By 1931 technological advances resulted in longer and heavier trains, making the 1894 bridge obsolete. The B&O built a new 1,400-foot bridge, which crossed the Potomac at an angle to reduce curvature for trains on the main line. Trains on the B&O Shenandoah subdivision to Winchester continued to use the 1894 bridge.

Between 1931 and 1936 there were three working bridges over the Potomac at Harpers Ferry. On March 17, 1936, flooding destroyed the 1837 bridge, which was still in service as a highway bridge. The flood also destroyed the road bridge over the Shenandoah River. As a result, the B&O allowed motor traffic to share the 1894 bridge with trains. This arrangement continued until the 1950s, when a replacement highway bridge was built for US-340 over the Shenandoah River.

In the 1980s, a pedestrian lane was added to the 1894 bridge. By sharing the bridge with CSX Winchester Branch trains, visitors could cross the Potomac between Harpers Ferry and Maryland. The 1931 bridge continues to carry CSX freight trains, Amtrak passenger trains between Chicago and Washington, and MARC commuter trains between Martinsburg, West Virginia, and Washington.

Center (NPS fee area) off US-340, where shuttle bus service takes visitors to the Lower Town. From the shuttle bus drop-off point, follow Shenandoah St. to the Point, and cross the bridge to Lock 33. 304-535-6371, www.nps.gov/hafe. The park is open daily 8 a.m. to 5 p.m. (closed Thanksgiving Day, Christmas Day, and New Year's Day). Harpers Ferry and the nearby town of Bolivar are the third and fourth "Canal Towns" along the towpath. Visit www.canaltowns.org for more information.

To access the Sandy Hook/Harpers Ferry Rd. from the east (MD), take US-340 until the two lanes merge and take an immediate left onto Keep Tryst Rd. If approaching from the west (WV/VA), take the first exit on the right after crossing the Potomac River bridge. Go about 0.25 mile and turn right onto Sandy Hook Rd. The road parallels the railroad and canal, becoming Harpers Ferry Rd. at the railroad bridges. Lock 33 is on the left after the road passes over the railroad at the downstream end of the tunnel and drops down under the railroad bridge.

Lock 33 has been frequently rebuilt after being damaged by pounding flood waters. Most recently, it has been stabilized by the NPS. According to the 1833 Engineers Report, most of the stone used in the lock is Virginia "flint"

HARPER'S FERRY—THE SCENE OF THE LATE INSURRECTION.

This 1859 *Harper's Weekly* illustration depicts the canal (foreground) and the covered bridge that connected Maryland and then-Virginia. The bridge was first destroyed during a Confederate evacuation of the town on June 14, 1861. It would be destroyed and rebuilt nine times during the war. *(Courtesy Harpers Ferry National Historical Park, Historical Photograph Collection, Catalog #HF 246)*

hauled 1.5 miles by wagon, crossing both the Shenandoah and the Potomac. A small portion of stone came from a Maryland quarry one mile away. There is interesting masonry in the elaborate stone arch bypass flume culvert.

William S. Elgin was the locktender and section collector in 1850, according to the canal company's 1851 annual report. According to John Penn Warren's biography of John Brown, John Cook, an advance man for Brown, arrived 15 months before Brown's raid, married a local girl, and tended the lock "across the river from Harpers Ferry" (presumably Lock 33). Photographs taken during canal operation show several buildings on the river side of the lock, including those from which the Reed family sold feed for mules and groceries to canallers for at least two generations.

The canal parallels Harpers Ferry Road for 0.9 mile. The road is separated from the canal prism by a beautiful stone wall that forms the berm bank.

Two wooden footbridges provide access to the Maryland Heights trails, which lead to ruins of Civil War breastworks and forts and a must-see view of the town below. CAUTION: These are difficult hikes, steep and rocky, and proper footwear is required. It is a most delightful short hike from Lock 33 to Lock 36. In 3.48 miles round trip, one sees four lift locks, an inlet lock, beautiful river scenes, the skyline of Harpers Ferry, a now-unique canal dry dock, parts of two dams, and the remains of three lockhouses.

The ruins across the Harpers Ferry Road from Lock 33 are often referred to as the "Salty Dog Tavern." This designation, however, is incorrect. Properly called the Stone House, it sometimes housed the locktender but was privately owned. A frame building that housed a tavern with an unsavory reputation in the 1930s and early 1940s was adjacent to the Stone House and was supposedly nicknamed the "Salty Dog" after a popular song of the time.

60.79 The towpath between Locks 33 and 34 has a hard-packed, smooth, clay surface on top of the riverbank. There are excellent views of the river and of the cliffs on the berm. Vines have been cleared from the high rock wall forming the berm side of the canal. The canal prism is wide here, allowing enough room for boats to tie up on the berm side while other boats pass through.

Canal Towns, Harpers Ferry & Bolivar

Here two rivers and three states converge to form a spectacular scene of nature steeped in dramatic history. From Civil War to the Civil Rights Movement, through natural, transportation, and industrial history, the town has something of interest for every visitor. And for those just seeking recreation or adventure, Harpers Ferry offers rafting, tubing, canoeing, fishing, biking, hiking, zip lining, and rock climbing. See www.canaltowns.org.

Peter Stephens, the first permanent settler and a squatter on Lord Fairfax's lands where the Potomac and Shenandoah Rivers cut through the Blue Ridge Mountains, established a trading post and crude ferries here in 1733. Robert Harper, house builder, millwright, and merchant, purchased "squatters rights" from Stephens in early 1747, and in 1751 he obtained a patent for 125 acres of land in "the Hole." In 1763 the Virginia General Assembly established the town of "Shenandoah Falls at Mr. Harper's Ferry." Thomas Jefferson visited on October 25, 1783, viewing the water gap from atop a rock formation now known as "Jefferson Rock." Visitors today can climb to this area and see the same view little changed in over two centuries. In 1785 Jefferson's description appeared in *Notes on the State of Virginia*: "The passage of the Patowmac through the Blue Ridge is perhaps one of the most stupendous scenes in nature."

In the summer of 1785, George Washington surveyed the area to determine the need for bypass canals to navigate the river. Almost a decade later, Washington championed Harpers Ferry for the site of a new federal armory and arsenal. The site had an abundance of waterpower and was just 60 miles from the new capital—yet remote enough to be protected from foreign invaders. In 1796 Robert Harper's heirs sold 125 acres to the federal government, retaining three-quarters of an acre on the "Ferry Lot Reservation" (the present-day area known as The Point), and the "Six-acre Reservation," which would become the commercial heart of the town.

Construction on the new armory began in 1799, and operations commenced three years later. In 1803 Meriwether Lewis stopped here to procure weapons and hardware for his transcontinental expedition. By 1810 the Harpers Ferry Armory was producing 10,000 arms annually. John H. Hall, a New England gunmaker, arrived in 1820 with a contract to produce 1,000 breech-loading rifles for the War Department. Over the next two decades Hall's Rifle Works along the Shenandoah perfected precision machinery for interchangeable parts, pioneering the factory system in America. Mills and factories sprang up along the Shenandoah, covering almost every available space on Virginius Island. In 1835 two young British travelers viewing "a most abominable village" from Jefferson Rock wrote of the "smell of coal smoke" from the factories, and wrote that "the clanking of hammers obtrude themselves on the senses and prevent your enjoyment from being unmixed."

The C&O Canal reached the shore opposite Harpers Ferry in 1833. The B&O followed a year later and opened its bridge across the Potomac in January 1837. The town became a major transportation hub. After major renovations between 1845 and 1854, the armory reached its zenith with 20 industrial buildings stretching 600 yards along the Potomac. By

1859 it employed over 400 workers and housed more than 15,000 weapons. Nearly 3,000 people resided in the bustling industrial town. Resident John E. Cook had arrived in 1858, married a local girl, and worked as a school teacher, book seller, and locktender. His fellow citizens had no idea that Cook was actually there to gather intelligence for abolitionist John Brown's planned raid on the armory and arsenal. The weapons at Harpers Ferry made it a prime target of Brown's war on slavery.

On the night of October 16, 1859, John Brown and 18 raiders advanced toward Harpers Ferry. By 10:30 p.m. they had seized the bridges over both rivers, the armory and arsenal, and the rifle factory on Hall's Island. At daylight, citizens alerted the nearby towns to a slave revolt. Townspeople began firing on the raiders, and by 10 a.m. local militia had blocked all escape routes. Gunfire continued throughout the day, killing raiders and citizens—including the mayor of Harpers Ferry. Brown and his surviving men were forced into the fire engine house on the armory grounds. U.S. Marines under the command of Col. Robert E. Lee surrounded the engine house that night. The raid ended the next morning when marines stormed the engine house. The trauma and fear inflicted on the town continued for the next six years.

John Brown's capture, trial, and execution propelled an already divided country toward war. When war finally came 18 months later, Harpers Ferry—on the border between North and South—immediately became a military target for both armies. The federal armory and arsenal was destroyed, wrecking the town's economy. Most of the citizens fled, but those who remained endured four years of destruction, occupation, deprivation, and fear. The town changed hands eight times; the B&O Railroad bridge was destroyed and rebuilt nine times. In the September 1862 Maryland Campaign, Gen. Stonewall Jackson surrounded and captured over 12,500 Union troops here—the largest surrender of the war. The Union army established

Lock 33 at Harpers Ferry was once a busy place. Note the covered bypass flume necessitated by the large head of water passing through from Dam 3 above.

supply depots at Harpers Ferry and Sandy Hook and used the canal and railroad to service the troops pursuing the Confederates. To support Union Gen. Sheridan's Shenandoah Valley Campaign in 1864, the canal was used to forward grain, forage, and stores to Harpers Ferry.

Harpers Ferry never recovered from the war. Most of the citizens who had fled never returned. The ruins of the armory were torn down—the fire engine house or "John Brown's Fort" being the only building to survive. Fire, flood, and epidemics continued to harass the town. The replacement of water power by electricity made it possible to locate industry above flood plains. Eventually Harpers Ferry was little more than a whistle stop on the B&O.

One thing, however, continued to draw curious visitors to the town: John Brown's Fort. Many argued that the fiery abolitionist's stand here ignited the Civil War. Frederick Douglass, W. E. B. Dubois, and other early civil rights leaders turned the little engine house into a symbol of freedom. During August 15–19, 1906, the Niagara Movement (the future National Association for the Advancement of Colored People) held its first public meeting in the United States on the campus of Storer College (one of the first colleges in the U.S. to teach African Americans) in Harpers Ferry. On June 29, 1944, Franklin D. Roosevelt signed legislation creating the Harpers Ferry National Monument, and in 1963 it was declared a National Historical Park.

Over the following decades meticulous research and restoration turned the Lower Town of Harpers Ferry into a replicate nineteenth century town. The town now offers museums, unique shops, galleries, restaurants, and a host of hotels, inns, and bed and breakfasts. Public transportation options include Amtrak, the MARC commuter train, and PANTRAN bus service.

For more information see: Jefferson County Convention and Visitor's Bureau, 37 Washington Ct., Harpers Ferry, WV 25425, 1-886-HELLO-WV, www.wveasterngateway.com; Appalachian Trail Conservancy Headquarters, 799 Washington St., Harpers Ferry, WV 25425, 304-535-6331, www.appalachiantrail.org; Harpers Ferry National Historical Park, 171 Shoreline Drive, Harpers Ferry, WV 25425, 304-535-6371, www.nps.gov/hafe.

John Brown's Fort in the restored Lower Town area of Harpers Ferry. *(Image courtesy National Park Service)*

According to legend, Native American tribes considered the meeting of the two rivers as a shared neutral zone. In early spring, Native Americans converged to spear and net the yellow sucker (also known as the northern hogsucker) as the fish made their annual run up the rivers to spawn. Dip net platforms, similar to the Native American structures, and frequent along the upper Potomac until about 1950, continue to be erected by fishermen across the Potomac on the Virginia shore.

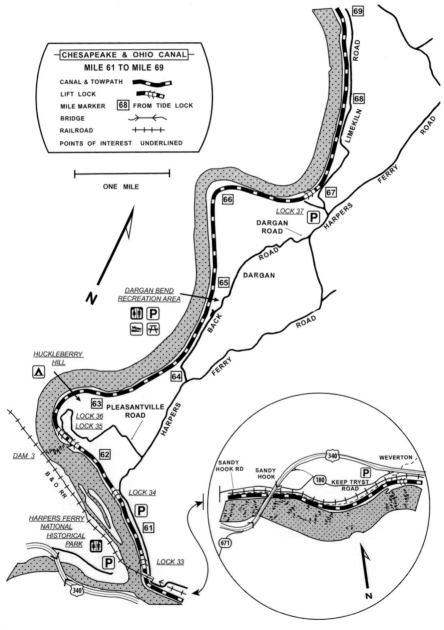

61.xx View across the river of the skyline of Harpers Ferry overlooking the Potomac from the former Hilltop House Hotel on the left to the "Crazy House" at right, where Civil War relics are embedded in the concrete. The long wooded island on the West Virginia side of the river is Byrnes Island. It was the site of an amusement park operated by the B&O Railroad as a destination for passengers on excursion trains.

61.07 A prominent rock ledge crosses the river in the direction of a former Potomac Edison hydroelectric plant. The building is not visible when trees are fully leafed out. An old military road leads to the Maryland Heights and Elk Ridge trails, passing the site of a Civil War naval battery. In 1862 sailors from the Washington Navy Yard lugged cannon—one weighing nearly five tons—up to this position to fortify the Union's defenses.

61.27 A footbridge to limited parking (39.329395, -77.731919) along Harpers Ferry Road (see mile 60.70) provides access to the Maryland Heights Trails by walking up the dirt fire road.

61.37 Evidence of a rock slide from the sheer cliff next to the road on the right. Broken rock 60'–75' long extends upward about 100'.

61.52 Intersection of Hoffmaster and Harpers Ferry Roads; a stream enters the canal from a ravine.

LOCK 34 (Goodhearts Lock)

61.57 (39.333430, -77.738577) Access: From the east (MD), take US-340 until the two lanes merge and take an immediate left onto Keep Tryst Rd. If approaching from the west (WV/VA), take the first exit on the right after crossing the Potomac River bridge. Go about 0.25 mile and turn right onto Sandy Hook Rd. The road parallels the railroad and canal, becoming Harpers Ferry Rd. at the railroad bridges. Continue 1.0 mile to Lock 34. There is a drop-off or pick-up lane and limited parking (three vehicles). A gate blocks vehicle access to the towpath. Drinking water and bench available. Steps lead to the river.

On October 16, 1859, John Brown and his men descended Harpers Ferry Road from their base at the Kennedy Farm for the raid on Harpers Ferry. The same road was used by Col. Benjamin "Grimes" Davis and 1,300 cavalrymen to escape Harpers Ferry the night before Gen. Stonewall Jackson captured 12,500 Union soldiers on September 15, 1862.

The lockhouse here washed away in the 1936 flood. A few remains of the stone foundation are visible. The lock was constructed of limestone with a few blocks of red sandstone at the upper end, possibly replacements.

One Christmas Eve, sometime before 1919, the locktender shot in self-defense a man by the name of Smith who demanded entry to the lockhouse and tried to force open the door.

After the 1936 flood, the last locktender, Willard "Coon" Goodheart, sat in a rocking chair that he had salvaged and commented, "We would swap belongings at flood time—lose some, gain some." He said in a 1946 interview:

> The lockhouse withstood many previous floods. Sometimes water came into the first floor and belongings were moved to the second floor. During the 1936 flood, water rose higher and higher and we moved our possessions to the second floor. Even the chickens were carried upstairs. It was a brick house with stone foundations and appeared to be firm against the swirling waters. However, we could hear the walls cracking, and we escaped by boat without our possessions before the house collapsed.

According to the 1822 river survey, the canal bed ahead was the location of the Patowmack Company's "Long Canal"—a skirting canal for passing the rapids in the river. The Patowmack Company built three skirting "canals" that consisted of a channel between the river bank and a low stone wall. They served to allow the Potomac gundalows (a form of narrow shallow boats used to carry limited cargoes down the river) to get safely past the rapids. This section may have been the one described in the survey: "a broad wall at foot of Rocky Mountains is used for a towpath along which the boats are dragged up." It should be noted, however, that the river boats were most often sold (likely for their wood) at their destination and not hauled back up the river.

61.61 A stream enters the canal on the berm. High bluffs begin.

61.68 Breaks in the towpath here were repaired with the towpath bridge with heavy rock and surfaced with crushed rock. Whitewater enthusiasts call the adjacent stretch of river "The Needles," as navigating the narrow rocky channels with sharp turns beginning below Dam 3 is compared to threading a series of needles.

61.91 Extremely steep bluffs and interesting rock formations plunge into the canal bed forming the berm bank in places. Round drill holes for early powder blasting can be seen.

62.20 The abutment of the New Armory unfinished dam. The dam was started in 1859 to replace Dam 3 for diverting water into a raceway for turning water power wheels in the Harpers Ferry Armory. With the destruction of the armory in 1861, and the decision not to rebuild it after the Civil War, the dam was no longer necessary.

The channel of the Patowmack Company's "Long Canal" likely began above the canal trail's bridge abutment.

FEEDER DAM 3 AND INLET/GUARD LOCK 3

62.27 A mule crossover bridge that carried the towpath over the feeder intake has not been rebuilt by the NPS, necessitating the diversion from the original towpath to a trail on the guard wall. (Note: the mileages given in this guidebook denote the original towpath.) The dam comes into view along the trail or guard bank parallel to the feeder canal and up to Inlet (Guard or Feeder) Lock 3. The trail crosses the upper end of the inlet lock, which has been filled in.

> WARNING! Canoeists should avoid unmarked Dam 3. Canoeing is not recommended between the US-340 bridge and Dam 3. This is an EXTREMELY DANGEROUS area.

The first dam was built in 1799 to supply water for the Harpers Ferry Armory and rebuilt in 1809 and 1820. Known as the "Government Dam," it was repaired frequently thereafter. Originally the C&O Canal Company had planned to build its own dam below the mouth of the Shenandoah, but by the time the canal reached Harpers Ferry in 1833, the company was experiencing severe financial problems. The federal government permitted it to tap the pool of water formed by its dam in order to fill the canal between that point and Dam 2 at Seneca. The designation of "Dam No. 3" comes from the dam's role as the third dam in the C&O Canal's system that was intended to include eight dams to impound river water to feed the canal. Ultimately, the

Feeder Dam 3 above Harpers Ferry, ca. 1936. Note the construction detail.

company did not have to build this dam (although they shared responsibility for its maintenance after the Civil War), and it ended up not building Dam 7. Consequently, the C&O Canal Company built only six of the seven dams it actually used.

By April 1, 1863, Union engineers had constructed a 450' double-track pontoon bridge above Dam 3. On July 5, 1863, Union cavalry destroyed it to prevent the Confederate army, retreating from Gettysburg, from possibly using it to cross the Potomac.

Locals residing here when navigation ceased on the canal in 1924 recall that canal barges loaded with rocks were sunk above the dam on the Maryland side around 1927 to divert more water to the raceway then serving the hydro-electric plant on the West Virginia side of the river.

As you proceed along the trail on the guard wall, note the ruins of the two-story brick lockhouse with a center chimney and fireplaces on each side. This house was for the locktender who tended both Lock 36 and the inlet lock. The house was destroyed in the 1936 flood. The last locktender was John W. Ault, grandfather of Lavenia Waskey Brus, who described the house as follows:

> Grandfather's house sat in a sort of semicircle. This high guard protecting it from the high waters of the Potomac River gave it a look of seclusion so different from the other lockhouses. A two-story house consisting of two bedrooms upstairs, a living room, large kitchen, and a frame summer kitchen built on. Also a porch the length of the house with many steps. A two-room size basement where grandmother stored all her canned vegetables, and pickles. Not to mention all the potatoes, apples, pears, etc. When viewed from the towpath, it presented a picturesque scene, with its unusual type of house, and scattered buildings, which housed chickens, hogs, a shed for garden plows, and tools. There was a pond alive with ducks, frogs and fish. A beautiful well-kept garden, fenced in from chickens. There was even a cow to provide milk and butter, and an old white horse which was a family pet and a source of enjoyment for my cousins and myself, when I was lucky enough to visit. To me this birthplace seemed like a small estate, secluded, yet homey. Verily a scene of tranquility.

The Potomac River above Harpers Ferry is said in many sources to have been called "Cohongoroota" by Native Americans. Various translations of the name are given, including that it means "River of Wild Geese," or is a derivation from the sound of honking geese.

LOCK 35

62.33 When headed upstream, Lock 35 and its dry dock can only be accessed via the guard wall trail to Lock 36 at mile 62.44. This is due to the missing crossover bridge at the feeder intake (see mile 62.27). If headed downstream, from Lock 35 one must backtrack to Lock 36 and take the guard wall trail to Harpers Ferry and points below.

Locks 35 and 36 are built of limestone brought five miles by water from Knotts Quarry on the opposite shore. These locks were known as "Two Locks" in the late 1800s. Immediately below the lock on the river side is the feeder canal, with water flowing from Inlet Lock 3 and the slackwater pool it forms above Dam 3.

A footbridge over the lock leads to the best example of a dry dock on the C&O Canal today. It was used extensively for repairing canal boats in the 1800s. There was an inlet with lock gates. Concrete beams supported boats when water was let out of the enclosure via a now-vine-covered drainway. Boats rolled on built-in trucks under the water. There was space enough for a man to stand and repair a boat's hull with tin and tar.

A member of the Cross family was locktender in the 1900s. John Kercheval was locktender for Locks 35 and 36 in 1850. The last locktender for Lock 35 was "Jap" Smith, who lived in a frame house on the hill above the lock. Only the foundation remains.

The dry dock at Lock 35 (shown here in 2010) was used extensively for repairing canal boats during the operating period. *(Image courtesy Steve Dean)*

LOCK 36

62.44 Access: Lock 33 at mile 60.70 or Dargan Bend Recreation Area at mile 64.89. From Lock 36, one can follow the original towpath route down to Lock 35 and the inlet channel. However, if headed further downstream, one must return to Lock 36 and follow the diversion trail on the guard wall.

Lock 36 has been filled in to keep it from collapsing. The frame house on the hill above the lock has been unoccupied since the late 1950s and was the subject of local ghost tales.

62.56 Cross concrete waste weir.

62.90 Huckleberry Hill Hiker–Biker Campsite. Nearest road access is Dargan Bend at mile 64.9. The campsite is situated on a river bend, exposed to brisk winds in winter and gentle breezes in summer.

63.05 Low cliffs along the berm support a beautiful rock garden of wildflowers. Fine sycamores surround the dry canal bed.

63.29 The canal rounds a rocky point where the river side of the towpath drops straight to the water.

63.68 A small stream flows into the canal from a forked ravine to the right. The canal bed may be swampy. The wetness of the bed varies widely in most sections of the canal, depending on the season or even the year, unless some persistent source of water feeds a particular area.

64.20 A stream enters the canal. Site of lost Culvert #95. A path leads across the canal bed to Back Road. Here, as elsewhere along the canal, it is inadvisable to drink from side streams because waste is sometimes dumped in the streams.

64.68 Culvert #96, Sawmill Run, 8' span, rebuilt ca. 1980.

DARGAN BEND RECREATION AREA

64.89 (39.364182, -77.740073) Access: From US-340 take exit for Keep Tryst Rd. Go 0.25 mile and turn right on Sandy Hook Rd. After 1.6 miles the road becomes Harpers Ferry Rd. Continue 2.3 miles and take slight left onto Back Rd.; continue 0.8 mile to parking area on left. The area can also be reached from Sharpsburg by taking Harpers Ferry, Dargan, and Back Roads. There is parking here for 25 cars; the 14 spaces in the upper lot are for vehicles with boat trailers. The vehicular bridge at the lower edge of the upper parking lot crosses the canal to an asphalt boat-launching pad. Dargan is one of many power boat-oriented recreation areas the NPS constructed along the canal in 1969–71. Camping is not permitted. The area has two picnic tables, two fire rings, and toilets. Summer and year-round houses are scattered along the floodplain on the West Virginia side of the river.

64.99 Culvert #97, 8' span. The arch of the culvert completely washed away; a stone abutment put in by the NPS also collapsed. The towpath narrows here due to the stabilization effort the park has in place here.

65.10 Beginning of the ruins of the Potomac Refining Company. The original quarry opened in 1876 and was started up again in 1908 by the newly formed PRC, which planned to process manganese, limestone, marble, and iron ore. Though mining began and elaborate claims of profitability were made in promotional materials, little was actually done by this company. It eventually collapsed in 1912 after company officials were accused of mailing false information about its profitability.

65.21 Two abandoned limestone kilns sit on the bank above the berm. O. J. Shinham operated the kilns until 1952. A dirt road upstream connected several quarries.

65.34 A slide has obscured the downriver entrance of a 50'-long tunnel associated with the mining activity in the area. The tunnel passes through a high ridge at the edge of the canal. The tunnel is unsafe and should NOT be entered.

65.37 A cave opening about 25' above the floor of the quarry can be reached via a properly equipped rock climb. The cliff rises above the opening.

65.38 A cave opening at the base of the quarry wall. Cave-ins near the entrance make it unsafe to explore.

65.60 Cabins and trailers can be seen along the floodplain across the river, with more substantial dwellings on the heights.

65.65 Open pasture dotted with red cedar. Stone foundations and a cistern are on the knoll 150 yards from the canal, but are undetectable with summer growth. Across the river a stream from a ravine drains a watershed surrounding Bakerton, West Virginia. The area has extensive abandoned manganese and limestone quarries.

65.78 Open field on the flat along the berm.

66.00 On the West Virginia side of the river is an extensive cut from which iron ore was obtained for the Antietam Furnace prior to the canal days. Also on the West Virginia side was Cow Ring Sluice, one of the Patowmack Company's river improvements.

66.02 Lower end of a half-mile, narrow island, 100 yards from the Maryland shore. Driftwood lodged on the shore indicates it is subject to overflow.

66.03 End of field on berm. The towpath beyond cuts across the upper end of Dargan Bend. The distance of the river from the towpath exceeds 100 yards in some places. Sycamores are predominant, with scatterings of beech, oak, silver maple and infrequent persimmon, wild cherry, and shadbush (also called serviceberry) and juneberry, which bloom in March and April. Paw paw, spicebush, honeysuckle, and grapevines provide an understory for taller trees.

66.30 The towpath rejoins the river.

66.32 The hillside along the berm rises; rocky outcrops protrude from the slope. The rocky hillside soon becomes a cliff.

66.61 A ravine enters the canal with drainage providing water to the canal for 100 yards downstream. A broad path leads up the ravine.

66.86 A path leads across the canal to a road ending at a limestone quarry.

LOCK 37 (Mountain Lock)

66.96 (39.385295, -77.734451) Access: From US-340 take exit for Keep Tryst Rd. Go 0.25 mile and turn right on Sandy Hook Rd. Follow Sandy Hook/Harpers Ferry Rd. 6.7 miles (0.3 mile beyond Dargan Village) and turn left onto Limekiln Rd. Take slight left onto Mt. Lock Canal Rd. and follow it to a small parking area.

Mountain Lock has one of most picturesque settings along the canal, with rocky slopes rising immediately behind the lockhouse and a panoramic view of the river in the foreground. The white-washed lockhouse is constructed of red brick; the attic has double windows in each gable. There is an outside entry to the cellar with small windows at ground level. A wooden lower extension in the rear has a large stone fireplace with a rock chimney extending 14' upward before it converts to a smaller 4' brick chimney.

The lock has a 9' lift and was extended downstream. A concrete bridge spans a waste weir; the rock wall on the upper river side has collapsed. Otherwise the stonework is in good condition. A footbridge crosses the lock. Blocks of limestone were transported from a quarry one-half mile away on the Maryland side. Capt. John Moore, Boat No. 9, stated that there was also a dry dock at Mountain Lock. Some coping stones retain towrope creases. Remnants of the lower gate survive.

In his August 14, 1872, report, W. R. Hutton, chief engineer for the canal company, advised that Mountain Lock was in need of repair. "A part of the masonry is loose, and the side walls have been pushed in at top, so that boats cramp in it." On May 31, 1873, Hutton reported that Mountain Lock had been rebuilt.

A wide basin extends north of the lock for about 75 yards before the canal narrows to its normal 40' width. The basin and canal have a built-up berm here as the canal crosses a stream valley beyond the berm.

Joseph Lewis operated a store at this location. When he requested a five-year extension of his canal land lease in 1876, he also asked to be able to control the towpath in the area as the sale of produce by peddlers who set up beside it was harming his business.

67.02 Informal overflow.

67.07 Culvert #100, 8' span.

67.15 Cross a concrete waste weir that controlled the water level between Locks 37 and 38.

67.37 The built-up berm stops, and the canal widens for the next mile, as hills and cliffs on the opposite side form a natural berm.

67.61 Quarry.

67.83 Fine spring but the water is not safe for drinking. Moderate cliffs along the berm.

67.93 Steep, dry watercourse to the right with "giant steps" that afford an interesting rock scramble.

68.25 In wet seasons a large spring forms a stream from the base of a hill on the berm side and north along the canal until it disappears in the canal bed.

68.45 Old ruins of a lime kiln on the berm mark the probable location of "Sharpless Landing" of early canal days.

68.52 Lost Culvert #101 (Briens Road). Former site of McShanes or Briens Ferry.

The Antietam Iron Furnace was located across the road from the lime kiln ruins. Traces of an old millrace that supplied a number of wheels may be discerned in the low-lying area opposite the kilns.

Antietam Village

This peaceful locale—today on the National Register of Historic Places—gives little hint of the teeming activity which prevailed here from pre-canal days through most of the nineteenth century. A handful of homes and the remnants of three lime kilns on Harpers Ferry Road are all that remain of an industrial hamlet that once extended one-half mile from the Potomac up both banks of the Antietam Creek.

The first iron furnace opened here in 1765. During the American Revolution craftsmen forged cannon, cast cannon balls, and turned out muskets. Products may have reached the lower valley by Potomac longboats. In 1786 metal parts were forged at Antietam for James Rumsey's experimental steamboat, which he demonstrated on the Potomac River at Shepherdstown on December 3, 1787. Blacksmiths also produced farm and other machinery. At various times the village included a rolling mill, slitting mill, nail factories, large grist mill, limestone crushing mills, spinning mills, hemp mills, flour mills, sawmill, shingle mill, cooperage factory, woolen mill, and stove works. Water power from the Antietam Creek raceway drove the wheels of industry. The dam, diverting water into the raceway, was 19.5' high. The water wheel operating the bellows for the furnace was 20' in diameter and 4' wide. The furnace produced 40 to 60 tons of pig iron a week. The forge's 21-ton hammer was operated by a 16' mill wheel. An iron rolling mill was operated by a 14' overshot wheel, and a 16' wheel in the nail factory drove 19 nail and spike machines, producing 400–500 kegs of nails per week. In its heyday, the ironworks employed over 250 workers, including some 60 slaves. This industry is hard to visualize today as one gazes across soft green pastures to the quiet present-day village.

As early as 1802, work was underway to develop Antietam Creek for boat navigation by the typical Potomac gundalow. After ground-breaking in 1828, C&O Canal construction made its way up from Georgetown. The Antietam Aqueduct was built in 1834 by Irish immigrants. Many workers died in the 1832–33 cholera epidemic and were reputedly buried in common graves in the area. The four-arch span bridge that carries Harpers Ferry Road over the Antietam Creek was built by John Weaver in 1832. Constructed of coursed local limestone, the bridge is an example of the type of bridge architecture prevalent in the area. Weaver also built the bridge now known as Burnside Bridge on the Antietam Battlefield.

In the September 1862 Maryland Campaign, Gen. Ambrose Burnside's forces passed through the village en route to Sharpsburg. A house atop the hill overlooking Antietam Creek was reportedly used as a field hospital during the Battle of Antietam.

The iron works suffered some damage during the war, but it was rebuilt and operated by the Ahl family until 1882. When it was sold, plans were discussed for additional furnaces and the construction of a railroad branch to Sharpsburg, but the development never occurred. The furnace and surrounding buildings eventually fell into disrepair. The National Register of Historic Places report summarized the demise of the industrial village: "The machinery was dismantled and the other mill buildings disappeared from the cultural landscape, leaving only the furnace stack, the store building, some foundations, and a handful of homes to reflect the heyday of this major western Maryland industry along the banks of Antietam Creek."

Antietam Iron Works, ca. 1822.

68.53 Limestone loading wharf.

68.85 Footbridge across the canal. After Culvert #101 collapsed, the Antietam Iron Works constructed a pivot bridge at this location, but even the pier on which the bridge pivoted has disappeared. This is Wades Landing, frequently referred to as Shaffers Landing, popular with fishermen and boatmen. Limestone for the Godey Lime Kilns on lower Rock Creek in Georgetown (see mile 0.36, page 6) was boated across the Potomac after quarrying on Knotts Island opposite. Berm stone wall beyond.

69.30 A probable stone-walled water gate through the berm served to water a small (two or three acres) basin. This was "O'Briens Basin" and the canal landing area for Antietam Village. A ca. 1877 map of the Sharpsburg area in the *Illustrated Atlas of Washington County 1877* shows a railroad connecting the village with the canal at this point.

ANTIETAM AQUEDUCT

69.36 (39.419001, -77.746573) Access: From the center of Sharpsburg take S. Mechanic St. (which becomes Harpers Ferry Rd.) for 3 miles. Turn right on Canal Rd. (just short of Antietam Village) and follow 0.2 mile to a camping area at the upper end of Antietam Creek Aqueduct. The road turns 90° to parallel the canal; there is a wide area for parking between the canal and road. The aqueduct can also be reached via Canal Rd. from Lock 38 at mile 72.80.

Several footbridges cross the canal bed to campgrounds between the towpath and river. This is a C&O Canal NHP Drive-in Campground equipped with grills, chemical toilets, and water. (See www.nps.gov/choh for current fees.) A volunteer campground host may be on duty in the summer. All campgrounds are open year-round.

Antietam Aqueduct is 200 yards downstream from the lower end of the parking lot. This beautiful 140' structure is the fourth of 11 stone aqueducts. Built of limestone from a quarry 0.75 mile away, it is 108' between abutments. The aqueduct has three elliptical arches with the two outside spans 28' wide and the center span 40' wide.

On July 6, 1864, during Gen. Jubal Early's invasion of Maryland, Confederate forces tore out the berm wall of the aqueduct down into the arches and removed the ringstone. On the towpath side, the Confederates tore out the aqueduct wall two-thirds of the distance toward the bottom of the canal.

Antietam Creek drains an extensive watershed reaching to Hagerstown and beyond into Pennsylvania, where it originates. The Burnside Bridge, which played a key role in the Battle of Antietam, crosses it four miles upstream. The creek includes some class I and II whitewater stretches.

69.48 Canal Road continues upstream along the berm to Lock 38 and connects with MD-34 opposite Ferry Hill Plantation. Downstream about 0.3 mile, on Harpers Ferry Road in Antietam Village, a beautiful stone arch bridge crosses Antietam Creek.

69.98 End of developed area; fields to the right.

70.38 Culvert #103, 8' span. The road bends over a natural spring outlet through the culvert. Houses line the berm road from here through the Millers Sawmill area.

Antietam Creek Aqueduct, ca. 2013. *(Image courtesy Steve Dean)*

70.52 Grassy area begins in front of the houses facing the canal. The view to the east includes the bulk of Elk Ridge, where fighting took place during the September 1862 Maryland Campaign.

MILLERS SAWMILL

70.68 Access: Via Canal Rd. from Lock 38 at mile 72.8; or, from Sharpsburg take Harpers Ferry Rd. 0.8 mile to Millers Sawmill Rd. Turn right and follow about 2.5 miles to parking spaces along Canal Rd.

Millers Sawmill was "Millers Basin" during canal days. The mill, run by Jacob Miller, supplied wood to the canal company during the 1833–35 construction years in this area. Subsequently, the canal supplied water to the mill

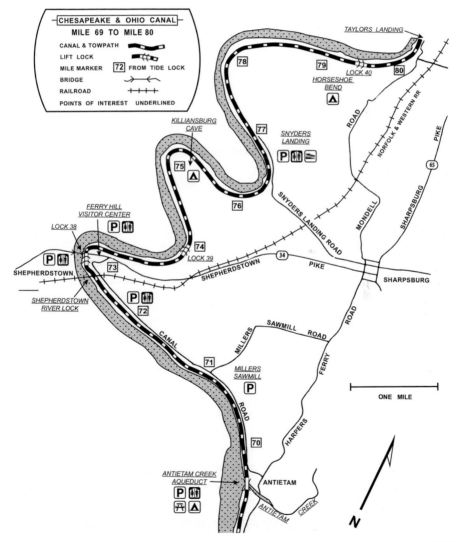

until the Civil War. From January 19 to May 14, 1862, troops occupied the mill. Following the Battle of Antietam, Union soldiers used the mill as a hospital and then as a pickets' rendezvous. When the soldiers moved out, they carried the doors, windows, partitions, garners, flooring, weatherboarding, chimney stove, and other movable materials with them. Even Miller's post and board fence had been cut down and burned. Union troops did heavy damage to the property based on Miller's reputed southern sympathies.

The wide area in the canal marks the location of a former wharf and warehouse.

70.78 Culvert #104, 4' span. The hillside behind the first house west of Millers Sawmill has an interesting geological formation consisting of a series of twisted anticlines. The grassy stretch of towpath here is marked by a fine line of large sycamores.

71.24 Cross a cleared area with a road leading up to the Conococheague Gun Club. The clubhouse was the fifth stop during the 1954 Douglas Hike.

PACKHORSE FORD

71.39 Access: From paralleling Canal Road directly on berm.

Note the irregular pattern of rocks forming a double "V" in the area of Packhorse or Boteler's Ford. South of the ford on the West Virginia side is Trough Road, the route of the Confederate retreat after the Battle of Antietam. Fighting that took place here September 19–20, 1862, is known as the Battle of Shepherdstown or Boteler's Ford, where Union forces attacked the rear of the retreating Confederate army. During the engagement, Union infantry took cover in the dry canal and fired over its embankment, using it as a breastwork.

71.55 Culvert #105, 4' span. The beautiful wooded shelf between the towpath and river was formerly used for camping.

71.63 The riffle running across the river here represents the remains of the old Boteler or Reynolds Dam, which supplied water to the millrace for Boteler's grist and later natural cement mill. Remains of the mill and kilns are sometimes visible on the opposite side of the river. Much of the cement for locks and other stone structures along the lower and middle sections of the canal was produced at this mill. First operated as a flour mill and then as a cement mill, it was burned by Union troops in the early morning of August 19, 1861. It was subsequently rebuilt and operated from 1888 to 1903 as part of the Potomac Mills, Mining, and Manufacturing Company. The next important cement mill was Round Top above Hancock. The dam, in addition to impounding water for the mill, created a slackwater pool that allowed boats to come and go across the river between the canal and cement mill using the river lock. Much of the mill's cement went to Washington for federal buildings. South of the old dam on the West

Virginia side is a beautiful example of a complete geological fold—a rare view caused by erosion over centuries.

71.73 The large abandoned cement kilns across the berm road (visible during winter months) were part of the Antietam Cement Company. There is active birdlife here year around. C&O Canal Association Level Walker Ken Rollins, assigned to this section many years ago, commented, "This must be the blackbird capital of the world."

71.75 A small culvert drains directly into the canal bed. Note the almost hidden cedar logs, which formed a timber cage filled with riprap for the wall of a landing, probably for the limekiln and cement company.

72.23 Two large pin oaks overhang the river. Oak trees generally are not common along the towpath.

72.4x Large parking area across the road from the canal (39.433927, -77.795512). A pedestrian crossing at the lower end leads to a path and footbridge across the canal. Toilets available.

72.48 Pass under the high trestle of the Norfolk Southern Railway. The trestle was built 1908–09 to replace an older bridge 500' upstream.

72.59 Atop the cliff across the river in West Virginia is Rumsey State Park. The James Rumsey Monument, erected in 1915, has a 75' high, granite Ionic column. (James Rumsey's remains lie in an unmarked grave in St. Margaret's churchyard,

Packhorse Ford

When the first settlers (Germans, Irish, and Scotch-Irish from Pennsylvania and Dutch from New York) began to push into Western Maryland in the 1730s, they followed an old Native American and packhorse trail from York, Pennsylvania. Those who wished to cross the Potomac River into Virginia found Packhorse Ford, one mile below the site of present-day Shepherdstown, West Virginia. The site was one of few good crossings for many miles east or west of it. The Maryland Civil War Centennial Commission sign along the road reads:

Blackford's Ford. Also known as Boteler's, Pack Horse, and Shepherdstown Ford. "Stonewall" Jackson's Command crossed here en route from Harper's Ferry to Sharpsburg. Here the entire Army of Northern Virginia withdrew into Virginia, Sept. 18–19, 1862, following Battle of Antietam.

The 1751 map of Virginia made by Peter Jefferson and Joshua Fry shows the Great Wagon Road from Philadelphia that ran north–south in the Great Valley (the Shenandoah Valley south of the Potomac River and the Cumberland Valley north of it) crossing the Potomac at Williams Ferry, where Williamsport is today. But it also shows a "Philadelphia Wagon Road" branching off to cross the Potomac in this area. It terminates on the map a short distance into Maryland, but there are indications that this was an important alternative route for those traveling between points to the northeast and southwest of this location.

London.) Rumsey (1743–92) was a pioneer of steam navigation and for about a year (1775–76), the first superintendent (chief engineer) of the Patowmack Company, a position for which he was recommended by George Washington.

Rumsey's famous steamboat, using a type of hydraulic jet-propulsion, made its debut in a gala public demonstration in a calm section of the Potomac at this point on December 3, 1787. Hundreds of spectators lined the banks when the craft set out from the Shepherdstown ferry landing and headed into the current. Onlookers were astounded as the steamboat made headway upstream at the rate of four miles per hour. By many, this is considered a true "first" for steam navigation. How far the boat traveled is uncertain, but one report indicates it may have gone a half mile above Shepherdstown, to a point opposite Swearingen's Spring, before returning and traveling for some distance below town.

72.63 Pass five stone piers of the old Shenandoah Valley Railroad bridge. The piers were built on wood cribbing, visible at low water. When the dam below was in place, the cribbing was protected by being submerged, but it is now rotting and the piers are tilting. The Shenandoah Valley Railroad was an extension of an earlier local railroad whose northern terminus was at Shepherdstown. It eventually became a division of the Norfolk & Western—which in turn became the Norfolk Southern. The bridge was built, and the line opened to Hagerstown in 1880. The piers today, topped by cedar trees, are quite picturesque.

Old canal scene below the Shepherdstown locks. Note the narrow planks that were used for getting on or off the canal boat.

This is the beginning of a 100'-wide section of the canal that serves Lock 38 and the Shepherdstown River Lock. Directly across the river is the wall for an old wharf area. The brick building beside the boat ramp at the bottom of Shepherdstown's North Princess Street was the Mecklenburg Tobacco Warehouse.

SHEPHERDSTOWN RIVER LOCK

72.65 Access: From Lock 38 at mile 72.8.

Boats entered the canal from the river slackwater formed by Botelers Dam below. This is one of three such river locks on the C&O, the others being near Edwards Ferry (across from Goose Creek) and across from Harpers Ferry.

The towpath crosses a filled-in portion of the river lock and continues on an embankment with a masonry wall on the river side. The towpath originally passed over the upper end of the lock on a high, arched bridge. This lock once admitted boats to the canal from Shepherdstown and the cement mill downriver. It operated until the 1889 flood and was reopened by late 1895. Directly across the river are the remains of a stone wharf where boats were loaded or unloaded at Shepherdstown. A March 27, 1858, *Shepherdstown Register* article reported:

> The boat "Susan Barker," George Harris, Capt., left the Chesapeake and Ohio Wharf at this place on Saturday, ladened with 4,000 bushels of corn, 200 bu. of wheat, 150 bu. oats, 128 barrels of flour, 56 bu. of timothy seed—the entire weight of which was 134 tons. The boat averaged 4 feet 6 inches of water in the bow, and 4 feet 5 inches in the stern. This is said to be the heaviest load ever known to leave the wharf of Shepherdstown upon the Chesapeake and Ohio Canal.

72.77 A concrete ferry ramp is on the river bank. The exact site of the original Blackfords Ferry is unknown.

72.78 Most of the piers of the old section of the Shepherdstown bridge that carried the road over the canal washed away in 1936. The low embankment in the canal bed running up to the lower end of Lock 38 is the remnant of an extension intended to allow two boats to be passed through the lock at one time.

> If you encounter a life-threatening emergency while visiting the park, please **call 911** or contact the Chesapeake and Ohio Canal National Historical Park's **Emergency Hotline 866-677-6677**.

Blackfords Ferry

When the Packhorse Ford no longer met their needs for crossing the Potomac River, first Thomas Shepherd and then Thomas Van Swearingen established a ferry in this vicinity. In 1765 the charge was three pence per person or horse. Shepherdstown maintained a road to the ferry landing on its side of the river, and Washington County, Maryland, constructed a road from Boonsboro through Sharpsburg to the Swearingen Landing on the Maryland side.

The ferry passed from Swearingen to his descendants. In 1816 Col. John Blackford (who had married into the family) purchased half interest in the ferry and franchise, boats and apparatus, and three tracts of land. He later purchased the remaining half, and with additional land acquired from Thomas Shepherd, among others, Col. Blackford established Ferry Hill Plantation. Blackford appointed two of his slaves "Foremen of the Ferry." They did the work themselves, called on other slaves to assist, and even hired free labor, both black and white, to assist in rush periods.

Construction of the C&O Canal resulted in a court case involving 1 acre, 3 rods, and 17 perches of the ferry lot. The Canal Company condemned the lot, and one cent in damages was awarded on August 30, 1832. Col. Blackford and five others retained three lawyers to appeal. In court they claimed the ferry business would suffer, as boats from Virginia could bypass the ferry and enter the canal via the river lock. The court ruled in favor of the Canal Company and confirmed the one-cent damages.

The ferry passed to Blackford's son Franklin in 1838, until he (or his brother Henry Van Swearingen Blackford) sold it to the Virginia and Maryland Bridge Company for $15,000. The bridge company abandoned the ferry in 1850, replacing it with a covered bridge that was burned by Confederates in 1861. The bridge was rebuilt in 1871, destroyed by the 1889 flood, and replaced in 1890 by an iron bridge—the piers of which are still evident in the river. The 1936 flood carried away that bridge, and the present concrete ramp was built when a ferry resumed operation. A fourth bridge was constructed in 1939 and was replaced by the current (and fifth) Rumsey Bridge, which was built on an alignment on the upstream side of the 1939 bridge and opened in July 2006.

Blackfords Ferry at Shepherdstown.

LOCK 38, SHEPHERDSTOWN

72.80 (39.436456, -77.799527) Access: From Shepherdstown take WV-480 0.4 mile from the center of town across Rumsey Bridge. Go 0.1 mile and turn right on Canal Rd. Follow downhill 0.2 mile to the small Lock 38 parking area. There is also a pedestrian sidewalk and bike lane across the bridge with a ramp down to the parking area. From Sharpsburg take MD-34 3.1 miles west and turn left onto Canal Rd. opposite the entrance gate for Ferry Hill. Follow downhill 0.2 mile to the small Lock 38 parking area. A larger parking lot with portable toilets is available 0.4 mile farther down Canal Rd. which parallels the berm. (See mile 72.4x.) There is a footbridge over the lock. No drinking water available. Shepherdstown is the fifth "Canal Town" along the towpath. Visit www.canaltowns.org for more information.

Lock 38 offers an excellent starting point for a nice 3.75-mile walk upstream to Snyders Landing or 3 miles downstream to the Antietam Aqueduct and Antietam Village.

The lower end of the lock shows the well-preserved covered bypass flume more clearly than the opposite end, which is mostly filled in. Lock 38 has an unusually short 5' lift (standard was 8'). The lock is in good condition. It was constructed of limestone from quarries on the opposite shore. A two-and-a-half story brick lockhouse stood opposite the upper end of the lock on the towpath side, approximately 40' from the lock wall. A frame feed store 40' long stood mid lock on the berm side of the lock wall. The lockhouse was lost in the 1936 flood.

An old inn constructed in 1775 by Thomas Van Swearingen was on the berm opposite the lock until about 1972. The inn may have been operated by

This ca. 1900 image of Lock 38 at Shepherdstown shows the Knode's feed store adjacent to the lock.

John Blackford and then by his son Franklin. It later was occupied by the Knode family which also operated the feed store beside the lock.

George Knode (of Shepherdstown) lived in the inn early in the twentieth century. He related how canal Level Walker Capt. Dan Soulders (of Sharpsburg) would stop or pass by around 7:15 each morning, carrying a little pack on his back as well as a pick and square-ended

145

shovel (for minor repairs) as he made his round from Sharpsburg to the canal at Snyders Landing, then down the towpath to Millers Sawmill and Mountain Lock, then back to Sharpsburg. In his pack he also carried letters and miscellaneous items for people living near the canal. He was a well-known figure for many years.

The community that existed here on the Maryland shore was known as Bridgeport.

Canal Town, Shepherdstown

Argued to be the oldest town in West Virginia (vs. Romney), Shepherdstown celebrated its 250th Anniversary in 2012. Today this eclectic college town is a mix of museums, restaurants and cafes, unique shops, and galleries. Visitors can find outdoor recreation, casual or fine dining, and cultural events such as film festivals and live theater, music, and dance. Whatever the interest, this quaint historic town draws thousands of visitors to its picturesque setting on the Potomac.

In 1734 founder Thomas Shepherd obtained a 222-acre land grant and laid out the town, which he named Mecklenburg, on 50 acres of that land. By 1739 Shepherd had established a grist mill on Town Run, the major stream through town. On November 12, 1762, the town was incorporated with Shepherd both owner and governing authority. In 1794 another charter granted the town self-government. In 1798 the name was changed to Shepherd's Town; after the Civil War the name was contracted to Shepherdstown.

In 1775 Capt. Hugh Stephenson answered Gen. George Washington's call for volunteers and mustered a company of troops here. The soldiers departed Shepherdstown on July 16, 1775, and made their famous "Beeline March" to Cambridge, Massachusetts, covering 600 miles in 24 days. Thirty-eight Revolutionary veterans are buried in Shepherdstown.

Following the 1862 Battle of Antietam, five to eight thousand casualties flooded the town. The residents of this small community tended to the wounded and dying, who filled every house, building, church, alley, and street. More than 100 Confederate soldiers died here and were buried in Elmwood Cemetery. The cemetery contains the graves of 285 Confederate veterans, including Henry Kyd Douglas, one of Stonewall Jackson's staff members. Douglas's home, Ferry Hill, is located just across the river from Shepherdstown. Elmwood Cemetery, located five blocks south of the four-way stop on Route 480, offers self-guided walking tours.

After the courthouse in Charles Town suffered damage during war, the county seat of Jefferson County was moved to Shepherdstown. From 1865 to 1871, the Town Hall (northeast corner of German and King Streets) housed the courthouse, until it was moved back to Charles Town. In 1872 the Town Hall Building was chartered as a "Classical and Scientific Institute." It became the first building of what is today Shepherd University; in 1927 it was named McMurran Hall in memory of Shepherd's first principal.

For more information visit www.canaltowns.org or the Shepherdstown Visitor Center, 304-876-2786, www.shepherdstownvisitorscenter.com.

Ferry Hill

On a high bluff overlooking the Potomac River and the C&O Canal, Ferry Hill was at various times a farm, restaurant, and Union troop encampment. Built by Col. John Blackford in 1813, Ferry Hill once encompassed 700 acres. Blackford owned 18 slaves and often hired part-time laborers. Blackford shipped his produce and timber overland to Harrisburg, Pennsylvania and Baltimore, Maryland, and to Georgetown via the C&O Canal.

Robert and Helena Blackford Douglas moved into the mansion with their four children in 1850. Their son Henry Kyd Douglas enlisted in the Confederate army in 1861 and served as Stonewall Jackson's youngest staff officer. Henry's enlistment cast suspicion on the family, and the Federals kept the Douglases under house arrest for most of the Civil War. During the war, Ferry Hill was used by both Union and Confederate troops as a headquarters and encampment site. Wounded Confederates were cared for here following the Battle of Antietam. Suspecting the Douglases of spying for the Confederates, the Federals arrested Robert and held him at Fort McHenry for several months.

In 1903 the property passed to the Beckenbaughs, who ran a pig farm from 1914 through 1928, then opened a restaurant in 1948. After the Beckenbaughs sold the property, it remained a restaurant but underwent extensive changes, including the addition of four imposing columns. In 1974 Ferry Hill was acquired by the National Park Service.

Once the headquarters of the C&O Canal National Historical Park, Ferry Hill now features exhibits and tours. The house is open seasonally; the grounds are open from dawn to dusk. Ferry Hill Place, 16500 Shepherdstown Pike (MD-34), Sharpsburg, MD 21782, 301-582-0813, www.nps.gov/choh/planyourvisit/ferry-hill-place.htm.

Ferry Hill Plantation, once the C&O Canal National Historical Park Headquarters, reopened as a visitor and interpretive center in 2012. Note: the columns were added after 1951. *(Image courtesy Steve Dean)*

72.82 Pass under the James Rumsey Bridge. An uphill trail here branches to a bridge overlook to the right or through the trees to the left to Ferry Hill Plantation.

The next 11.6 miles to Dam 4 is an area rife with Civil War history, pretty river scenes, fine berm cliffs, and interesting caves. The beauty of this section can be rivaled by few others. Though close to main roads, it seems far away from congestion.

73.07 The towpath comes directly onto the riverbank and remains so to Lock 39, with interesting stone paving designed to maintain the towpath during flood periods. The berm rises steeply as the canal runs along the base of a cliff. Here begins a very beautiful stretch of berm cliffs, extending for the next mile.

73.29 Two small caves 20' up the berm wall.

73.46 Culvert #107, 4' span. The berm wall is broken by a ravine.

73.89 The cliff reaches a height of 100'.

73.9x Stone paving of footway ends about 100 yards below Lock 39.

Canal Town, Sharpsburg

Once a rich hunting ground frequented by Native American tribes, the town of Sharpsburg, Maryland, survived the bloodiest day in American history to become a quaint Main Street town just two miles east of the C&O Canal. Though Antietam National Battlefield draws thousands of visitors a year, Sharpsburg manages to maintain its historic heritage and small town charm.

Following the roads settlers used to travel west, Joseph Chapline chose this site for a town because of the "great spring" of water nearby. Chapline founded the town on July 9, 1763, naming it Sharps Burgh, after his friend, Governor Horatio Sharpe. Farmers and herdsmen established flourishing farms while the town thrived as a commercial community. The arrival of the C&O Canal in the late 1830s provided many construction and canal operating jobs. By the 1860s, the town's population was 1300.

Gen. Robert E. Lee invaded Maryland in September 1862, bringing the Civil War to Northern soil. Following fighting in nearby Harpers Ferry and South Mountain, Union Gen. George McClellan pursued the Confederate army to the banks of Antietam Creek. On September 17, 1862, thousands of soldiers clashed in cornfields, along a sunken road, and finally across a stone bridge on the Antietam Creek. When the battle ended, over 23,000 men were dead, wounded, or missing. The residents of Sharpsburg were left with the devastation, but were able to overcome the hardships left in the wake of the battle to rebuild their town.

In addition to Antietam National Battlefield, nearby attractions include Crystal Grottoes Caverns (www.crystalgrottoescaverns.com), South Mountain, the Washington County Rural Heritage Museum (www.ruralheritagemuseum.org), and Washington Monument State Park.

Battleview Market is open daily from 7 a.m. to 11 p.m., 111 East Main St., Sharpsburg, MD 21782, 301-432-5813, www.battleviewmarket.com. See www.canaltowns.org for a list of inns and bed and breakfasts. For more information visit Town of Sharpsburg, 106 East Main St., PO Box 368, Sharpsburg, MD 21782, 301-432-4428, www.sharpsburgmd.com.

LOCK 39

74.00 Access: From Lock 38 at mile 72.8 or Snyders Landing at mile 76.65.

The level between Locks 38 and 39 was known by boatmen as the "One-Mile Level" or "Foot of Sharpsburg Level." The lock was known as "Mitchels Lock" in 1838.

There is evidence of an old road to the lock on the berm. At one time a store was located at the lock, suggesting the location served residents in the area as well as canallers. A portion of the former lockhouse foundation remains on the berm at the upper end of the lock. Some original iron work remains in the stonework. The lock had a stone and concrete bypass flume. There is a high cliff at the downstream end of the lock, and beyond the lock is a wooded ravine with an intermittent stream.

74.04 Culvert #108, 6' span. A good example of fine masonry work done on canal culverts.

74.07 Cross a concrete waste weir that serves the level between Locks 39 and 40. Earlier construction of a masonry weir can be seen below the concrete. An old map shows a "mule drink" (informal overflow) in this area of the towpath.

74.2x A 40-yard stone wall on the berm was probably used for a two or three-man repair scow based in this area of the canal, as well as for loading or receiving products being shipped on the canal. The ruins of an 18' x 33' two-and-a-half story canal company frame section house are at the upper end of the wall. The Zimmermans, Lock 39 locktenders from 1916 to 1924, likely maintained the house for repair scow quarters. The foundations of a stable and root cellar are above the company house, and two buildings appear on old maps.

74.28 Culvert #109, 5' span, carries a small stream from the ravine on the berm. A faint trail leads up the ravine to a road that connects with MD-34 on each side of the Norfolk Southern Railway overpass. On old maps this trail appears as a road that continued upstream along the berm for a half mile. An Osage orange (*Maclura pomifera*) hedge, still visible, marks its route.

74.30 Pumping station.

74.60 The next mile contains cedar-dotted cow pastures on the berm, with stretches of hedgerows and a wooded floodplain with many fine trees on the riverside. Cliffs line the far side of the river.

75.29 Killiansburg Cave Hiker–Biker Campsite. The closest access is from Snyders Landing at mile 76.65.

The berm side becomes rocky slopes and cliffs. The towpath berm forms a river wall.

75.61 On the berm side is one of several caves known as the Sharpsburg Shelter Caves. The lower two caves, which form an interesting rock formation, have openings about 20' apart, and are accessible from the edge of the canal bed.

Caves are muddy, slippery, and dangerous, so use caution! The next cave upstream has a winding crawlway reaching back 200'.

75.73 Very interesting cliff, 75' high, with overhangs and a curious twist. There are two shallow caves here. The first, Killiansburg Cave, is reached via a steep climb 50' above the towpath on the cliff face. The cave is about 20' high x 30' wide x 35' deep, with a shallow opening obscured by growth in summer. Visitors should not build fires in caves or deposit trash in them. The second shallow cave is near the canal bed level. Published documents on the Battle of Antietam report that during the fighting the citizens of Sharpsburg took shelter in caves along the canal, including Killiansburg Cave.

> Park mines, tunnels, and caves along the canal used by hibernating bats may be closed to minimize the spread of White Nose Syndrome. See the General Information section for more on this disease.

75.78 The towpath is supported on the riverbank by a stone wall. There is a long straightaway in the canal here.

75.8x Another shallow cave is about 30' above the towpath. At least 20 caves are found in the cliffs between miles 75.61 and 76.58.

75.9x The riverbank is cleared here, providing an unobstructed view of the river.

75.95 An abrupt cliff is on the berm; more spectacular cliffs are ahead.

76.24 Another shallow cave is on the berm, with very interesting cliffs about 120' high, followed by a steep ravine.

Killiansburg or Killing's Cave was a place of refuge for Sharpsburg citizens during the Battle of Antietam. (*The Soldier in Our Civil War, Frank Leslie*)

76.5x The river is 75 yards from the canal. The intermittent stone wall ends. Grove's stone warehouse once stood here on the berm.

76.58 The cliff ends and the canal enters a populated area with a road along the berm.

SNYDERS LANDING

76.65 (39.465270, -77.777313) Access: From Sharpsburg at junction of MD-34 and MD-65, turn north on MD-65. Take next left onto Chapline St., crossing a short metal grate in the road. Go two blocks to Snyders Landing Rd. (Pass the Antietam Guest House on the right, which has a Sharpsburg Heritage sign indicating the birthplace of C&O Canal Boat Captain Raleigh Bender, who boated for 35 years on the canal.) Follow Snyders Landing Rd. about 1.6 miles to Snyders Landing Potomac River Boat Ramp, where there is a rock wall retained by a wire grid. There is limited parking here. Snyders Landing was previously known as Sharpsburg Landing. Homes appear on the berm. Cross Culvert #111, 6' span. NO CAMPING is allowed here. Barron's Drinks & Snacks Store houses C&O Canal memorabilia and serves ice cream. It is open on weekends, weather permitting, from May through September.

76.73 The Snyder coal and grain warehouse here washed away in the 1936 flood. A footbridge rested on concrete supports early in the park's history. The supports were once part of a swinging pedestrian bridge high enough over the canal for boats to pass beneath it. Steep, ladder-like steps on both sides gave access to the single rope-suspension span.

77.24 For the next two miles to Lock 40, the canal and towpath run parallel to the river (150 yards away) as it makes a long curve known as Horseshoe Bend. Several large fields, farm houses, and barns are visible on the berm. Large numbers of sycamores and maples line the canal.

78.15 Culvert #112, 2' diameter pipe.

78.4x A stone wall begins on the berm. This property line fence continues to mile 79.15.

78.60 Listen for the rushing rapids here, as the towpath nears the river. A grove of paw paw trees is also here, with fruits often found on the towpath.

78.84 Prominent cliff on the West Virginia side of the river.

LOCK 40

79.41 Access: From upper Snyders Landing at mile 76.65.

Lock 40 has a proliferation of golden aster (*Chrysopsis mariana*) and yellow jewelweed (*Impatiens pallida*) flowers. There is also a Witness Post Survey Marker that has grown into and is part of a very large tree across from the lock.

In this little-frequented section, Andrew McKoy was listed as locktender in 1839 and was still the locktender in an 1851 report. Faint remains of the lockhouse foundation (lost in the 1936 flood) as well as the remains of an old well and stone cellar are on the berm. The lock has a concrete bypass flume, and its stones are in good condition. A wood-and-earthen dam is at the upper end.

Boatmen sometimes damaged locks. For example, on May 5, 1879, Capt. Jacob Hooker ran the boat "W. J. Booth" into the gates at Lock 40 and was fined $40 in damages.

79.65 Cross a concrete waste weir (over an original masonry waste weir).

79.68 Horseshoe Bend Hiker–Biker Campsite. Access from Sharpsburg via MD-65 to Taylors Landing at mile 81.0.

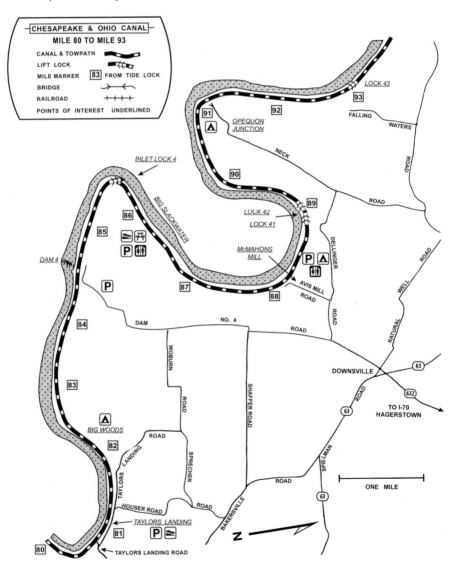

The Cholera Epidemics

This portion of the canal was severely impacted by the Asiatic cholera epidemic in 1832, when construction was just beginning between Dams 3 and 4. The period from August through September was commonly known as the "sickly season" in the Potomac Valley and represented the time during which waterborne diseases were most common every year. However, a truly terrible catastrophe arrived in the summer, with the spread of cholera southward from eastern Canada and the U.S. ports on the St. Lawrence River and Great Lakes. Panic spread among the Irish immigrants, and work stopped as laborers scattered throughout the countryside. Canal engineer Thomas Purcell, writing from Sharpsburg on September 11, said:

> Men, deserted by their friends or comrades, have been left to die in the fields, the highways, or in the neighboring barns and stables. In some instances, as I have been told, when the disease has attacked them, the invalid has been enticed from the shandee [sic] and left to die under the shade of some tree. Excited by the sufferings of the miserable victims of the disease, the citizens of this place [Sharpsburg] have administered to their wants, and sought to soothe their dying moments, but unfortunately for the cause of humanity, nearly every person who has been with the dead bodies or has assisted in burying them have paid the forfeit with their lives, and it is now scarcely possible to get the dead buried.

The canal company tried to calm the panic and remove the sick from the crowded shanties. Among other measures was a rough "hospital" set up at Harpers Ferry and operated on funds obtained by a form of group insurance in which workers contributed 25 cents monthly through payroll deductions. The epidemic dramatically slowed construction and contributed to the canal company's and contractors' bleak financial situation. While 1832 saw the worst cholera epidemic on the C&O, an outbreak in 1833 was also severe. Subsequently, cholera joined the list of diseases that spread along the canal line, especially during the "sickly season."

79.77 An old map shows an informal overflow built in the towpath.

79.98 Culvert #114 (Roses Culvert), 4' span.

80.55 Culvert #115 (Mondell), 6' span. A stream runs from the valley on the berm. Paved Mondell Road comes down the valley on the far side and continues along the berm to Mercersville. Pass ruins of a 60' x 25' stone structure. There are numerous cross paths between the river and the houses. Trees are removed from the canal bed and grass is neatly cut to mile 81.6x.

80.95 Community of Mercersville. Taylors Landing Road continues along the berm, with occasional houses and frequent cross paths to the river. The walled portion on the berm here is the site of Harris and later Boyer Warehouse and wharf of early canal days.

Mercersville was named after Charles Fenton Mercer, the primary force behind the organization of the C&O Canal Company and its first president. Today, the area is better known as Taylors Landing. John William (Jack) Taylor was born and spent 80 years here until he died in 1948. Taylor, superintendent of this section of the canal, operated a general store for 50 years in the basement of his stone house. His obituary described him as one of the best known and beloved characters along the canal.

81.0x Taylors Landing Boat Ramp (39.499645, -77.767866). Access: From Sharpsburg at junction of MD-34 and MD-65, turn north on MD-65. Go 2.2 miles and turn left onto Mondell Rd. Follow Mondell Rd. 0.6 mile and turn right onto Bowie Rd. Follow Bowie Rd. 0.7 mile until it merges with Taylors Landing Rd. Boat ramp area will be ahead to the left. A vehicle bridge over the canal leads to an informal parking area (limited to two or three vehicles).

81.62 Culvert #116 (Marsh Run), 10' span. Marsh Run gives the appearance of a rushing mountain stream. In a short distance, Taylors Landing Road crosses Marsh Run on a low bridge that can be flooded by even localized storms that drop large amounts of rain on the ravine and farmlands to the north. Taylors Landing Road continues uphill and can be followed to access Dam 4 via its connection to Woburn and Dam No. 4 Roads. The area was known in the early canal days as Middlekauffs Basin. Fields occupy the berm side; large trees border the towpath.

81.87 There appears to be a collapsed culvert here. There are rocky wooded bluffs on the West Virginia side of the river.

81.93 A stone house and barn are visible in winter months on the open slope on the berm. Corn fields and pastures on the slope continue for some distance.

82.11 Possible informal overflow.

82.24 An old road parallels the towpath for 0.3 mile. Bluffs are now steep on the West Virginia side.

82.46 Big Woods Hiker–Biker Campsite. Best access is from Taylors Landing Road at mile 81.0x. Fine woods stretch between the canal and river, with tall trees in the canal bed and fine sycamores between the towpath and canal bed. A water pump is located 50 yards below the campsite.

82.75 The river comes into view here, opposite the lower end of Shepherds Island. The berm rises to a heavily-wooded hill and then into cliffs.

83.13 Shallow ravine on the right. The towpath is on the riverbank. The river here has been slackwater for some time, containing few rapids.

83.21 Head of Shepherds Island. Cliffs on the berm reach 100'. The stone wall on the berm was the location of a wharf for the quarry directly behind.

DAM 4 CAVE (Bergen Cave)

83.30 Access: From Dam 4 parking lot at mile 84.4.

There is a large entrance to the cave at canal level. This interesting cavern extends about 200' back into Conococheague limestone, with offsets, side passages, a flowing stream, and two pools. From the entrance, the floor and stream rise to a 20' pool. The passage offsets to the right, then continues as a 4' x 4' corridor to a low-ceilinged room. From this room, take a 2'-high passage to a pool, or take a narrow fissure to the right that leads into a 30'-high chimney. At one end of the offset a side passage leads up to a similar chimney, which connects with the other chimney by a narrow fissure passage. Stalactites and flowstone are in the chimneys, along with deposits of river gravel that have worked down from the gravel terrace atop the hill above the cave. A good description of Maryland caves can be found in *Caves of Maryland* by William Franz and Dennis Slifer (Maryland Geological Survey, 1976). Several smaller caves are in the vicinity between here and Dam 4.

83.37 Shallow ravine on the berm. Ahead is a straightaway section with several small ravines on the berm. An earthslide beyond exposes a cave opening at the top left.

83.47 Site of lost Culvert #117.

83.51 Sediment-collecting basin on the berm.

83.70 An abandoned stone farmhouse is beyond the old road at the top of a steep ravine.

83.75 Fine cliffs on the berm with cedars along the ledges.

83.88 Nice cliff with a stone wall and terrace. Dam 4 comes into view ahead; listen for it as well. Several boulders have fallen into the canal bed.

83.99 Culvert #118 (Hensens Culvert), 6' span, from a wooded ravine. This is a nice picnic area a short distance from Dam 4.

84.23 Paved Dam No. 4 Road leads uphill.

84.35 Cross a concrete waste weir. Magnificent view of the masonry structure of Dam 4.

FEEDER DAM 4, BIG SLACKWATER

84.40 (39.496001, -77.826266) Access: From Hagerstown take I-70 Exit 28, MD-632 South to Downsville Pike. Continue about 5.0 miles to intersection of MD-63. Cross MD-63, and Downsville Pike becomes Dam No. 4 Rd. Continue approximately 4.4 miles to the parking area. A sign reads: "Big Slackwater Recreation Area and Boat Ramp 1 Mile." Access to Dam 4 is via a footbridge over the canal and towpath alongside the winch house. There is a picnic area with grills, tables, and toilets, but no water. NO CAMPING.

CANOEISTS MUST PORTAGE ON THE MARYLAND SIDE.

The first dam was begun in 1832 and opened in 1834. By using slackwater above the dam, boats were able to reach Williamsport 15 miles upstream. The original dam was of rubble-filled wooden cribs covered with heavy planking. However, it suffered flood damage and continued seepage. The loss of water was critical in dry years and at least twice caused suspension of navigation below the dam. To correct this, the canal company contracted for a completely new masonry dam in 1856, said upon completion to be one of the finest in the country. Yet the disastrous November 1877 flood tore a 200' breech in the masonry. The dam was also badly damaged in 1936.

During C&O operating years, machinery in the winch house over the canal operated the guard gate. The gate closed the canal opening in the guard wall that extended from the Maryland abutment to the hillside where the road to the recreation area is today. This guard wall protected the canal should flood waters get into the line of the canal above, between it and the inlet lock. The guard gate at mile 13.7 above Lock 16 is the only other gate of this type on the C&O Canal.

Note the rope burns at each end of the guard gate pier on the towpath side. The present dam was begun in 1906 and began operation in 1909. The electrical generating plant across the river in West Virginia uses tandem, multiple

The winch house at Dam 4 housed machinery that lowered this large gate for protection against floods.

runner, horizontal shaft turbines connected by a rope drive to horizontal shaft generators. The Historic American Engineering Record states that this plant is probably the last commercially-operated rope-driven plant in the U.S.

The current towpath from Dam 4 to Inlet/Guard Lock 4 (1.22 miles upstream) is on a high guard wall protecting the canal below. The original towpath alongside the canal is an alternative but less-maintained route. Guard walls exist at all the dam and inlet/guard lock locations on the canal, but vary with the design of the structures and the surrounding terrain. They are necessitated by the fact that at such locations the canal or inlet channel must be at river level and thus must be protected from frequently severe floods. The guard wall here is the longest and highest of any because, among other reasons, the inlet/guard lock is more than a mile above the dam.

Late in 1861, Confederate Gen. Stonewall Jackson sent a force under Turner Ashby to attempt to breach Dam 4. On December 11 Confederates opened a cannonade on the dam and on Union positions on the Maryland side of the river. After some time it appeared that the Southerners had withdrawn from the area. When a small party of soldiers from the Twelfth Indiana crossed the river to investigate, Confederate cavalry emerged from the woods and captured them. Another skirmish erupted before the Southern horsemen left the river with eight prisoners, but having made no damage to the dam.

The canal dams all served to create a reliable pool of water to feed the canal through a lock below the dam. Such locks can be referred to in several ways, such as feeder or inlet locks because they feed water into the canal, or guard locks because they pass through the guard wall and thus have exceptionally high gates at the upstream end of the lock. In the case of this lock, ordinary miter gates were in the upper end but were much higher than the lock, extending up to the top of the guard wall. A final important feature of these locks is that they must function as do river locks, allowing for normal fluctuations in the level of the river.

85.21 Sheer cliffs across the river that drop directly to the water can be viewed from the high trail on the guard wall.

85.35 A wooden bridge carries the berm road diagonally across the canal and towpath to the recreation area. The bridge was rebuilt in 2014.

85.40 Big Slackwater Boat Ramp (39.501346, -77.845385). Access: From Hagerstown take I-70 Exit 28, MD-632 South to Downsville Pike. Continue about 5.0 miles to intersection of MD-63. Cross MD-63, and Downsville Pike becomes Dam No. 4 Rd. Continue approximately 4.4 miles to Dam 4 parking area. Stay left and follow the access road 1.0 mile to a large parking area. A 30'-wide boat ramp descends into the river. A picnic area at the end of the parking area has tables and grills. Toilets are available. NO CAMPING.

85.5x The new and improved surface begins in this area, but due to limited escape routes in high water, it is recommended that you do not use the towpath in high river levels in the slackwater area from Dam 4 to Falling Waters. New interpretive signs at the end of the parking area and just beyond indicate a former lockhouse foundation and the guard lock and control gates near the inlet weir that was used as a supplemental source of water in addition to the inlet lock.

INLET/GUARD LOCK 4

85.62 Access: From the parking lot at mile 85.4, via the original towpath beside the canal or on the current trail on top of the guard wall. The head of the lock has been sealed with a concrete wall where the lock gates would have been. An earthen berm on which bushes have grown beside the river protects the inlet/guard lock and canal below from the typical flood levels. The foundation for the lockhouse can be seen on the hillside just up from the lock.

The canal actually stops at this point where boats entered the 14-mile-long quiet or "slackwater" pool that is created by the dam. The canal resumes 3.28 miles upstream at Lock 41, mile 88.9. Boats followed the riverbank along which a towpath had been constructed. There was once a pivot bridge at the lock built ca. 1835.

85.68 A concrete bridge carries the towpath over a canal water supply inlet. There is a pool between the inlet and a control gate that allowed canal employees to control the amount of water passing into the channel beyond the gate and into the canal below the lock on the berm side. This inlet made it possible to feed water into the canal independently of the lock. This would have been desirable

The Big Slackwater Restoration

On October 13, 2012, a 2.7-mile stretch of the towpath that had been closed for over a decade reopened to an enthusiastic crowd of hikers and bikers. In 1972 this section had been severely damaged by the flood following Hurricane Agnes. Further damage from the 1996 flood forced the National Park Service to close the towpath here. Visitors were detoured 4.5 miles along a dangerous, narrow road, which saw 35 car accidents in a five-year period.

The Big Slackwater towpath upgrade was completed with funds from the 2009 American Recovery and Reinvestment Act that were appropriated for this "shovel-ready" project in 2010. The state of Maryland, Maryland bond bills, NPS recreation fees, and donations from the C&O Canal Association also funded the $19 million project. Park Superintendent Kevin Brandt stated this was "the largest construction contract since the canal was built."

The new section starts at the inlet weir above Dam 4. A wall was built along much of the next two miles and much of the path itself is a suspended concrete walkway which measures 10' wide and is anchored in the stone of the cliff embankment. To the delight of users, the towpath now runs unobstructed from Georgetown to Cumberland.

whenever the lock gates were closed, such as when boats were being locked through or when conditions made it advisable to keep gates closed.

86.00 This NPS milepost, which was missing for many years, was replaced during the 2011–12 Big Slackwater Restoration. Several log piles in this area also attest to the massive amount of clearing done during the restoration. The next two miles are now passable and in some areas are paved.

86.25 Vehicle turn-around point followed by a plastic drain culvert to divert water.

86.55 A yellow and red DANGER sign announces the new concrete sections of towpath ahead. An interpretive sign on the cliff side of the towpath provides information about river navigation. Across the river, an open white pavilion and large flat level of land is used for summer recreation. Two boat ramps on the West Virginia side can also be seen in this area.

86.61 The towpath is on an old road that comes in diagonally on the berm. There is an intermittent spring, hill, and then a rocky cliff beyond, followed by a steep gully.

86.83 Fern-decked cliffs. Presence of much lip fern (*Cheilanthes lanosa*) testifies to the limestone character of rock.

86.94 The "improved towpath" formerly ended at approximately this point, just short of the cliff. Concrete "bridges" alternate with the towpath supported by dry stone walls from here to McMahon's Mill. While the bridges are not historically accurate, the dry wall sections of towpath are.

The $19 million towpath reconstruction at Big Slackwater (shown here after it reopened in 2012) was "the largest contract since the canal was built." (*Image courtesy Steve Dean*)

86.96 The towpath is supported on a masonry wall as it rounds this rocky point, known locally as "Bass Rock" with a fine view of the river palisades. Beyond are several ravines and steep, dry watercourses. The towpath is very picturesque as it clings to cliffs with nice views of the river edge.

87.04 An eight-ton boulder on the towpath was removed during the Big Slackwater project in 2011–12. The higher wall ahead at McMahon's Mill can be spotted from this view. This area is concreted now and allows for close examination of the rocks that make up the cliffs. Note a boat ramp and floating docks across the river.

87.19 Towpath is a ledge at the foot of a vertical cliff.

87.64 The towpath ledge widens at the foot of a ravine where Berkson's Run cascades to the towpath level. The concrete towpath now crosses the stream and covers the former stonework that created a waterfall (during low water) where creek water joined the river. Several large concrete blocks from private docks remain. An NPS survey marker is on the cliff side of the towpath opposite the concrete blocks.

87.76 Several small caves are in this area. McMahon's Mill, now less than a half mile upstream, is within view. The towpath is a concrete sidewalk in this formerly difficult area.

87.8x A narrow cave is in the cliff just before reaching the mill and road access point. Nice views both upstream and downstream from this slight turn in the river.

88.xx Reach the end of the Big Slackwater Restoration section. This site served as the access point for major construction cranes and barges, which were brought in to construct concrete sections of the towpath from approximately mile 86 to mile 88.

McMAHON'S (CHARLES) MILL

88.10 (39.530654, -77.823522) Access: From Hagerstown take I-70 Exit 28, MD-632 South to Downsville Pike. Continue about 5.0 miles to intersection of MD-63. Cross MD-63 and Downsville Pike becomes Dam No. 4 Rd. Take Dam No. 4 Rd. 0.8 mile and turn right on Dellinger Rd. Continue 0.5 mile, turn left on Avis Mill Rd., and follow to McMahon's Mill recreation area. McMahon's Mill offers tent and RV camping with shower and toilets, a museum (open by appointment only), and Potomac fishing, boating, and swimming. McMahon's Mill, 7900 Avis Mill Rd., Williamsport, MD 21795, 301-223-8778, www.mcmahonsmill.com.

The mill is just ahead on the berm. A mill was built on Downey Branch in 1778 to produce flour, feed, and plaster. The mill—much changed over time—was finally closed in 1922 due to floods. A wooden overshot wheel was replaced by a steel wheel in the 1920s, when waterpower was used to generate

McMahon's (Charles) Mill.

electricity here. The mill has been known by various names: Shanks, Charles, Avis, Shaffers, Old Flouring, Galloways, Cedar Grove, and more recently, McMahon's Mill.

This Charles Mill is not to be confused with the two Charles Mills located at mile 108.13, Dam 5. Most grist mills along the Potomac in the nineteenth century from Harpers Ferry to Big Spring were operated by the Herr, Charles, Middlekauff, and Peacher families, all of whom intermarried.

The river sometimes rises to the foundation of the mill and above during spring floods, so plan your passage carefully depending upon weather conditions in this area. McMahon's Mill is one of the few places in this section of the river where vehicles can get close to the water's edge for observation or rescue operations.

CAUTION! The towpath along the cliff above here is at a low level and sometimes floods when the river is high, necessitating a detour on local roads to Locks 41 and 42. For up-to-date park closures call 301-582-0813 or visit www.nps.gov/choh/planyourvisit/closures.htm.

88.12 Cross a concrete bridge over Downey Branch. The cliffs here are a veritable rock garden of wildflowers, with sedum (*Sedum*) and moss pinks (*Phlox subulata*) predominant, some gaining nourishment from unbelievably small cracks in the rock. The towpath has been rebuilt for a short distance at the base of the cliff, but passage should not be attempted when water covers this low-lying section of the trail.

88.28 Howell Cave with one entrance (on right) in a beautiful grotto. One of two Howell Caves, this one is sometimes referred to as McMahon's Mill Cave. (Note: caves in this area have high, small openings and may be difficult to access.) A large underground stream issues from the cave, and another to the right is the reappearance of a stream that descends into a sinkhole 700 yards north. The limestone cave opens into two large rooms, one 20' x 60' x 12' high. The end of the room is blocked by a rockfall but is reputed to lead into a passage running to the sinkhole. Numerous small cave openings exist in the cliffs to the area below Lock 43.

88.52 Interesting overhang, with flowstone formed below a small cave opening. The towpath traverses a rough rocky area. The cliff face gives the appearance of an enormous, shallow grotto.

88.59 An opening to the Little Howell Cave is 20' up the cliff and is best seen looking backward. The towpath here has views of the river bend in both directions.

88.6x Round, steep, rocky cliff. The towpath here is under water when the Potomac floods. Note the drill marks and rope burns from tow ropes.

88.68 Cross the mouth of a narrow ravine with a normally-dry watercourse and path leading 300 yards up to Dellinger Road. The towpath ledge widens into a honeysuckle-covered area.

LOCK 41

88.90 Access: From McMahon's Mill at mile 88.10.

The canal resumes after slackwater navigation through this lock. The most exposed surface of the lock structure is concrete, representing later repair work. This lock functioned as a river lock, with the number of feet a boat would have to be lowered or raised depending on the level of the river at the time. The maximum lift here is 10'. When the river was extremely low, a boat may not have been able to be safely lowered into the pool at the foot of the lock. If the river was quite high, a boat coming into the lock would not have to be raised very much to get it onto the level between Locks 41 and 42. The canal resumes at this point—or, from the point of view of a downstream boat, ends here, requiring the boat to enter the river and its mules to take the path along the shore for the 3.5-mile length of Big Slackwater.

A small stone foundation is to the right of the lower end of the lock. A cleared area is above the upper end of the lock on the berm. One has the choice of using the towpath (on the berm) or the road-like path along the riverbank to Lock 42, which gives a good view of the canal and river. The towpath proper remained on the land side of the canal to Lock 42.

89.01 Several foundations here—including one on the berm—represent a small community with a road once running along the berm and ascending the hill to present-day Spring Dell Road and the Dellinger School on Neck Road.

LOCK 42

89.04 Access: From McMahon's Mill at mile 88.10.

As with Lock 41, there is much concrete work in this structure. This second lock—just above Lock 41, which was at river level—has a 9' lift. The two locks together raise the canal about 15' above the typical river level, which is enough to protect it from low or moderate floods.

Neither Lock 41 nor 42 had a bypass flume as there was no canal beyond these two in which the water level needed to be maintained when the lock gates were closed. Also, any boat lowered in Lock 42 would likely pass down immediately to Lock 41 and be lowered to river level, so the level between the locks would receive a large supply of water when the water in Lock 42 was released to lower the boat.

A very old foundation on the berm was probably that of the lockhouse for both locks. There is another foundation beyond the opposite head of the lock. The towpath once crossed the lock on a former mule cross-over bridge at

Boat leaving Lock 42 and heading downstream in the canal operating days.

the downstream end of the lock, but now crosses above the lock and continues through a wooded area 25 yards from the river. There are numerous cabins on the West Virginia side.

89.1x An old foundation is on the berm, about 20 yards beyond NPS milepost 89.

89.21 Culvert #118-1/2, 4' span, carries a stream from the fields to the berm. (Culverts #118–136 were built in 1835.) A beautiful Colonial stone farmhouse (ca. 1825) is one of nicest houses along the canal. The towpath beyond is lined by cedar trees that also provide beautiful borders to the rolling fields in this area. The canal bed has some growth and Osage orange trees (*Maclura pomifera*).

Early C&O Canal Association Level Walker Victor Conrad commented that some of his most enjoyable hikes have been in cold, windy weather, as hills, cliffs, and great trees provide shelter from wind, allowing one to walk along in comparative calm, listening to wintry blasts roaring through branches high above, imparting a sense of security and peace.

89.63 Begin a broad section of canal bed, formerly the half-mile-long pool known as Dellinger Widewater. Note the interesting cliffs across the river on Whitings Neck—another of the long necks caused by the meandering course of the Potomac. The river can appear a beautiful green color on cloudy winter days.

89.78 In April this region is a sea of purple as bluebells (*Mertensia virginica*) come into bloom.

90.24 Upper end of Dellinger Widewater. There is a long straightaway in the canal. A line of silver maples borders the grassy towpath, giving the appearance of a little-used country lane.

90.52 Good picnic site at grassy area to left.

90.94 Opequon Junction Hiker–Biker Campsite. Access: from Lock 43 at mile 92.96 or McMahon's Mill at mile 88.10.

Near here was the site of Foremans Ferry, which crossed the Potomac River to the mouth of Opequon Creek, visible just ahead on the opposite side of the river, where the West Virginia Izaak Walton league now runs a boat ramp and clubhouse. The small campground lies between the towpath and river on a narrow (about 10 yards) terraced area.

Initially, canal company engineers had planned to end the slackwater navigation behind Dam 4 here, so that there would be a river lock near Virginia's (now West Virginia's) Opequon Creek—a 64.5-mile waterway through an agriculturally rich area with a number of mills along its shores. When they decided on May 30, 1833, to extend the canal two miles farther downriver to the present location of Lock 41, they lost the support of Virginia, whose financial assistance was contingent upon a river lock opposite the mouth of the Opequon.

The Potomac here is still part of the pool behind Feeder Dam 4, so the river is quiet and wide. On summer weekends, however, the river attracts a lot of boating activities including waterskiing. Cliffs on the opposite shore drop sharply into the river. The worn groove of a very old road runs down the slope, probably the original route to the ferry. Cliffs resume beyond.

91.xx Towpath is wooded on both sides. The Potomac immediately on the left remains about 15' below the canal. Cliffs rise abruptly on the berm and are dotted with columbine (*Aquilegia vulgaris*) and gnarled tree growth. On a cool and calm December day, one may see red-bellied woodpeckers, downy woodpeckers, chickadees, mockingbirds, ducks, and hawks. Deer tracks are common on the soft towpath surface.

91.13 A long straightaway of the canal.

91.19 Cliffs recede for a wide ravine then resume, with long slanting folds rising from right to left that are well decorated with wildflowers and shrubs.

91.46 Cliffs drop back to a rocky wooded hillside. A power line crosses the river.

91.66 Culvert #119, 4' span. A ravine breaks into the hillside.

91.70 A summer cabin community once stretched for a half mile on the opposite side of the Potomac; beyond is rolling pasture land.

92.xx Cliffs in this section—90' to 100' high—have beautiful folded strata and shrub and tree growth.

92.05 A good, fast-flowing accessible spring issues from the foot of a cliff on the berm side of the canal. There is a lush growth of watercress in the pool made by the spring in the canal bed. The ravine contains rare calcareous tufa deposits—a variety of limestone, formed by the precipitation of carbonate minerals from ambient temperature water bodies. Also highly rare snow trillium (*Trillium nivale*), on Maryland's endangered list, are found only at Dellingers Spring within Maryland.

92.11 A steep-sided wooded ravine breaks the cliff, with a cascade of water coming down into the canal bed over a lush growth of green moss and cress. A trail leads across the canal prism and up into the ravine along the stream, but within 35' may be blocked by a private-property fence. Dellingers Cave is found farther up the ravine at the top of the cliff.

92.25 Exact mid-point of the canal. The inlet lock at Cumberland is 92.25 miles upstream, and the tide lock in Washington is 92.25 miles downstream.

92.56 A usually-dry cascade interrupts the cliff. Just beyond is a fast-flowing spring at the foot of the cliff on the berm side. In the canal operating period, boatmen sometimes took water from this spring by means of a bucket attached to a boat hook. The canal is partly filled with water from the spring. There is a good growth of cress here. Approaching the spring is difficult across the soft and wet canal bed.

92.63 The cliffs end and recede to a steep wooded slope beyond. There formerly was an overflow in the towpath here.

92.73 The towpath crosses a concrete waste weir. Water from a spring flows in a narrow stream in the canal prism and is joined by another stream flowing downstream from above Lock 43. Together they pass through a drain into the Potomac.

LOCK 43
92.96 Access: From McMahon's Mill at mile 88.10.

Just before the lock area, a hill on the berm side recedes and is interrupted by a narrow ravine. The hillside beyond is approximately 35 yards from the canal. This limestone lock (in good condition) was scheduled to be extended at one time but shows no sign of any actual extension being done. A stream flows through the lock. A brick lockhouse stands 10 yards back from the lock on the berm side. It was reconditioned during the park's early years. A locktender's shanty once stood at the upstream end of the lock.

93.02 Culvert #120, 6' span. Pass through an area with extensive lawn that is part of the Potomac Fish and Game Club.

93.29 Begin a 1.5-mile stretch of private homes and property. This extensive recreational community at Falling Waters has rights to use the towpath as an access road for some of the properties at the downstream end. Towpath users should be cautious of vehicles.

93.56 Culvert #121, 6' span. The road leaves the towpath and parallels it to mile 93.88.

93.88 The recreation area's road crosses the canal and becomes a paved road connecting with Falling Waters Road. This access to the recreation area is privately owned by the Potomac Fish and Game Club and is not a public access point to the towpath. There is no public access between McMahon's Mill and Williamsport.

94.0x The double row of cabins and recreational vehicles ends.

FALLING WATERS
94.44 Pass the stone piers of a bridge over the canal that was washed out in the 1936 flood. It served a ferry that operated to the village of Falling Waters, West Virginia. The village is reached by car via US-11, 5.0 miles south of Williamsport.

95.05 Culvert #121-1/2, 6' span. There is a path to the river on the downstream side of the culvert.

95.20 Cumberland Valley Hiker–Biker Campsite. Access: from Williamsport, Lock 44 at mile 99.30.

Geologists, like early settlers, refer to the valley between the Appalachian ridges here as the Great Valley. Today it is known as the Shenandoah Valley south of the Potomac and the Cumberland Valley north of the Potomac. The latter was named after Prince William, Duke of Cumberland (1721–65).

95.66 Culvert #122, 6' span.

96.24 Culvert #123, 5' span, rebuilt by the NPS.

96.72 Culvert #124, 4' span. An access road is marked "Funkstown Rod and Gun Club—Private." The towpath is on the riverbank in this area.

96.89 Culvert #125, 4' span.

96.97 Culvert #126, 4' span, rebuilt by the NPS.

97.15 This area has many fine shagbark hickory trees and paw paw trees along the towpath. Numerous large walnut and sycamore trees grow along the riverbank.

97.42 Masonry wall.

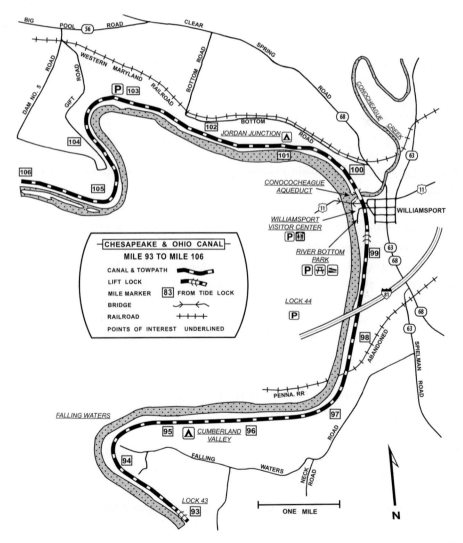

The Gettysburg Retreat

The canal at Falling Waters was the scene of intense military activity in July 1863 during Gen. Robert E. Lee's withdrawal after the Battle of Gettysburg. Lee's engineers, sent ahead to prepare a crossing of the Potomac for the retreating army, found the river swollen from heavy rains, and the pontoon bridge there destroyed by Union troops. At Williamsport, Confederate engineers quickly began taking lumber from canal boats and pieces of warehouses and wood from lumberyards to reconstruct the bridges, floating them downriver to Falling Waters. The Confederate army established a line from Hagerstown to Downsville, Maryland, north to south. Gen. George Meade's Federal troops soon set up a parallel line some miles to the east. While Lee's engineers rebuilt the pontoon bridge at Falling Waters, and small groups crossed using ferries at Williamsport, a major battle seemed imminent. However, Meade failed to attack.

On the night of July 13, in a continuous downpour, some of Lee's forces may have moved down the towpath from Williamsport and crossed the river at Falling Waters, while others traveled over local roads. Others crossed over the fords at Williamsport. Early on July 14, Union Gen. Judson Kilpatrick attacked the rear guard of the Confederate army on Falling Waters Road, taking many prisoners, but arriving too late to prevent the withdrawal of the Southerners. When Meade finally advanced in force on July 14, he found his enemy safe beyond the river.

97.44 The stone wall with timbers on the berm represents the remains of a wharf where canal traffic made a connection with the Cumberland Valley Railroad. Piers in the river mark the location of the bridge built 1871–72 by the railroad, when it decided to extend its rail line south from Hagerstown to Martinsburg. In 1914 the railroad built a newer bridge a short distance upstream. The bridge is currently owned by the Winchester & Western Railroad. A siding on the downriver side of the old bridge led to a track along the berm, where transshipment of coal from canal boats to railroad gondolas was made by a crane, for shipment to nearby points in Pennsylvania and West Virginia. This operation continued until the canal closed to navigation in 1924. The concrete foundation of the crane may still be in evidence. An interesting piece of curved masonry work can be seen on the abutment of the old railroad bridge.

97.95 Culvert #127, 4' span, repaired in 1985.

98.4x A spring drains from under the towpath through a French drain of fitted stone.

98.5x Pass under the highway bridges of I-81. A steep hillside with rocky outcroppings continues to mile 99.

98.82 Pass under a transmission line coming from the power plant at Williamsport, Maryland (shut down in 2012). A canal watering project from mile 98.78 to mile 99.80 was completed in 1996.

98.92 Cross a concrete waste weir for the level between Locks 43 and 44.

99.12 Culvert #128, 4' span.

This 2012 image of Lock 44 and the lockhouse at Williamsport shows its appearance following the mid-1990s restoration and re-watering project. *(Image courtesy Steve Dean)*

99.16 Old quarry on the berm.

99.23 Sewage disposal plant in fenced area on the river side. A horse race course was located on a tract of land between the canal and river, extending from the mouth of Conococheague Creek to the waste weir below Lock 44. Jousting tournaments and community picnics were also held there. At the close of the Civil War, baseball was played on the same tract of land, which Gen. Abner Doubleday could see from his observation post on what is now known as "Doubleday's Hill" at the north end of Riverview Cemetery.

Canoeists must portage on the West Virginia side of the river around the power plant's unmarked dam.

LOCK 44, WILLIAMSPORT

99.30 (39.595037, -77.824712) Access: From the center of Williamsport at the intersection of Potomac and Conococheague Sts. (US-11 and MD-68), take Conocoheague St. three blocks south and turn right onto W. Frederick St. Take slight left onto Canal St.; turn left onto Main St. and follow to the parking lot at Lock 44.

Lock 44 was an extended lock and is in good condition due to the extensive restoration done for the re-watering project in the mid-1990s and again in 2013. It is watered from here to the Cushwa Basin at mile 99.72. In the summer the NPS sometimes offers launch boat rides in this watered section of the canal.

A footbridge across the lock and its elaborate bypass flume lead to a well-preserved, large wooden-frame lockhouse.

99.35 R. Paul Smith Power Station that operated from 1927 to 2012.

99.38 Masonry wall once used by Steffey & Findlay Coal Company and the Darby Mill on the berm.

99.59 A high wooden fence directly on the towpath encloses the former coal yard of the power plant, now a grassy field. On the berm side is Riverview Cemetery where Williamsport founder, Otho Holland Williams, is buried. The cemetery grounds sit on Doubleday Hill, where Gen. Abner Doubleday installed an artillery battery to defend the canal and river during the Civil War. The town's Civil War cannon were refurbished and placed on authentic carriages on the top of the hill in 2013.

99.65 Pass under a wood and iron bridge carrying W. Salisbury Street over the canal to River Bottom Park, where the canal and Conococheague Creek meet the Potomac. This is a popular picnic, beach, and fishing area with a boat ramp.

A pony-Pratt iron truss bridge was constructed in 1879 by Baltimore engineer Wendell Bollman's (1814–84) Patapsco Bridge and Iron Works company. Along with Squire Whipple and Albert Fink, he introduced the system of bridge trussing using iron in all the principal structural members, beginning the great age of the metal bridge. Of perhaps 100 Bollman bridges, the one at Savage,

The towpath passes beneath the Western Maryland Railroad bridge at Williamsport. The bridge lifted the railway tracks for passing canal boats. *(Library of Congress, Prints and Photographs Division, HAER, Reproduction Number MD, 22-WILPO, 1--13)*

Maryland, was thought to be the sole survivor of Bollman's early unique truss design. Mule tender George "Hooper" Wolfe decided to take a closer look at this bridge over the canal after reading an article on the Bollman bridges. After dusting off the cast-iron name plate and applying a bit of red paint, he discovered that it read "1879–W. Bollman Baltimore." The bridge was rebuilt with a pedestrian bridge ca. 1990. The road beyond to the river once led to a ferry across the Potomac.

99.69 The Western Maryland Railway spur crosses the canal on a lift bridge built in the early months of 1923 by the Potomac Public Service Company. The bridge is significant as a rare surviving example of a short-span railroad vertical lift bridge. It is now owned and maintained by the NPS, having been donated by Potomac Edison.

99.71 Pass under the US-11 highway bridge that crosses the Potomac River.

CUSHWA BASIN AND CONOCOCHEAGUE AQUEDUCT

99.72 (39.600996, -77.826927) Access: From the center of Williamsport follow US-11 (W. Potomac St.) to the NPS Visitor Center parking lot at the bottom of the hill. The visitor center offers canal boat rides seasonally. Exhibits and restrooms are available. C&O Canal NHP Williamsport Visitor Center, 205 W. Potomac St., Williamsport, MD 21795, 301-582-0813, www.nps.gov/choh/planyourvisit/williamsportvisitorcenter.htm.

The Cushwa basin is the only restored historical basin on the C&O Canal, having been excavated and rebuilt in 1994. The Cushwa warehouse is one of the oldest buildings along the canal—some parts of it pre-dating the canal's construction. Adjacent to the basin on its downstream side was the Cushwa wharf, which, along with the Steffey and Findlay wharf near Lock 44, made Williamsport the most important coal shipment point on the canal above the Federal District.

99.76 Upstream end of Cushwa Basin. A causeway path leads from the towpath to the visitor center parking lot and provides access to the town center.

99.80 The Conococheague Aqueduct, over Conococheague Creek, was completed in 1834, and is the fifth of 11 masonry aqueducts on the canal. Built of limestone obtained "from quarries within 3 miles" according to early engineering reports (the primary source likely having been High Rock Quarry, now known as Pinesburg Quarry), the aqueduct has three equal 60' arch spans extending 196' between abutments. Note rope burns in the wood at the top of the railing. The letters "C. S." and date "1877" are carved in the stone of the first arch's pier.

During the Civil War raids against the Conococheague Aqueduct were committed by both sides. During the Battle of Antietam, Union cavalry attempted but failed to damage the aqueduct or destroy the bridge over the canal.

Lithograph of the Conococheague Aqueduct, C&O Canal basin, and the Embrey and Cushwa Warehouse, ca. 1872.

When the Confederates invaded Maryland beginning June 15, 1863, pioneers were immediately dispatched to tear apart the aqueduct. Stone was torn out of the four corners of the aqueduct down to the bottom of the canal, and a 10' gap was made in one of the arches. On August 5, 1864, Confederate Gen. Jubal Early sent troops across the river at Williamsport to distract attention away from Southern cavalry that had burned Chambersburg, Pennsylvania, and threatened Cumberland. During this occupation of the town, minor damage was inflicted to the aqueduct.

The berm wall collapsed early on the morning of April 20, 1920. Boat No. 73 was headed for Cumberland with Captain Frank Myers steering the boat and his step-son, Joseph Davis, driving a three-mule team. Around 5 a.m. Myers saw the east end of the berm wall waver, possibly due to the wall's already increasing instability. Myers called to his step-son—who was almost at the western end of the aqueduct—to cut the mules loose. When the wall broke and the rushing water pulled the boat toward the breach, Capt. Myers leapt onto the eastern end of the berm parapet. The boat fell into the Conococheague Creek and remained there until the 1936 flood carried it down the Potomac. It sat on the towpath downstream until subsequent high waters caused it to break up and float away. A wooden wall replaced the stone and remained until 1924. Though stabilized by the NPS, the aqueduct has not been restored to its original condition.

The restored/re-watered portion of the canal prism terminates at the causeway between the parking area and the basin.

99.84 Upper end of aqueduct.

99.85 Former boat basin for the nearby tannery.

172

Boat No. 73 stranded in the Conococheague Creek after the aqueduct berm wall collapsed on the morning of April 20, 1920.

Canal Town, Williamsport

Williamsport is the seventh of nine Canal Town partners along the C&O Canal. Visit www.canaltowns.org to learn about points of interest, services, and food sources in these towns.

The Conococheague settlement here was the first in what is now Washington County, Maryland. Native Americans, fur traders, and settlers all traveled through here long before the first land grants were given in 1739. That year Jeremiah Jack settled 175 acres called "Jack's Bottom," and Charles Friend received 260 acres named "Swede's Delight." In 1744 the Virginia House of Burgesses permitted a ferry to cross the Potomac between Virginia (now West Virginia) and Maryland. The ferry—operated by Evans Watkins and known as Watkins Ferry—landed about 50 yards downstream from what is now US-11 on the West Virginia bank of the river and at the foot of what is now the west end of Salisbury Street in Williamsport.

The Conococheague settlement was an important point during the French and Indian War (1754–63). Gen. Edward Braddock used Springfield Farm as a depot during his ill-fated expedition in 1755. The owners of Springfield Farm were Joseph and Prudence Williams. Their son Otho Holland Williams grew up to be a general in the Continental Army, fighting in the American Revolution. In 1787 he purchased Springfield Farm and the surrounding land and formally established Williams Port.

River trade had been important to Williamsport long before construction of the C&O Canal. The Patowmack Company's skirting canals and river improvements allowed a lively commerce to develop through small river boats and rafts. Boats carried varied products to Georgetown and Alexandria, and sometimes brought payloads back, although the arduous return trip was difficult enough for empty boats. Rafts carried much trade, and were dismantled and sold for firewood at the lower end of the journey.

In 1834 the first canal boats reached Williamsport via slackwater navigation from Dam 4. The canal itself was in operation to the town basin the next year, initiating a period of intense activity and prosperity. In the busy Cushwa Basin tons of coal were unloaded, especially after 1850. In 1873 a branch of the Western Maryland Railroad from Hagerstown reached the Williamsport wharves, dramatically increasing demand for coal here. Williamsport was perhaps the most typical "Canal Town" and the most major port except for Georgetown and Cumberland on the C&O.

Several Civil War battles and skirmishes were fought in and around Williamsport. In May and June 1861 the Williamsport Home Guard skirmished with the Confederates posted opposite the town. On September 19, 1862, following the Battle of Antietem, Confederate Gen. J. E. B. Stuart crossed back into Maryland at Williamsport and skirmished with Union forces before withdrawing the following day.

On July 6, 1863, during the Confederate retreat from Gettysburg, the Battle of Williamsport, also called the "Waggoners Fight," occurred between Union cavalry and a ragtag collection of Confederate forces supplemented with the walking wounded and a force of teamsters who had volunteered to fight. The Confederates held off the Union horsemen in the last named engagement.

During the Maryland Campaign of 1862, damage to the canal at Williamsport included the burning of the bridge over the canal, the lock gates and locktender's house at Lock 44, and twelve canal boats. A year later during the Gettysburg Campaign of 1863, the Conococheague Aqueduct was badly damaged; two rows of stone were removed from Lock 44; four roads were built through the canal walls; and an unspecified number of boats were burned.

In 1864 Confederate troops under Gen. Jubal Early burned the lock gates, breached the towpath, and inflicted minor damage to the aqueduct. An undetermined number of boats were burned in and around town.

Floods left their mark on the Williamsport basin. The 1889 flood (the same year as the Johnstown Flood) augmented by a local tornado, did tremendous damage, reaching an all-time high and transforming the area around the aqueduct into a huge lake. The 1924 flood, which ended navigation on the canal, and the devastating flood of 1936 pounded the area unmercifully.

Williamsport survived the Civil War, natural disasters, and the closing of the canal, and has been transformed into a charming stop along the towpath. For more about its history and what it currently offers in recreation, dining, and lodging, visit www.canaltowns.org or www.williamsportmd.gov. Bike repair and supplies are available at River City Cycles, 16 ½ N. Conococheague St., Williamsport, MD 21795, 301-223-6733, http://rivercitycyclesinc.com/.

Irish Woes at Williamsport

Construction of the C&O Canal was not without incident, and two dramatic episodes forever linked the history of the canal to the history of Williamsport.

First, between 1832 and 1835 the cholera epidemic that had already claimed hundreds of workers' lives downstream made its way to Williamsport. Irish victims of the disease were first buried in a Catholic cemetery in Hagerstown, but citizen protests forced the priests to move the bodies closer to the canal. Due to lack of funds and the difficulty in hiring grave diggers who were willing to risk exposure to the plague, many were buried in a mass grave in what is called Hospital Hill.

The second incident unfolded when the rivalry between two factions of Irish laborers erupted into armed clashes during the idle winter months. The worst battle occurred in January 1834 between the Corkonians, who were working near Dam 5 above Williamsport, and the Fardowners (or Longfords), who were located near Dam 4, below town. Each hoped to oust the other from the canal workforce and therefore eliminate competition for labor and wages.

A preliminary clash near town resulted in several deaths before militia restored order. Williamsport townsmen set up patrol over the unfinished Conococheague Aqueduct to keep the factions apart. A week later, 300 Fardowners marched up the canal armed with guns and clubs and persuaded the aqueduct guards to let them pass. Above the aqueduct they were joined by 300 or 400 more. They met the vastly outnumbered Corkonians on a hill near Dam 5, defeated them in a short-pitched battle, and returned to their shanties downriver. Federal forces were finally dispatched to maintain peace along the line.

Work along American canals sometimes slowed as laborers were victims of disease, accidents, and infighting.

99.93 An unpaved extension of Fenton Avenue leads from the canal bed to MD-68/ Clear Spring Road. Here a number of canal workers who died in the cholera epidemic are buried in a plot of ground known as Hospital Hill (not visible from the road).

100.23 Culvert #129, 6' span.

100.51 A path across the canal leads up the edge of a field to Bottom Road.

100.69 Culvert #131, 4' span. Small picnic area.

101.00 A footbridge leads across the canal to the foot of cement stairs ascending a levee around the R. C. Wilson Water Filtration Plant. A path on the river side leads to steps down to concrete intake gates on the riverbank. Duck Island is visible near the far shore.

101.10 On the berm side a graded, flat area adjoins the levee around the filtration plant. There may have been a basin here.

101.15 Site of Culvert #133 or #132—now a concrete pipe. End of the intensive 1957 canal clearing area.

101.28 Jordan Junction Hiker–Biker Campsite. Access from the Williamsport Visitor Center at mile 99.72 or parking area at 103.26. Cornfields stretch along the berm side.

102.00 Culvert #134, 6' span.

102.20 The towpath comes onto the riverbank, built up with a protective wall. There is an outcropping of rock on the berm.

102.26 A sharp cut in the hill on the berm side leads to an active quarry previously known as "High Rock." Stone for Conococheague Aqueduct was probably taken from here. Other nearby quarry activity is visible. The berm rises from a steep slope to a cliff.

102.45 Interesting sheer cliff on berm. The boulder in the canal bed is a result of blasting from the nearby quarry.

> USE CAUTION NEAR CLIFFS. BLASTING FROM NEARBY QUARRIES MAY CAUSE LOOSE ROCKS TO FALL.

102.65 Culvert #135, 6' span. Cliffs resume beyond.

102.90 A narrow ravine cuts between the cliffs on the berm. Near the top of the cliff on the left of the ravine is the entrance to Pinesburg Cave, approximately 75' long. The cave was closed by the owner in November 2009.

103.02 A limestone cliff on the berm has bare blocks of rock interspersed with cedar trees.

103.26 Gift Road Parking. (39.616863, -77.888503) Access: From I-70 take Exit 18, MD-68 East/Clearspring Rd. Continue 1.8 miles and turn right onto Dam No. 5 Rd. Go another 0.9 mile and turn left onto Gift Rd. Follow another 0.9 mile (the last 0.2 mile is unpaved) to the NPS parking area. Parking is limited to two or three vehicles.

103.xx Culvert #135-1/2, 4' span. A stream from the wooded ravine flows directly into the river.

103.45 Remains of a two-story wood house that housed canal maintenance workers. CAUTION: this house is in an extremely poor and dangerous condition and should not be investigated. A basin and dock once present here were likely used for maintenance boats.

103.53 One mile of cultivated fields on the berm.

MILLERS BEND

104.38 Cliffs on the West Virginia shore recede to the sheer limestone cliffs of the abandoned Nestles Quarry. A well-known landmark during canal operating days was Indian Church Cave—a shallow cave entrance shaped like a church with a spire on the north side of the quarry wall. According to legend, Native Americans slept on dry, recessed platforms on each side of the cave during stormy weather. Sometime after World War II, relic searchers excavated clay shelves down to rough-edged bedrock. Trees growing from the quarry floor now obscure distant views of the cave entrance. The lack of sun exposure has made the cave damp, and it is no longer a comfortable shelter. The "Sun and Moon" limestone spring gushes from a quarry wall near the present housing development.

104.41 A clearing on the river side of the canal provides spectacular views of the cliff on the West Virginia shore.

104.61 Breakwater.

104.8x Concrete piers of a former railroad bridge across the river. The line belonged to the Williamsport, Nessle, and Martinsburg Railway, a subsidiary of the Western Maryland Railway. The line was built to carry limestone from quarries in the West Virginia panhandle to Charlton, Maryland, where it connected to the WM. The line was intended to extend to Martinsburg and Charles Town, West Virginia, and then further to the Potomac Yard in Virginia, but the bridge was destroyed in the 1936 flood.

105.xx Culvert #136 (Little Conococheague Creek), 24' span, built 1833–34. A path on the berm leads to ruins of the Charles (Middlekauffs) Mill. Another path on the river side leads to the riverbank.

106.21 The path across the canal bed leads to Dam No. 5 Road. The brick house across the road belonged to the miller of Charles Mill. Also known as Middlekauffs or Coultons Mill, it began operating in pre-canal days. Beyond the house are foundation stones and other evidence of the mill, which was badly damaged by floods.

106.26 The canal widens here, possible evidence of a basin.

106.61 Concrete waste weir for the Lock 44 to Dam 5 level.

FEEDER DAM 5 AND INLET (GUARD) LOCK 5

106.80 (39.607079, -77.921117) Access:: From I-70 take Exit 18, MD-68 East/Clear Spring Rd. Continue 1.8 miles and turn right onto Dam No. 5 Rd. Follow approximately 3.2 miles to the Dam 5 parking lot. Canoeists must portage on either side of the dam.

A footbridge crosses the canal bed. A one-and-a-half story lockhouse sits on the hill above the lock. Construction of the Potomac Edison Power Plant at the far side of the dam in West Virginia began in 1917 and was completed in 1918. The power plant, now owned by Harbor Hydro Holdings, has a total installed capacity of 1210 kilowatts. The dam was constructed 1833–35 of stone-filled timber cribs covered with heavy planks.

A temporary lock was constructed around an abutment of the dam in 1833 to permit continuation of river trade while the dam was being built. The stretch of canal between Dams 4 and 5 opened in 1835, and that between Dams 5 and 6 (27 miles upstream) opened to navigation in April 1839.

Construction of an 18' masonry dam began in 1857, but most of the dam was still a crib dam when the Civil War began. Early in the war the Confederates made a number of attempts to breach Dam 5. Before evacuating Harpers Ferry on June 8, 1861, Gen. Joseph E. Johnston sent a party of soldiers to the dam, where they spent several days trying to detonate a powder charge in it. The structure was defended by the Clear Spring Home Guard, and no damage was done. Confederate Gen. Stonewall Jackson first tried to breach the dam December 6–8, 1861. His troops attempted to divert water around the dam and to cut the cribs of the structure, but were prevented by Union riflemen behind the northern abutment of the dam and on the bluffs overhead. Jackson tried again December 17–21. After several days of frustration, he sent his force at the

Inlet Lock 5 as it looked in the heyday of the canal.

dam toward Little Georgetown with boats, a ruse that caused the Union force to follow, and which gave a Confederate work party an evening to cut the cribs without being fired upon. Convinced that they had made a significant breach, they withdrew. The damage was minor, however, and canal boats were moving the next day. On a third attempt January 2–3, 1862, Jackson's men worked in the river, widening the breach. The damage was still not significant enough to halt boat traffic. After the war the conversion to a masonry dam was completed.

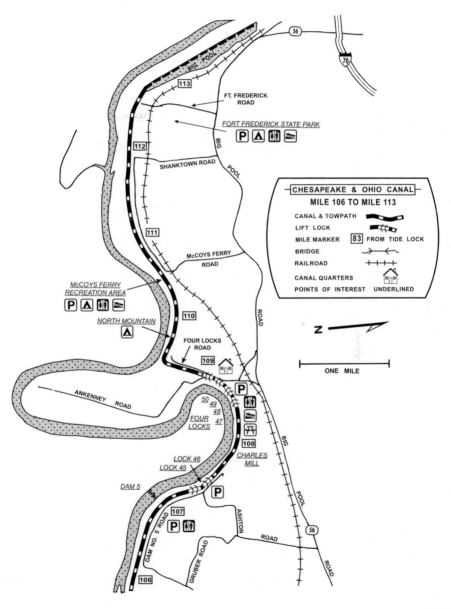

Dam 5 north of Williamsport, 2011. *(Image courtesy Steve Dean)*

106.82 A mule crossover bridge was located at the upper end of the inlet lock to carry mules to the berm side of the lock. Here the towpath ran along the riverbank, as the boats switched to slackwater navigation between here and Lock 45, one-half mile upstream. The towpath follows ledges that were directly alongside the river during the canal's operating years.

106.86 A high water medallion on a berm-side rock reads: "1942/217.43." The widened towpath runs along a canal-like ditch that once formed a channel between a long island-like strip of land and the towpath. This strip of land protected light boats from the main body of the river on the other side. The channel continues to the other end of the protective island 0.2 mile up from the inlet lock.

107.13 The previously bare-ledged towpath that veers around a rocky point was leveled, widened, and given a concrete surface to allow for NPS service vehicles. An overhanging cliff was also altered by the widening.

107.15 About 30' above the towpath were the entrances to three small caves, known as Two Locks Caves, which may have been altered by the blasting of the cliff. The opening to the left is a crawlway, floored with river gravel, extending 30' south. The second cave is a fissure, its entrance in a small hollow 150' south. It apparently connects to a third cave with another crawlway extending 100' into Stonehenge limestone and with a few small side passages at the rear.

107.19 Old tow rope marks were obliterated when part of the beautiful rock cliff was blasted to widen the towpath around rocky points here.

LOCK 45

107.27 Access: Lock 46 at mile 107.42.

The canal resumes at this lock after a half mile of slackwater navigation. Included in the lift-lock numbering system, this lock is nevertheless also a river lock, as it raises and lowers boats to and from the river and the level of the canal at the upstream end of the lock. The towpath remains on the berm between Locks 45 and 46. An overgrown path leads to a strip of land above Lock 45 to Lock 46. The locks are known as "Two Locks," as is the nearby housing community. The lock has a 7' lift.

LOCK 46

107.42 (39.615866, -77.926626) Access: From I-70 take Exit 18, MD-68 East/Clear Spring Rd. Continue 1.8 miles and turn right onto Dam No. 5 Rd. Follow approximately 3.8 miles; an unpaved road turns left down a steep hill to a small parking area near the lock.

The upper of the "Two Locks," Lock 46 also has a 7' lift. A two-and-a-half story brick and stone locktender's house served both locks. The waste weir is filled in. The towpath formerly crossed back to the river side of the canal via a mule crossover bridge at the lower end of the lock. Stone piers of the bridge remain. Tunis "Bud" Newkirk's Store and Steel's warehouse were located here. Newkirk also rented and sold mules for canal use.

Here at Dam 5 loaded boats came down the river outside the narrow strip of land and light boats went up the narrow channel in the river.

Mule "cross-over" bridge at Lock 46, ca. 1900.

107.48 The bluestone, widened towpath that began at Dam 5 continues to Four Locks at mile 108.64. During winter months impressive rock formations on the berm are visible from the towpath.

107.62 The stonework here indicates a semi-formal overflow. The path on the berm leads to an old log house in a small valley where there was once a basin and canal company boat repair facility.

107.69 According to records there was a culvert in the present location of a pipe. Work was extremely difficult and expensive between Locks 46 and 47, as the embankments of the canal were made in the 20'-deep river.

107.73 Cliffs on the berm side.

107.93 Culvert #137, carries a stream from a broad ravine in a 2' pipe. Culverts #137 through #197 were built in 1839.

108.13 Culvert #138 (Camp Springs Run), 8' span. On the berm are ruins of the Benjamin F. Charles Mill and the remains of a former milling community. Charles Mill, built in 1807, operated until 1924. The mill contained both a plaster and grain mill. Some walls and the millwheel remain; the millrace washed out. Cliffs resume on the berm beyond the culvert.

108.40 Fine 75' sheer cliff on berm. Drill marks can be found on the cliff, especially when sunlight hits the rocks.

108.49 A former basin here provided a maneuvering space for barges and a docking area for the loading and unloading of goods. Beyond the canal bed overgrown and rocky cliffs resume on the berm side; houses appear on the cliff.

FOUR LOCKS

108.xx (39.615311, -77.947494) Access: From I-70 take Exit 18/Clear Spring Rd. into the center of Clear Spring. Turn left at traffic light onto US-40 west. Go one block and turn left onto Martin St. Follow Martin St. approximately 3 miles; the road goes under I-70, turns into Big Spring Rd., and then joins MD-56/ Big Pool Rd. Continue on MD-56/Big Pool Rd. 0.6 mile and take a slight left onto Four Locks Rd. Go 0.6 mile and take a slight right onto Starliper Rd. and follow it to a large parking area. The Four Locks Recreation Area has a boat ramp that provides access to a seven-mile slackwater lake, an extensive picnic area, water, and toilets.

The canal here leaves the river to take a half-mile shortcut across Prather's Neck, thus bypassing a four-mile bend of river. The locks here raised the level of the canal to avoid an otherwise expensive cut. All four locks have an 8.25' lift. The level from Lock 50 to Lock 51 is the longest on canal at 13.72 miles. There were several houses in the Four Locks community. The large stone house on the berm is the Hassett House, whose early owner was closely associated with canal affairs.

108.64 Lock 47, the first of the Four Locks. The canal bed between each of the four locks is grassy and well maintained. Remnants of a dry dock for repairing boats can still be found in the bushes between the road and the bypass flume around the lock.

Lockhouse at Lock 49 at Four Locks near Clear Spring in the winter of 2013. *(Image courtesy Ed Kirkpatrick Photography)*

108.70 Lock 48 with bypass flume. The road on the berm side of the canal was once designated as "Birm Road," on a country road sign. Part of the upper gate remains. A solid foundation for this lock was never achieved, and the ground under it was subsiding, making the lock unstable and likely to collapse until the NPS filled it in.

108.74 Culvert #139, 12' span, carries an often-dry stream and Four Locks Road under the canal to the recreation area between the canal and the river. Ankenny Road continues down Prather's Neck to the Prather's Neck Maryland Wildlife Management Area near the bottom of the neck, where there is a small parking lot for about 10 cars. Road culverts such as this provided access for vehicles and pedestrians to places on the river side of the canal.

108.80 Lock 49. A footbridge across the lock leads to Birm Road. Note the opening in the masonry for a flume. The canal shortcut across Prather's Neck begins. This area of Four Locks was the headquarters for Union troops defending the canal in 1861 and early 1862, particularly during Stonewall Jackson's raids against Dam 5.

The two-and-a-half story brick house on the berm was the locktender's house for all four locks. Locktenders at Four Locks were often residents of the community living in their own homes, and those using the lockhouse were often paid to hire local people as assistants. It was occupied until 1970 by four generations of the Taylor family. This lockhouse is available for overnight rentals via the Canal Trust's Canal Quarters program, 301-745-8888, www.canaltrust.org/quarters.

108.87 Lock 50, the uppermost of the Four Locks. The barn is a careful reconstruction of the original barn used to house mules on a short-term basis or over the winter months by boatmen who had made arrangements with local people

for their care. Note the locktender's "wait" house (also known as a lock shanty) at the upstream end of the lock. A reconstruction, it is the only example of a wait house along the canal and replicates a relatively small and simple one. Many were larger, and the most comfortable would have been large enough for a table and chair, a cot, and a small stove for heat and minimal cooking.

The old mule barn at Four Locks.

109.32 Cross concrete waste weir and emerge on the riverbank at the upper end of the shortcut. The two wickets are in perfect condition. Note the remains of a stone wall on both the berm and towpath sides of the canal prism between Lock 50 and the waste weir.

109.60 The towpath is high above the river flat.

109.90 Culvert #140, 10' span, road culvert built 1836–37. The canal here is 48'9" above river level.

110.00 North Mountain Hiker–Biker Campsite. The nearest access is from the McCoys Ferry Drive-in Campground at mile 110.42.

110.10 Culvert #141, 4' span, built 1835–37.

110.29 The 17' x 20' stop gate here was constructed 1835–37. It is the first of four stop gates along this nearly 14-mile level, which passes across terrain subject to sinkholes, such as the ones that can be seen in the prism here and there along the level. When a section of the canal began to lose integrity—or actually did so due to a sinkhole appearing—the stop gates made it possible to hold water in the canal above the area needing repairs, thereby limiting the amount of water that would be lost.

McCOYS FERRY

110.42 (39.609261, -77.970065) Access: From I-70, take Exit 12, MD-56 E/Big Pool. Follow Big Pool Rd. 2.6 miles and turn right onto McCoys Ferry Rd. Pass through culvert beneath a former Western Maryland Railway trestle (adjacent to Green Spring Run), and continue to the McCoys Ferry Drive-in Campground. (See www.nps.gov/choh for current fees.) Campgrounds include grills, water, chemical toilets, and a boat ramp. The towpath passes over the road leading to the recreation area. From the towpath, a footpath crosses the canal to McCoys Ferry Road.

Culvert #142 (McCoys Ferry), 12' span, constructed 1837, rebuilt in 1839. The Western Maryland Railway trestle #1018 was built in 1892.

At 2 a.m. on May 23, 1861, in the absence of the Clear Spring Guards, some Virginians seized the ferry boat and headed for the opposite shore. Home guards discovered the theft when the boat was halfway across the river. They called out three times and fired. The Virginians abandoned the boat and reached the opposite shore in a skiff. At dawn the home guards retrieved the ferry boat. Here on October 10, 1862, Confederate Gen. J. E. B. Stuart crossed the Potomac on his second ride around McClellan's army. On July 24, 1864, a portion of Confederate cavalry in the McCausland–Johnson Raid crossed the river at this ford on its way to Chambersburg, Pennsylvania. The cavalry burned the town when residents refused to pay a ransom.

> *We have come a way from the hustle and bustle of Georgetown, skirting the Great Falls of the Potomac, hiking through deciduous woods of the Piedmont to the foothills of the Blue Ridge Mountains and beyond, passing historic towns—Harpers Ferry, Shepherdstown, Sharpsburg, Williamsport—and sensing in the distance the larger valley towns of Frederick and Hagerstown, enjoying the slackwaters of the Potomac River, constant companion of the canal, marveling at the natural wonders of the valley and hills and the physical accomplishments of the builders of the canal—dams, lift locks, aqueducts, culverts—to this point, where we enter first a rather placid section, somewhat marred by a paralleling interstate highway ahead, but still a restful prelude to the adventures which await us in the mountainous region ahead. –Thomas Hahn*

110.45 Culvert #143 (Green Spring Run), 6' span. A road runs along the berm; the canal bed is cleared of growth. Long trains occasionally pass on the former Western Maryland Railway (now CSX's Lurgan Subdivision that runs from Cherry Run, West Virginia to Chambersburg, Pennsylvania). Green Spring Iron Furnace—built in 1850 on the site of a ca. 1770 furnace—ceased operations in 1873. Lancelot Jacques and Thomas Johnson built the original furnace. C&O Canal boats carried furnace products 1850–73.

110.80 Railroad ties lashed together and lying in shallow water form a path across the canal to an abandoned farm.

110.83 Culvert #144, 6' span. A wide, open valley with views of West Virginia's North Mountain.

111.20 This section of the towpath was once used as part of a farm. The berm road leads to Fort Frederick State Park. Begin a long straightaway in the canal.

111.28 Former boat basin on berm.

111.38 Culvert #145, 6' span, built 1837–38.

111.68 A small stream enters the canal from a large group of evergreens. From this point the canal borders Fort Frederick State Park.

112.05 Culvert #147, 4' span, built 1837–38.

112.23 Culvert #148, 6' span, built 1837–38.

FORT FREDERICK STATE PARK

112.40 (39.605391, -78.005041) Access: From I-70 take Exit 12, MD-56 E/Big Pool. Follow Big Pool Rd 1.1 miles and turn right onto Fort Frederick Rd. Park at the visitor's parking lot or continue on Fort Frederick Rd. to limited parking at the towpath. CAUTION: At the edge of the canal, the road crosses the CSX Lurgan Subdivision (former Western Maryland Railway) track on a curve with poor visibility. Listen for locomotive whistles.

The park offers period reenactments and other interpretive and educational programs, picnic areas with tables and grills, a picnic pavilion (permit required), a playground, camping between the canal and river, a boat ramp, boating and fishing at Big Pool Lake, trailer spaces, water, and toilets. Captain Wort's Sutler Shop has concessions, souvenirs, and camping supplies in season. The museum contains Indian and pre-Revolutionary War relics. The visitor center is open 8 a.m. to sunset, April–October, and 10 a.m. to sunset, November–March. Fort Frederick State Park, 11100 Fort Frederick Rd., Big Pool MD 21711, 301-842-2155, dnr2.maryland.gov/publiclands/Pages/western/fortfrederick.aspx.

Fort Frederick was built in 1756 by Gov. Horatio Sharpe to protect the frontier after Gen. Edward Braddock's defeat in the French and Indian War. It was part of a chain of colonial forts stretching along the entire eastern side of the Allegheny Mountains. The fort occupies a dominant position on North Mountain, 100' above the Potomac River. George Washington visited in July 1756 and June 1758. It was used as a detention camp for British prisoners during the Revolutionary War. In late 1861 and early 1862 it was garrisoned by Union troops to protect the canal during Confederate Gen. Stonewall Jackson's raids against nearby Dam 5. In 1922 the fort was deeded to the Maryland Department of Forests and Parks. The Civilian Conservation Corps (CCC) restored the fort's walls and built two barracks (reconstructed in 1975).

The stop gate beside the bridge on the road from the fort to picnic areas along the river provided a means of retaining water in Big Pool when the canal was drained in the winter. This avoided the necessity of filling the

A canal boat being towed in Big Pool above Fort Frederick, ca. 1903–23.

large lake when the canal was re-watered. The stop gate is a simple masonry structure of two parallel walls 18' apart, with 7" masonry wings on the upper and lower ends. The stone base indicates a pivot bridge that rested on the lower berm wall and was used for both pedestrians and vehicles. The stop gate probably had machinery for lifting a drop gate. Stones in the lock wall appear to be rough-cut granite. A dig at this site ca. 1972 revealed the circular pivot mechanism in place. A wooden bridge later replaced the pivot bridge. There was also a high pedestrian bridge here ca. 1900 with ladder-like steps on both sides.

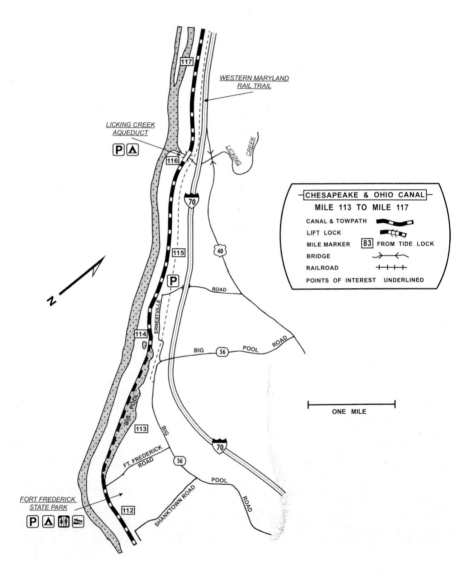

BIG POOL

112.50 This fine pool of water, extending 1.5 miles along the canal, was the result of the engineers' decision to connect a series of natural ridges for the towpath berm rather than follow the contour of land. This towpath surface enclosed a low-lying area creating the small lake.

112.85 Extensive cultivated fields between the towpath and river.

113.15 The high and deep walls here mark the location of a masonry waste weir (now filled with earth) used to control the water level of Big Pool. An elaborate 121' masonry spillway adjoins the waste weir. These may have been improved in the 1890–91 repairs, as the towpath was washed out in the 1889 flood, draining Big Pool. Mules walked through shallow water here, while pedestrians used a plank walkway that rested on stone piers placed 20' apart. Additional ruins are below the bank. The "Star of Big Pool" boat operated here in the late canal period.

113.48 Houses on the far side of the lake are part of the village of Big Pool.

113.89 The marshy pond here is an excellent bird area. In April, yellow spicebush (*Lindera benzoin*) and Dutchman's breeches (*Dicentra cucullaria*) add color, and grackles fuss in thickets. Chisel marks of pileated woodpeckers are visible on tree trunks and limbs.

113.94 Big Pool ends in a berm marsh.

Stop gate with pedestrian bridge at the lower end of Big Pool in the early 1900s. Note the pivot bridge to the right for vehicular traffic.

Western Maryland Rail Trail is a 23-mile-long, paved path paralleling the towpath from Big Pool (mile 113.7) to Lock 56 at Pearre (mile 136.2). Connections between the WMRT and the towpath exist at many places along the route. Parking is available at Big Pool, Mile Marker Lane, Little Pool, Hancock, and Pearre.

Today's bike path follows the right-of-way of the Western Maryland Railway (WM). The WM built its extension from Big Pool to Cumberland between 1903 and 1906. The extension required the construction of six bridges across the Potomac and three tunnels. Undoubtedly, WM management coveted the C&O Canal's water-level route to Cumberland. They could have drained the canal, laid tracks on the right-of-way, and avoided the construction of new bridges and tunnels. However, the B&O controlled the canal during this time period and wouldn't have been interested in making life easier for a competitor. The WM was acquired by the B&O in 1968. The B&O abandoned most of the WM Cumberland extension in 1975.

113.98 Pass under trestle of the former Western Maryland Railway track that extends along an embankment and crosses the river on a steel bridge to connect with the former B&O mainline at Cherry Run, West Virginia (now the southern end of the CSX Lurgan Subdivision). The trestle provides less than 9' clearance over the towpath. The WM ended across the river at Cherry Run until it was extended after 1904. The state of Maryland converted the section of the abandoned WM between Big Pool and Pearre (mile 136.2) to a paved hiking/biking trail now called the Western Maryland Rail Trail (WMRT).

114.15 Stop gate constructed on concrete over old masonry. The original parallel masonry walls were about 18' apart. This is the third of the four stop gates along the nearly 14-mile level between Locks 50 and 51.

114.21 Culvert #149, 6' span, 4'-high sidewalls, carries a stream from fields on the berm.

114.43 Culvert #150, 12' span, 7.6'-high sidewalls, carries a stream issuing from Ernstville. This was formerly a road culvert that gave river and ferry access to Cherry Run.

114.52 Ernstville Road (39.632970, -78.028951) Access: From I-70 take Exit 12, MD-56 E/Big Pool. Follow Big Pool Rd. 0.1 mile and turn right onto Ernstville Rd. After 0.3 mile take a slight left to stay on Ernstville Rd. Continue another 0.5 mile to a very limited parking area (do not block the gate). From the towpath the road leads across the canal 0.7 mile to the village of Big Pool or 1.0 mile to MD-40 west of Indian Springs.

114.83 Culvert #151, 6' span, built of gray limestone with 4' sidewalls.

115.02 Culvert #152, 4' span, carrying a small stream, is buried to the spring line on the outflow side. Built 1836–37.

115.50 Culvert #153, 4' span, nearly completely covered. Built 1837.

Licking Creek Aqueduct, April 2009. *(Image courtesy Steve Dean)*

LICKING CREEK AQUEDUCT

116.30 (39.655987, -78.053946) Access: From I-70 take Exit 12, MD-56 W/Big Pool toward US-40/Indian Springs. Go 1.4 miles and turn left onto US-40 W/ National Pike. Continue 2.5 miles and turn left onto Mile Post Ln. Follow to parking area.

Licking Creek Forge was built by James Johnson in 1775 at the mouth of Licking Creek to use pig iron from Green Spring Furnace. A 1795 survey lists Jacques Forge on Licking Creek near the Potomac River. When the furnace was shut down, the forge was sold to Mr. Chambers of Chambersburg, Pennsylvania, who ran it with pig iron from his Pennsylvania furnace.

The aqueduct has a single arch, 90' span, 15' rise, 180' wing-to-wing—said to be the largest single masonry arch built in this country at the time of its construction. It was constructed 1835–39 of Tonoloway gray limestone and Conococheague limestone by Enos Childs. Stone also came from a Licking Creek quarry one-half mile north on Licking Creek and from Prather's Neck quarry. The parapet and coping are 7' high, with the coping being 34' above creek level; the waterway is 21' wide. The berm parapet was replaced with a wooden trunk in 1874. An 1870 canal company report advised that the inferior stone used during construction had cracked in every direction and that stones had fallen. The walls bulged, but have been secured with iron ties and clamps extending entirely through the aqueduct. The towpath parapet has moved 8" out of line. Arch stones have fallen on the berm side. Up to five ringstones in the arch above all skewbacks are failing from overload and are badly fractured from shear stresses. The wooden trunk has rotted and fallen. One panel of the aqueduct's ornamental fence remains in place on the downstream, towpath wing wall. Notice the single remaining cast iron post finial. Former WM bridge #1076, steel on concrete piers, now carries the WMRT over Licking Creek upstream from the aqueduct.

Licking Creek Hiker–Biker Campsite is located here.

116.67 (NPS milepost 117.00) A service road parallels the canal from Licking Creek to this point.

116.76 Culvert #160, 6' span. Ringstones are made of cut limestone. The parapet rises 2.5' above the keystone. From here to Hancock, I-70 parallels the canal and the roar of traffic is almost constant.

117.17 Parkhead Station, Maryland (historical). The area gave its name to the Parkhead sandstone formation first identified in the nearby WM railroad cut exposure. Deposited in the Devonian period, the formation consists of gray and red sandstone interbedded with buff shale. This sandstone is made up mostly of conglomerates, bluish-black when fresh, buff or reddish when weathered. Parkhead sandstone ranges 400'–800' thick and is especially well exposed in the highway cut beyond the railroad.

117.30 Spring at edge of towpath.

117.75 Approximate location of buried Culvert #162.

117.90 The high, steep slope on the berm is the end of Orchard Ridge (formerly Pigskin Ridge), which runs north to the Pennsylvania border at Licking Creek.

118.09 Culvert #164 replaced with 6' corrugated-steel pipe in 1965; the original culvert is 20' to the east and covered with fill.

118.20 Loading dock on the berm.

118.40 The towpath comes directly onto the riverbank. Across the river, the mouth of Sleepy Creek may be visible below the end of a wooded island. Interesting rock strata are exposed in the canal wall and railroad cut.

118.46 Culvert #166 and waste weir, 8' span, 4' rise. The ringstones are of cut limestone; the rest of the culvert is rubble masonry. The weir on the berm side has a concrete frame, three vertical openings, and wooden planks for spillway control. A 10'-square well is between the berm face of the culvert and the culvert under the WMRT to the north. The well is constructed of matched blocks of gray and red sandstone (Parkhead sandstone, Devonian period). Historically it may have been Waste Weir #20. The wings extend 70 yards upstream and 180 yards downstream.

118.90 Site of the village of Millstone (Millstone Point). Approximately 100 people lived here in 1910. Millstone Point was owned by Dr. L. Jacques, a surgeon in the Revolutionary Army. This was a stagecoach stop on the National Pike.

Moffet Station on the Western Maryland Railway was presumably named for William Moffet, owner of Millstone Point in 1882. A turning basin is filled with silt. An old stone wall and foundation are visible on the berm side. A flour mill and tavern served both the road and canal. For a half mile at Millstone Point the canal was dug in the roadway of the National Pike, and the canal company had to make a new road at considerable expense.

On August 8, 1837, a stage coach plunged 40' off the new road into the canal, and a female passenger, her daughter, and a man were killed. Four others were injured. The accident was said to have been the result of the driver falling asleep. When Confederate Gen. Stonewall Jackson threatened Hancock in the first days of 1862, Millstone Point was headquarters for Col. John Kenly's First Regiment Maryland Infantry (Union), which helped defend the border and the canal. The old hotel here was destroyed by I-70 construction.

119.51 Culvert #170, 8' span, and berm-side waste weir, rebuilt 1975–76. This is one of five waste weirs on this level.

119.70 Interesting vertical strata in rock on the berm side.

119.91 Informal overflow.

119.71 Stop gate near the lower end of Little Pool, used to retain water when the canal was drained for winter or when water below needed to be withdrawn or lowered for repairs. This is the fourth of the four stop gates on the nearly 14-mile level between Locks 50 and 51. This simple structure, made of well-cut red shale and gray limestone, consists of two parallel walls 18' apart with 12' wings. Date of "March 6 1917" is found in the gate pockets.

119.84 Little Pool (39.684430, -78.103796) Access: From I-70 take Exit 5, Millstone Rd. to the four-way intersection at Hollow Rd. Turn left at Hollow Rd., following the sign for I-70 E/US-40 E. Cross I-70, curve left with Hollow Rd. for a short distance, and turn right at the Western Maryland Rail Trail parking area. A path and steps lead down to a wooden bridge that crosses the canal.

This nearly one-mile-long body of water is similar in nature to Big Pool. The normal water level is 398' above sea level, the towpath having risen that much from the tide lock in Georgetown. The pool and adjacent wooded areas are good bird-watching localities. Little Pool was formed by using a long narrow island paralleling the shore to form part of the towpath berm in this area. As a result the low area between the towpath and the higher land on the berm filled with water and formed the pool. A flood on April 1, 1886, washed out 50' of towpath.

120.60 Little Pool Hiker–Biker Campsite. Access from parking lot off I-70 at mile 120.20.

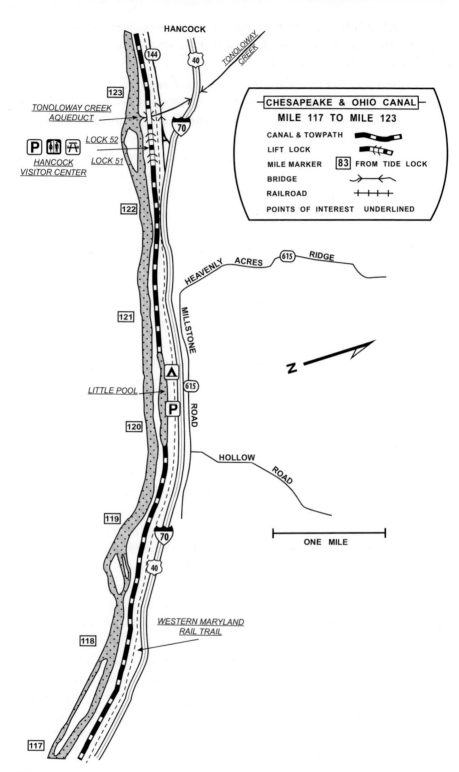

HANCOCK

144

40

TONOLOWAY CREEK

123

TONOLOWAY CREEK
AQUEDUCT

70

LOCK 52

LOCK 51

P

HANCOCK
VISITOR CENTER

CHESAPEAKE & OHIO CANAL

MILE 117 TO MILE 123

CANAL & TOWPATH

LIFT LOCK

MILE MARKER   83   FROM TIDE LOCK

BRIDGE

RAILROAD

POINTS OF INTEREST   UNDERLINED

122

HEAVENLY ACRES   615   RIDGE

121

MILLSTONE

N

615

LITTLE POOL

ROAD

P

120

HOLLOW   ROAD

119

70

ONE MILE

40

WESTERN MARYLAND
RAIL TRAIL

118

117

194

120.75 Upper end of Little Pool where the long island ended. A levee carries the tow-path to a point where it continues along the river shore.

121.19 Culvert # 172, 6' span, 3' sidewalls.

121.57 Culvert #173 (Barnetts Ditch Run), 8' span. Rebuilt by NPS.

122.11 Culvert #174, 6' span, and waste weir. The structure was rebuilt 1974–75. The waste weir spillway and culvert drop inlet are located on the back side of a berm dike of the canal.

122.49 Culvert # 175, 4' span. This is a 3' x 4' rectangular culvert, one of two found on the canal.

LOCK 51

122.59 (39.695110, -78.153670) Access: From I-70 take Exit 3, MD-144 to Hancock. At the end of the exit ramp turn right onto E. Main St., and then take the first left to the C&O Canal National Historical Park Visitor Center. The parking lot provides access to Locks 51 and 52 and the Tonoloway Aqueduct. The visitor center in the historic Bowles House is open seasonally. Hancock Visitor Center, 439 East Main St., Hancock, MD 21750, 301-745-5877, www.nps.gov/choh/planyourvisit/hancockvisitorcenter.

Lock 51 was completed by William Storey in the fall of 1838. The limestone lock walls are in good condition, with some coping stones out of place. The upper berm wing wall makes an uneven "u-turn" and parallels the lock walls for about 8'. There it abuts the bypass flume. Water spilled down on a pile of rocks to prevent undercutting. An extra 6" in the lower half of the gate pocket perhaps allowed the gates to be fully opened without shutting the wicket gates. The one remaining gate gooseneck is a type of slotted loop.

Note the rope burns on the upper section of the post. The post is 8'5" from the inner surface of the towpath wall and 16' from the upper end of the lower gate pocket. There were usually two of these posts 6'–9' from the lock walls; the lower one seems to have been about 16'6" above the lower gate pocket, and 16'–24' below the lower end of the upper pocket.

Most of the upper three courses of stone in this lock seem to have been replaced. The lower towpath quoin coping stone shows a date that may be "Feb., 1918." Most of the hardware is gone from the lock. The entire lock shows much rebuilding.

The compass orientation of the lock is N79°W, pointing straight at Lock 52. The bypass flume is little more than a wide shallow ditch parallel to the lock walls and lined with rubble stone. The faces of the lower wing walls were whitewashed in operating days, and traces remain. While most of the stones in the lock are a poor grade of limestone, there are four apparently unused quoin stones of excellent quality lying on the river side of the towpath just above the lock that were probably intended for replacements.

The lockhouse ruins sit beside the towpath at about mid-lock. The one-and-a-half story house was constructed of a mixture of limestone and dark red shale over a full stone basement. Only the first floor was plastered inside; the roof and floors are gone. The house measured 18' x 30' and had a narrow porch on the towpath side and a short porch on the downstream side. The first floor had a center chimney with back-to-back fireplaces. Inscribed in stone between the window and door is "Upton Rowland March 29 1843." Another stone, much more formal, is located near the ground in the center of the north wall. It has a formal xxx border, within which are several stars and the words "D. R. 1843." A stone above it is inscribed "Jonathan." Canal company annual reports list Upton Rowland as locktender for Locks 51 and 52 from 1840 to April 1, 1848, for which he was paid $200 per year—$50 more than paid to those responsible for only one lock. He was replaced by J. Miller.

122.85 Bowles House (Hancock Visitor Center, open seasonally). The house was built in the 1780s—originally a one-story structure overlooking the Potomac. The parcel of land here, known as "Sarah's Fancy," was transferred from Lord Baltimore to William Yates around 1775. The Yates family occupied the house during canal construction until 1875, when it was acquired by the Bowles family. The Bowleses remained here until 1905 when the house and surrounding property was purchased by the Little family. The Littles resided here until the NPS acquired the land in the 1960s.

LOCK 52
122.89 Access: Lock 51 at mile 122.59.

Lock 52 gives the appearance of being part of a continuous structure with the Tonoloway Aqueduct, as stone walls extend from the lock to the aqueduct. Robert Brown was contractor for Lock 52 and the Tonoloway Aqueduct, completing both in the summer of 1839. The contract for the walls connecting these structures was completed by William Storey by October 1839. The limestone lock walls are in fairly good condition. The towpath lock wall continues to the aqueduct and becomes part of the river side portion of that structure. The upper berm wing wall returns to form an entrance to the lock side of a bypass flume. The wide bypass flume has an earthen bank on the lock side, but a 4'-high, battered, well-laid stone wall of dark red shale is on the back side.

The foundation of a small building is beside the towpath at mid-lock measuring 18'11" x 16'7". It may have been the store the canal company permitted to be built here in 1865 by A. B. Taney for a fee of $36 a year.

Above: The Historic Bowles House, now a seasonal visitor center, during an unusual October snowfall in 2011. *(Image courtesy Steve Dean)*

Below: View of Lock 52, ca. 1903–23.

TONOLOWAY CREEK AQUEDUCT

122.96 Access: Lock 51 at mile 122.59.

This aqueduct appears as "Great Tonoloway" on earlier maps and as the "Bowles Aqueduct" on an early postcard. The stream here is sometimes called "Great Tonoloway" to distinguish it from the "Little Tonoloway" at the western end of Hancock (mile 124.38). The 110'-span aqueduct appears to be constructed of slaty rock. The aqueduct's single arch is irregular, with the spring line at the top of the abutment, 4' above the stream on the west, but on the east it is on a rock ledge 16' above the stream. Both parapet walls are gone, though the general supposition is that the stones were removed to within one course of the top of the barrel (curving part of the arch) stones. The reason probably is that when the flume was leaking badly and the arch so weakened, the stones were removed to help correct the problem. The bed of the canal was then replaced with concrete and heavy timber sills that supported the wooden flume as well as a wooden towpath bridge. A modern wooden walkway provides safe crossing. The spillway of an aqueduct waste weir is located in the lower berm parapet wall that is built on solid rock; the floor of the spillway is formed of stone set on the edge. This waste weir is another three-opening one where concrete was used, seemingly identical to the original timber sizes. It was stabilized by the NPS 1979–80.

123.56 Unmarked town line of Hancock.

123.84 Hancock Basin. The Taney Warehouse and dwelling, and the P. T. Little Warehouse and store were located on the berm. Only the foundations now remain.

123.95 Culvert #179, 12' span. This road culvert provided river crossing access for Hancock until the first crossing bridge was built.

Tonoloway Creek Aqueduct.

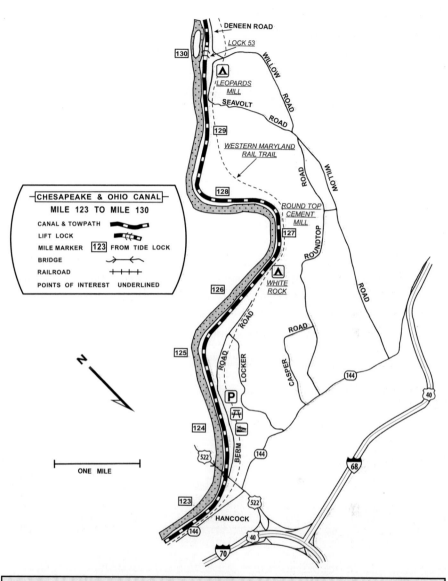

CHESAPEAKE & OHIO CANAL
MILE 123 TO MILE 130

CANAL & TOWPATH
LIFT LOCK
MILE MARKER 123 FROM TIDE LOCK
BRIDGE
RAILROAD
POINTS OF INTEREST   UNDERLINED

N

ONE MILE

DENEEN ROAD
LOCK 53
130
LEOPARDS MILL
SEAVOLT
WILLOW ROAD
ROAD
129
WESTERN MARYLAND RAIL TRAIL
128
ROAD
WILLOW
ROUND TOP CEMENT MILL
127
ROUNDTOP
WHITE ROCK
126
ROAD
ROAD
125
ROAD
LOCKER
CASPER
144
P
40
124
BERM
144
522
144
68
123
522
HANCOCK
144
40
70

Many boatmen carried horns to alert the locktenders to open the lock gates by the time the boat arrived. Horns were all sizes and shapes. Some were straight and a few were twisted like French horns. The average length was 2'–3', and rather than blowing through a reed the sound was made by lips.

HANCOCK

124.10 (39.698253, -78.181036) Access: From I-70 take Exit 1, US-522 south, Hancock; on US-522, take exit the first possible exit, signed as "To MD-144," onto Limestone Rd. Go about 0.2 mile and turn left onto MD-144/Main St. Continue 0.4 mile and turn right onto Williams St. Williams St. ends at Canal St., where there are large parking lots and easy access to the towpath for a quarter-mile in central Hancock. This paved street runs along the berm, with the backs of buildings facing the canal. Several streets perpendicular to Main St. also lead to the canal.

124.33 The berm street continues past the buildings to a parking and picnic area with a boat ramp. The canal is watered for recreation and fire protection. Drinking water is available in the picnic area. NO CAMPING.

124.38 Culvert #182 (Little Tonoloway Creek). The culvert is the largest on the canal, having a 36' span. It has sometimes been called "the culvert that wanted to be an aqueduct." This marks the western town line of Hancock. Old maps called this Tonoloway Creek, designating the larger stream one mile below Hancock as "Great Tonoloway." Samuel Rinehart owned a sumac mill located here. Using water purchased from the canal company, sumac leaves were processed into a leather tanning extract. (Possible remains of the mill are about 100' downstream of the culvert near the towpath.) There was also a bone mill and a sawmill at this location.

Hancock, Maryland, ca. 1900.

Canal Town, Hancock

This small town boasts a rich history due in part to three unique aspects of its location: it is the most northern point of the Potomac River; it is the westernmost town in Washington County; and it is located at the narrowest point in the state of Maryland. It is the eighth Canal Town. Visit www.canaltowns.org to learn about points of interest, services, lodging, and food sources in these towns.

Europeans settled in the area as early as the 1730s. Charles Polke (ancestor of future U.S. President James K. Polk) operated a trading post along the Potomac, in an area known as both "Northbend" and "Tonoloway Settlement." Polke, the "Indian Trader of the North," offered lodging to a young surveyor named George Washington.

The town is named for Edward Joseph Hancock, Jr., a ferryman who later fought in the Revolutionary War. Hancock came to life as a stop for travelers on the National Pike. Even before the pike officially opened through Hancock in 1818, the area was intersected by wagon roads and known for its taverns. John Donovan opened his tavern, Sign of the Ship, in Hancock before 1790. Other early taverns were named Sign of the Cross Keys, Sign of the Green Tree, Union Inn, and Sign of the Seven Stars. Each displayed an appropriate and sometimes elaborate sign. Gambling and horse racing were reportedly popular during frontier days.

Before and after construction of both the C&O and B&O, Hancock remained an important road center. Most freight and passengers passed between Hancock and Cumberland by stagecoach and freight wagon until about 1850, when the railroad gained momentum and traffic on the National Pike dwindled.

On January 4, 1862, Confederate Gen. Stonewall Jackson appeared across the river and began shelling the town in retaliation for the Union bombardment of Shepherdstown earlier in the war. The next day Jackson demanded the surrender of the town under the threat of another cannonade. The Union commander occupying the town, Gen. F. W. Lander, told Jackson's messenger that the Confederate general could "bombard and be damned! If he opens his batteries on this town he will injure more of his friends than he will of the enemy, for this is a damned secesh place, anyhow." Artillery rounds were exchanged for several hours, but Hancock remained in Union hands. Jackson left the river two days later.

On July 31, 1864, Confederate horsemen in the McCausland–Johnson Raid occupied Hancock and attempted to extract a ransom from the small town. Marylanders in the expedition protested, pointing out that many Southern sympathizers lived there. The Confederates burned canal boats but fled before they could collect the ransom.

At the turn of the twentieth century, apple and peach growing was a major part of the town's economy. Some of the abandoned orchards and packing plants can be seen from the towpath.

Amenities in Hancock today include museums, restaurants, lodging, hiking, biking, and a 48,000 square-foot antique mall. Bicycle rentals, sales, and service is available at C&O Bicycle, 9 South Pennsylvania Ave., Hancock, MD 21750, 301-678-6665, candobicycle.com.

124.59 Pass under the steel and concrete US-522 bridge across the Potomac, connecting Maryland and West Virginia. The Pennsylvania Turnpike at Breezewood is 26 miles north; Berkeley Springs is six miles south. The curious shape of Maryland is emphasized by mileages here: the Pennsylvania state line is 1.7 miles north; the West Virginia line is at the end of the bridge to the south. The shoreline across the river is actually not West Virginia, but Maryland— one of many odd points where the original river channel changed, leaving the state boundary on dry land 0.1 mile from the present shoreline.

125.11 Culvert #183, 4' span.

125.27 Culvert #184, 4' span, carries a stream beyond the WMRT, which parallels the canal from here to Pearre at mile 136.21. The canal is watered from this stream. There is a NO TRESPASSING sign for the Shalom et Benedictus Wildlife Sanctuary. Railroad ties provide access to the berm road.

125.66 The berm road swings back from the canal to follow the WMRT. The towpath follows the edge of an open field beyond, with broad views in all directions. Across and up the river, along the CSX track, is the U.S. Silica Quarry (formerly the Pennsylvania Glass Sand Company). Upstream from the plant, the end of Warm Springs Ridge rises to cliffs. The prominent Roundtop Mountain is directly ahead on the canal, with the long line of Tonoloway Ridge behind it.

126.00 An abandoned orchard is between the towpath and the berm road, now one-half mile away on the far side. A broad, overgrown field continues on the opposite side.

126.32 Locher House on the berm is associated with the Round Top Cement Mill.

126.42 Culvert #185, 10' span. Two miles of open fields end here. An abandoned orchard is on the berm side.

126.43 White Rock Hiker–Biker Campsite. Nearest access is from Hancock at mile 124.10.

126.84 Culvert #186, 4' span, with an old waste weir opening at the side, carries a stream from the abandoned orchards. The berm beyond becomes a natural, low rock wall with hillside fields beyond it.

127.10 A flat silted area in the canal gives the appearance of a basin. The towpath is on the riverbank. Pleasant view of the river, the West Virginia shore, and the mountain ahead.

127.24 "Devil's Eyebrow," a large and beautiful fold in the strata on the berm. This frequently photographed anticline is of shale, sandstone, and limestone in the Silurian Bloomsburg formation. Vegetation here and at the cement mill just ahead was removed in 1974. The upper portion, 15' above the canal, forms a spacious shelter cave. The canal prism is very narrow.

The Round Top Cement Mill burned and was rebuilt three times in its history.

ROUND TOP CEMENT MILL

124.70 The ruins of this important old mill, its attendant kilns, the many fine folds in the rock strata, the numerous "caves," and the general appeal of the surrounding area make this one of the towpath's most fascinating sections. One of the finest exposures of Wills Creek Formation in Maryland can be seen in the cut of the WMRT behind the cement mill.

127.4x Stone wall 30' above the berm bank. The debris in the canal bed is probably from construction of the railroad directly on the berm high above the canal. Hikers and bikers on the WMRT can frequently be seen and heard.

127.56 Opening of a mine shaft or cave between the canal and rail trail. Another entrance is a quarter mile from the cement mill interpretive signs; both entrances are blocked by metal grates. The steep curved slope of Roundtop Hill is above and ahead.

127.9x A high concrete wall supports the WMRT.

127.95 A concrete structure here was used to store and pump water to a former sand glass mining operation.

128.18 A wooded flat begins as the river and canal swing away from the foot of the steep slope. The towpath is built up on this repaired section.

128.52 An informal, quarter-mile path runs from the towpath, across the prism, and then up the hill to mile 15 of the WMRT.

128.53 A short, informal access path leads to the Potomac River.

128.57 Culvert #188, 4' span. The small stone foundation of a sediment trap is at the far side of the berm at the culvert inflow. Debris that entered the canal was a problem historically, and the canal company attempted to route watercourses draining land on the berm side of the canal under the canal through a culvert. However, in some places, especially in this upper, mountainous part of the canal, this is not possible, and streams feed water into the canal. The canal bed ahead is wide and watered.

129.xx The unseen river is approximately 200 yards away.

129.44 The 25' rock wall on the berm exhibits attractive horizontal bedding.

Round Top Cement Mill

The cement plant began operations in 1837, and much of the cement and mortar used in the canal structures' masonry was produced here. George Shafer discovered a good grade of limestone for producing cement in 1837 and began construction of the first mill in 1838, after arranging with the canal company for water and land rental. The mill burned in May 1846, but Shafer rebuilt it and in 1863 sold it to Robert Bridges and Charles W. Henderson. These early mills stood between the towpath and river, with a high bridge across the canal to the berm where the kilns were (and still are) located. The mill burned a second time in September 1897, and this time the new mill was built on the berm, on the upstream side of the kilns. The high smokestack dates from this mill. A third fire in May 1903 burned the mill to the ground, but the Maryland Geological Survey indicates that it was rebuilt a final time with a daily capacity of 300 barrels. The date for its closure and abandonment is unknown at this time.

The kilns were fired by coal shipped downstream via canal boat. Material came from four natural cement beds west of the plant at Roundtop Hill. The side of Roundtop Hill had five tunnels—two that went all the way through the hill—and all were constantly in work.

The hydraulic nature of the stone was discovered in 1837, when workers were making a cut for canal construction. Canal water was transported by a flume to an overshot wheel, 16' in diameter and width, equipped with 13 buckets, each 13" in depth. The four French burr stones used for pulverizing were 5' in diameter. The capacity of the plant was 2,200 barrels per week. Shipments were made by both the C&O and B&O. Cable cars shuttled cement across the river for loading and storage in a warehouse, the ruins of which can be seen along railroad tracks across the river.

Austin Mater of Bolivar, West Virginia, recalled working with Round Top Cement in 1908. He was working for the B&O Railroad, building concrete retaining walls to stop rocks from obstructing the tracks in areas prone to rock slides. The cement was packaged in waterproof sacks bearing the name "Setter Brand," with a picture of a setter dog on the sacks. When mixed with water, the cement immediately started to set. Mater recalled, "One of us would push the wheelbarrow and the other would stir vigorously with a hoe all the way to the retaining wall." Portland-processed cement with a slower setting rate came into use later. The history of this site is included in *Cement Mills Along the Potomac River* by Thomas Hahn and Emory Kemp (West Virginia University Press, 1994).

129.77 The berm rock wall is a garden of wildflowers.

129.87 Cross a concrete and stone waste weir for the level between Locks 52 and 53.

129.88 Leopards Mill Hiker–Biker Campsite. The nearest access is at mile 130.03. Additional camping near the towpath is available at Happy Hills Campground, 12617 Seavolt Rd., Hancock, MD 21750, 301-678-7760, www.happyhillscampground-md.net.

An old cement mill is shown on a historical map as being located between the shore and a small island in the river; however, there are no remains. The origin of the ruins in the stream is not known.

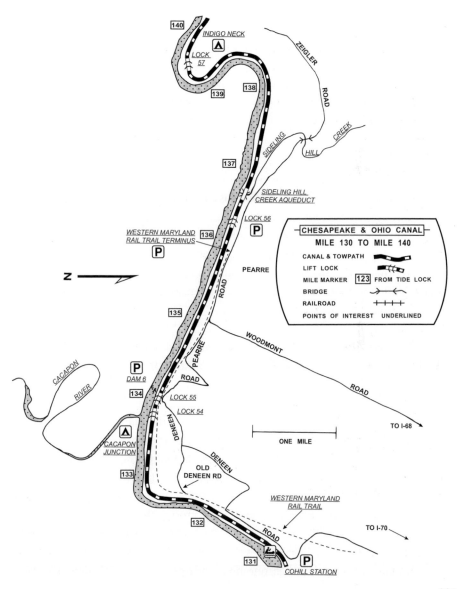

LOCK 53

129.96 Access: Cohill Station at mile 130.70.

Lock 53—known as "Irishman's Lock"—was completed in 1838 by Patrick McGinley. Only the lockhouse foundation remains. On the West Virginia side of the river is Sir John's Run, named after Sir John St. Clair, quartermaster to Gen. Braddock.

130.03 Culvert #192, 10' span, carries a stream from the valley beyond the WMRT. A berm road parallels the canal ahead.

130.70 Cohill Station (39.645446, -78.251711) Access: From I-68/US-40 take Exit 77, MD-144 E/Western Pike. Go 1.1 miles and take the second right onto Willow Rd. Continue 4.4 miles to Deneen Rd. and a small parking area on the left at Cohill Station. A pedestrian footbridge crosses over to the towpath.

130.72 Culvert #193, 10' span, carries a stream from the railroad underpass and follows the berm ahead. This area appears in early canal data as "Leopard's Mill." There is an informal overflow at mile 130.93. Deneen Road is on the berm.

131.24 Culvert #194, 4' span. Canoe ramp.

131.75 The road, railroad, and canal pass around a point of land. Cacapon Mountain is in full view across the river. The view from the berm road shows the railroad, canal, and river below. Possible fish traps or weirs are in the river just below this point and at miles 132.20, 132.90, and 133.50.

131.99 Culvert #195, 4' span, carries a stream from a large wooded ravine. Deneen Road beyond shows a good view of the canal, then bears away uphill to a shortcut across the river bend toward Dam 6.

132.10 A cemetery with unmarked graves for canal workers lies between the canal and the WMRT.

132.40 Culvert #197, 4' span, almost silted in, with a 135' informal overflow.

132.46 The river is 25 yards away; the wide canal bed is silted in. "Prospect Point," a popular viewpoint from West Virginia Route 9 on Cacapon Mountain, is across the river.

132.89 Fine folded strata in rock on the berm.

132.99 A large anticline is exposed in the cliff above the railroad, 200 yards above NPS milepost 133. The WMRT is directly on the berm.

133.17 Concrete waste weir for Levels 53–54 with pool below. Interesting strata in the reddish rock continues. Many trains pass on the West Virginia side of the river.

133.55 A beautiful four-arched railroad bridge crosses the mouth of the Cacapon River in West Virginia. The town of Great Cacapon begins on the West Virginia side. The 75-mile-long Cacapon River originates as the Lost River, where it flows more than one mile underground near Wardensville, West

Virginia, then emerges as the Cacapon. A half mile from its mouth are the Fluted Rocks—extremely sharp folds in the strata on the east bank, frequently pictured in geology textbooks. They are best seen in the winter months by following the road from Great Cacapon upstream on the west side of the river toward the power plant.

133.6x Cacapon Junction Hiker–Biker Campsite. The nearest vehicle access is from Deneen Road (a rugged, unpaved road) near Lock 54 at mile 133.96.

133.94 Cross a feeder canal from Dam 6. The towpath previously crossed a mule bridge (the abutments of which still stand) but now goes between the feeder and the canal to the dam. In a 1962 interview, the lockhouse occupant said the bridge over the feeder canal washed out in the 1924 flood.

LOCK 54

133.96 Access: See Lock 55, mile 134.06. Follow the towpath 0.1 mile downstream to Lock 54.

The badly damaged lock walls are collapsed on the upper berm side. In 1974 the lock was filled with earth to preserve it. Lock 54 was probably completed 1848–50. The lockhouse burned in 1981.

FEEDER DAM 6, GUARD LOCK 6, AND LOCK 55

134.06 (39.628174, -78.298262) Access: From I-68/US-40 take Exit 77, MD-144 E/ Western Pike. Take the first right onto Woodmont Rd. and continue 6.3 miles. Turn left onto Pearre Rd. and follow it to a small parking area. Do not block gate. Walk 0.4 mile east on the WMRT to a footpath that leads down to Lock 55 and Dam 6.

This is an interesting area in the history of the canal, for it was at this point that canal construction came to an end in 1842 while the crucial financial struggle for funds to complete the work went on. Eight years elapsed, with Dam 6 as the head of navigation, before the difficult section upstream—the "Fifty Miles"—would be completed and the goal of reaching Cumberland would be met at last.

Lock 55 was completed by Henry Smith in 1840. The crumbled lockhouse foundation sits on the berm side between the lock and bypass flume. Note Benchmark 6 of the 1878 Transcontinental Leveling on the downstream end of the berm wall.

A 475' structure, extending between surviving abutments, Dam 6 consisted of wooden cribs, filled with loose rocks, and covered with heavy planks. Because there was no high bank on the then-Virginia side of the river against which the abutment could be anchored, two guard banks were built, one parallel to the river, and the other continuing south from the dam to higher land. The latter had a gate allowing Long Hollow Run, which ran north into the Potomac just west of it, to pass through the guard bank during periods of heavy flow. However, this system proved inadequate. Part of the guard wall along the Run was breached in the 1852 flood. Subsequently, the company removed the guard bank along the river and replaced the one running south with a substantial masonry wall that today extends nearly to the CSX Railroad's right-of-way.

Dam 6, completed in April 1839, may be the only dam that burned. The fire, started by fishermen on August 31, 1936, burned into and spread through the wood-planking and cribbing timbers. Floodwaters have washed rock rubble into corkscrew rapids in which, however, there is a clear channel favored by canoeists. Guard Lock 6 adjoins the dam abutment. The extensive masonry work here is particularly interesting.

Floods never failed to leave their mark on Dam 6. On November 24, 1877, a flood seriously damaged the abutments; a freshet tore a hole in the center of the dam on April 1, 1886; and the 1889 flood virtually destroyed the structure, completely washing away 100' of the breast wall. But the dam was back in service by 1891. The 1924 flood—which ended canal operation—did little damage. The great floods of 1936 and 1942 (combined with the 1936 fire damage), however, turned the structure into the pile of rubble one sees today.

This photo from the early 1900s shows a boat departing Lock 54 to the right, the feeder canal from Dam 6 to the left, and Lock 55 ahead.

Old view of Dam 6 and Guard Lock 6. During the Civil War, the dam was the objective of several Confederate raids, especially a purported plan to destroy it on October 20, 1861, when the canal management found itself suspected of "lukewarmness" in its defense measures.

The Fifty Miles

In the fall of 1843, when Dam 6 was the head of navigation, an agreement was reached with the B&O Railroad, whereby coal from Cumberland was carried by rail to a point on the opposite shore for two cents a ton per mile. It was to be transferred to canal boats that would cross the river behind the dam and pass through the guard gate into the inlet channel that flowed into the main canal just below Lock 54. In reality, the agreement was terminated in the spring of 1845, and the amount of coal shipped under this arrangement was inconsequential to such a degree that the canal company did not include it in statistics published in 1878. Those statistics on the Cumberland coal trade reviewed the division among common carriers from 1842 to 1878.

Locks 54 and 55 were not used until the "Fifty Miles" were opened to navigation. Dam 6 represented the upper end of the "Hancock Division" at the height of the canal operating period; the "Cumberland Division" began above Lock 55.

When construction came to a halt here in 1842, $10 million had been spent on construction, plus another $2 million for interest and losses. The 1827 estimates of $4.5 million by two experienced Erie Canal engineers for the cost to build the canal to Cumberland had rapidly become obsolete in the face of the unpredictably large increase in the cost of land, labor, and materials. The national economic downturn brought on by the panic of 1837 and its subsequent recession also impacted costs. And still ahead were the increasingly rugged terrain, a growing scarcity of building stone, twenty locks, four aqueducts, two dams (one was later omitted), and a daring proposal to tunnel through a mountain. Actually, much work upstream was already done. Only 18 miles remained to be finished, but it was in scattered small sections and always the most difficult ones. The "Cost to Complete" was estimated at $1.5 million, and the books of the desperate canal company showed liabilities of $1.2 million in excess of assets. It was little wonder that many people doubted "The Fifty Miles" would ever be built.

134.23 Mouth of Long Hollow. The canal crossing of this stream, Resley Run, is unusual. Resley Run drains Long Hollow, a steep valley, and the proximity of the canal to the hillsides and river did not lend itself to a large culvert. The engineers solved the problem by allowing the towpath berm to impound the water to the level of the canal, creating a pool known as Polly Pond, which extends back up the hollow. To carry away high waters, a 60'-long spillway was constructed in the towpath berm with piers to support a bridge carrying the towpath across it. Downriver cement boats turned around here, passing under a railroad trestle to reach the pond. The spillway was substantially rebuilt in 1992.

134.25 Two 22'-long formal masonry spillways flank shallow, double waste weirs carrying Resley Run into the river. They were rebuilt by the NPS in 1991.

134.35 Exposed strata in the hillside and along the railroad cut represent one of the best exposed sections of Lower Jennings Formation in Maryland. A wooden bridge carries the towpath across a double-pipe culvert installed by the NPS in 1981 to drain the canal. The old stone wall has been replaced.

134.62 A fork of the berm road leads uphill to Woodmont Lodge, a former rod and gun club founded in 1870. Guests to the 3,400-acre club included Presidents James Garfield, Chester Arthur, Grover Cleveland, Benjamin Harrison, Herbert Hoover, and Franklin Delano Roosevelt, and also Babe Ruth and Gene Tunney—all of whom sat on the club's antique hickory chair adorned with wildcat skins. Stuffed game birds and animals peer at diners from the walls and overhead. Henry P. Bridges was the guiding spirit of the club for many years, and hosted members of the Douglas Hike in 1954. Bridges, after expressing disappointment that the Prince of Wales (then the Duke of Windsor) had not been a guest, dedicated a name plate to Justice William O. Douglas.

134.94 Culvert #199, 6' span, built in 1840. Woodmont Road comes downhill on the berm side and becomes Pearre Road, allowing an approach to the towpath at any point in the next mile.

135.06 Foundation of a high pedestrian suspension bridge dated 1914 and built by the Woodmont Club to provide access to the river.

135.10 Culvert #200, 10' span, carries a stream from the valley that includes Woodmont's Lake Jenkins above, formed by a small dam. (A second lake above Lake Jenkins is now a wetland after its dam was breached during a local flood.) Originally built in 1840, the culvert was rebuilt 1974–75.

135.30 Narrow field on the left, with a fine view ahead of the steep end of Sideling Hill Mountain in West Virginia. The houses are part of the scattered village of Pearre (pronounced pair-EE).

135.71 Culvert #201, 10' span, carries a stream from a deep ravine.

Outflow of Culvert #200, 2012. Note the wooden timber foundation and the few wooden planks serving as the mooring. *(Image courtesy Steve Dean)*

135.90 Terminus of the Western Maryland Rail Trail. (39.636480, -78.323262) Access: From I-68/US-40 take Exit 77, MD-144 E/Western Pike. Take the first right onto Woodmont Rd. and continue 6.3 miles. Turn right onto Pearre Rd. and follow it 0.9 mile to the large WMRT parking lot on the left. An informal path crosses the canal prism to the towpath.

136.01 Culvert #202, 6' span, built 1847–50.

LOCK 56, PEARRE/SIDELING LOCK

136.21 (39.637868, -78.328302) Access: Park at the WMRT lot (see 135.9 above), or from I-68/US-40 take Exit 77, MD-144 E/Western Pike. Take the first right onto Woodmont Rd. and continue 6.3 miles. Turn right onto Pearre Rd. and follow it 1.3 miles to a small parking area on the left.

Lock 56 was begun in 1837 but due to abandoned contracts and financial difficulties, it was not completed until 1848 or 1849. It has a 7.7' lift. A two-and-a-half-story frame lockhouse sits on the towpath. A general store sat over the bypass flume. The NPS stabilized the lock in 1985. The paved WMRT ends at the small parking lot for Lock 56.

If you encounter a life-threatening emergency while visiting the park, please **call 911** or contact the Chesapeake and Ohio Canal National Historical Park's **Emergency Hotline 866-677-6677**.

Note the asymmetrical span of the Sideling Hill Creek Aqueduct. *(Library of Congress, Prints and Photographs Division, HABS, Reproduction Number HABS MD, 1-HAN.V.1--1)*

SIDELING HILL CREEK AQUEDUCT

136.56 Access: Lock 56 at mile 136.21 or WMRT parking at 135.90.

Sideling Hill Creek Aqueduct, completed in 1845, is the eighth of 11 stone aqueducts on the canal. The single 110' span is supported by steel bracing. The upstream parapet collapsed at some point, and parts of the iron railing are missing, but the balance of the structure in is good condition. Limestone was used for the cut masonry of the arch and the inside of the parapets and coping. The arch is asymmetrical, the downriver end being closest to the keystone. On the berm rises the precipitous southern end of the Pennsylvania–Maryland portion of Sideling Hill, while across the river towers the equally abrupt end of Sideling Hill, West Virginia. This creates a narrow water gap crowded by the river, canal, road, and two railroads. Slackwater from Dam 6 backs up beneath the aqueduct a short distance into the bed of Sideling Hill Creek. This stream rises far to the north in Bedford County, Pennsylvania, and as it traverses Maryland it is marked by many entrenched meanders, producing much rugged and beautiful country well worth exploring on foot. This tortuous water-course is the Washington–Allegany County border.

Sideling Hill is a syncline—it represents the bottom of folded strata rather than the top of the fold. The narrow crest both north and south of the river is capped by Purslane Sandstone, a massive white sandstone and quartz conglomerate more resistant to erosion than the surrounding formations. Although Purslane was in the trough of the fold, it now marks the highest point of the mountain. Contrary to what a canal observer would expect, the strata on the east side of the mountain dip to the west, and strata on the west side dip east. A walkway near I-68 allows a closer look at the mountain cut.

136.9x The canal prism narrows.

137.20 Fine rock exposures in the railroad cut. Rock debris along the towpath is from railroad construction and continues for some distance as an embankment between the towpath and the river.

137.7x The sharp left curve in the river is Turkey Foot Bend. The canal ahead passes through strata of Jennings-Catskill Formation (Devonian period); flat slabs above the railroad show alternating layers of red and yellow sandstone. A hollow at about mile 138 was known as "Clapper's Hollow."

138.06 East portal of Indigo Tunnel. The former railroad cut through the spur of High Germany Hill for nearly one mile. Both portals of the Indigo Tunnel—reported to be the largest bat hibernaculum in Maryland—are fitted with bat gates and closed to the public. The tunnel is home of the Eastern Small-Footed Bat, an endangered species due to White Nose Syndrome. The canal bed is completely filled with debris from the railroad cut.

138.20 The cleared area enhances a fine view ahead, across the river bend to Sideling Hill, West Virginia. The berm side has a natural rock garden of wildflowers and fern, with steeply dipping strata running into the canal. A Parkhead Sandstone formation begins 150' east of the tunnel portal and continues 775' to a point where Woodmont Shale begins.

138.63 When not in drought, the canal bed becomes a swamp—sometimes 6'-8' deep. This is typical of many wild sections in the next 40 miles. Opportunities abound for nature study or for absorbing the refreshment of virtual solitude.

LOCK 57

139.22 Access: Fifteenmile Creek Drive-in Campground at mile 140.77.

Lock 57 is the last of the masonry locks for some distance, as the next 13 locks upstream were composite locks, due to lack of funds and suitable native building stone. The upper half of the lock wall on the river side has been repaired with concrete. The lower berm gate is standing, while the towpath-side gate is in the floor of the lock chamber. Most of stone-lined bypass flume remains. The lock was completed late in 1840 by James Wherry. Stone from the river side of the lock is piled above the remains of a two-and-a-half-story, log cabin lockhouse. The canal ahead is known as the "Five Mile Level."

139.2x Indigo Neck Hiker–Biker Campsite.

139.40 The steep cascade on the berm side follows the cliff face strata for an interesting effect. Beyond, the berm consists of fine flower-covered cliffs.

140.03 The former railroad emerges onto the berm from the west portal of the Indigo Tunnel. This was the approximate location of "Marten's Hollow."

140.66 A railroad crossing to the right, where the road from Pearre and other points comes down from High Germany Hill and continues ahead between the canal and the former railroad.

140.77 Fifteenmile Creek Drive-In Campground (39.625648, -78.385868) Access: From I-68 take Exit 68. Follow Orleans Rd. south for 5.5 miles. Turn left onto High Germany Rd. and continue 0.1 mile, passing under the railroad overpass, to a T-intersection. Turn right and follow the road a very short distance to the campground. Parking is available alongside the railroad embankment on a nearby paved road. Campsites include fire rings, grills, water, chemical toilets, and access to a boat ramp. (See www.nps.gov/choh for current fees.)

Supplies, canoe rentals, food, and drinks are available at Little Orleans Grocery Store/Bill's Place, 12719 High Germany Rd., Little Orleans, MD 21766, 301-478-2701. Lodging is available at Little Orleans Lodge, 12814 Appel Rd., Little Orleans, MD 21766, 301-478-2102, www.littleorleanslodge.net. Additional camping near the towpath is available at Little Orleans Campground & Park Area, 31661 Green Forest Dr., SE., Little Orleans, MD 21766, 301-478-2325, www.littleorleanscampground.com.

This is the canoe and float take-out point for the 21-mile trip through the Paw Paw Bends. Rock ledges stretching across the river in this area were once converted to fish traps by Native Americans according to archaeologists. A rough road route to the Paw Paw Tunnel and Oldtown is via the Oldtown gravel road through Green Ridge State Forest.

One of the best-known landmarks along the C&O Canal is Bill's Place, a unique country store, restaurant, and bar—a spot hikers, bikers, fishermen, and hunters return to year after year.

A general store had been located adjacent to the canal since 1896. A warehouse (later converted to a garage) had a beam equipped with a large pulley extending over the canal. Driven by mules, the pulley system brought cargo from canal boats to a wharf. After the turn of the twentieth century, the store and warehouse were moved from the banks of the canal for the construction of the Western Maryland Railway.

In the 1960s, Bill Schoenadel and his wife Ethel began operating the store. The original store burned to the ground in 2000 but was rebuilt. Bill's hospitality, humor, and colorful accounts of local history made this a favorite stop for towpath users. Though Bill died on January 5, 2013, he will be remembered as one of the most colorful characters along the canal.

Little Orleans

The little village is now separated from the mouth of Fifteenmile Creek by the Western Maryland Railway berm. The creek was named in colonial times for its location on the road (actually, little more than a trail) about 15 miles from Hancock and 15 miles from Town Creek on the Oldtown Road. Native American campsites have been located on both sides of the mouth of the creek and north of the railroad tracks above the aqueduct. Early references indicate Kings Tavern was operating here in 1795 and Mrs. O'Queen's Tavern in 1841.

A road formerly extended down to the river and crossed a ford diagonally downstream to Orleans Cross Roads, West Virginia, which at one time was the post office for both settlements. The Oldtown Road was the main route from Fort Frederick to Fort Cumberland for many years. A variety of traffic—horseback, supply wagons, and stage lines—passed this way as the years went on, until the more direct route across the summits of the mountains was opened.

A riot between canal construction workers erupted near Little Orleans on May 17, 1838. Following a period of non-payment from the canal contractors, Irishmen organized a work stoppage. When German laborers were hired to replace them, hostilities escalated. A German worker was almost clubbed to death with swinging shillelaghs, and another German was thrown into a bonfire and almost burned to death. Fifty duck guns were ordered from Baltimore and distributed to Irish workers from Little Orleans to Paw Paw. After another riot near the Paw Paw Tunnel in August, three state militia companies from Baltimore confiscated and destroyed the guns, burned Irish shanties, confiscated whiskey, and suppressed the rebellion. Non-rioting whiskey owners sued, and the court ruled that the militia had acted illegally and exceeded its authority in confiscating privately-owned whiskey.

Violence returned in August and September 1839 when militia from Allegany and Washington counties seized firearms, tore down 50 shanties and shops, and arrested 26 prominent leaders, who were taken to Cumberland for trial.

On a knoll across the creek from Little Orleans is St. Patrick's Catholic Church, surrounded by a cemetery that predates the present church. The earliest burial date noted was 1802. The cemetery contains many unmarked graves of Irish canal construction workers and their descendants. The church gable facing the river features a round window with a green shamrock.

FIFTEENMILE CREEK AQUEDUCT

140.90 Access: Fifteenmile Creek Drive-in Campground at mile 140.77.

Completed 1848–50, the ninth stone aqueduct on the canal is similar to Sideling Hill Creek Aqueduct. The 110' single-span structure is in comparatively good condition with the exception of the upstream spandrel. The waste weir at the upper end of the aqueduct is fed by a stream that falls into the creek. Fifteenmile Creek rises in Pennsylvania and flows through a wild, mountainous region, cutting deep water gaps directly through Green Ridge State Forest. The U.S. Geological Survey mark in the southeast corner of the aqueduct notes the elevation as 459' above sea level. Cement used in the aqueduct was from Lynns Mill at Cumberland and Shafers Mill near Hancock.

141.33 Interesting fold in strata on berm side. The berm is a fine rock garden of wildflowers and ferns. A special feature along the towpath in April is the extensive growth of Dutchman's breeches (*Dicentra cucullari*) and squirrel corn (*Dicentra canadensis*). The canal prism becomes very narrow.

141.7x First of many sharp river bends.

142.04 Informal overflow.

142.25 The broad river terrace ends; the berm again becomes a rock wall with nearly vertical strata. Rocks throughout the area are a part of the Jennings Formation, consisting of slate-gray shale and buff, sandy shale, including Parkhead sandstone, through which the canal passes periodically. Some terrace gravels, indicating the former levels of the river bed, are 250' above the present river level.

142.75 Purslane Mountain, a rocky finger across the Potomac, produces one of the big bends or loops in the river. Beyond the river flat on the West Virginia side is a deep ravine, Doe Gully. The B&O met a grade construction challenge here by using the gully and constructing the Randolph Tunnel at the west end, where the gully ends. The line emerges at almost river level, having avoided the five-mile river bend. Two additional tracks were later added to a deep surface cut north of and parallel to the tunnel.

Fifteenmile Creek Aqueduct.

143.05 Rock folds in the berm are particularly interesting. The cliff is festooned with moss pinks (*Phlox subulata*), mayflower (*Epigaea repens*), and wild ginger (*Asarum canadense*) in the spring.

143.33 A worn path leads to the Western Maryland Railway grade that provided access back to Little Orleans. Towpath users are advised to stay off the old railroad bridge ahead—VERY DANGEROUS.

143.40 Pass under the Western Maryland Railway trestle (rebuilt 1917). The abandoned railroad crosses the river and continues upstream. This is the first of three crossings in this section. At one time a 5'-high beaver dam backed water up to Lock 58.

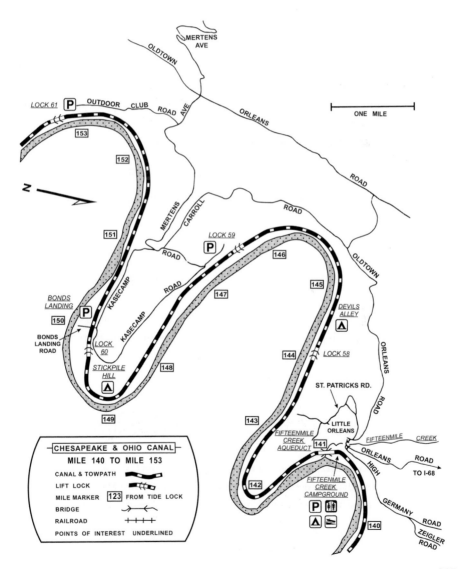

"The Largest Apple Orchard In The Universe"

An interesting history winds along the remote country road, Mertens Avenue. At the turn of the twentieth century, 3,000 acres between the Town Hill and Green Ridge mountain ranges became the setting for an unusual, visionary real estate development.

In the 1880s and 1890s, the Mertens family of Cumberland, Maryland, cleared much of the forest here. Around 1895 plans blossomed to develop what they foresaw as "the largest apple orchard in the universe." In addition to more than 200 ten-acre orchard plots, the land would include villa sites, a commercial area, trolley line, school, and post office—a utopian society where a wealthy investor could leave the "burdens of cultivation and business" to the Green Ridge Valley Orchard Association and "devote himself to leisurely recreation." The convenient location of the B&O, C&O, and Western Maryland Railway promised investors easy access to markets on the East Coast. Many of the lots sold, most purchased by non-residents who made arrangements with the orchard company for clearing, planting, and picking apples.

Unfortunately, by 1918 poor business practices and improper cultivation of the trees led the Mertens into bankruptcy. In 1931 the state of Maryland began purchasing the old lots, and today the land is part of the 44,000-acre Green Ridge State Forest. Here and there an old apple tree remains, not yet completely choked out by the pines. The Mertens name persists, monument to an all-but-forgotten dream.

For more read *A History of Green Ridge State Forest* by Champ Zumbrun (The History Press, 2010).

143.51 Canal widens into attractive birch-bordered pool.

143.65 In 1983 an active beaver lodge sat right on the towpath.

LOCK 58

143.96 Access: Fifteenmile Creek Drive-in Campground at mile 140.77 or Lock 59 at mile 146.56.

Lock 58 is in a remote stretch of the canal. It is the first of 13 upper locks that used a double layer of kyanized (treated) wood planks fastened to vertical beams on the rubble-stone lock walls. This system was a substitute for the costly finished stone locks because the stone available in the area simply broke apart when quarried and could not be worked into rectangular blocks. Wood created continuous maintenance problems. As this one shows, the wood lining in many of these locks was largely replaced with concrete during the receivership era (1891–1924). The foundation of a wood-frame lockhouse constructed over a stone basement remains. Across the canal a side trail leads into the extensive network of trails in the Green Ridge State Forest; one can follow these trails for over 21 miles, rejoining the towpath at Lock 67.

Remains of upper lock gate at Lock 58, 2008. *(Image courtesy Steve Dean)*
Below: Lock 58 above Little Orleans, ca. 1903–23.

144.54 Devils Alley Hiker–Biker Campsite. Access from Little Orleans at mile 140.77 or Lock 59 at mile 146.56. The canal makes a long curve around a spectacular rocky cliff. The towpath is on the riverbank.

145.52 A hook-shaped fish trap was located in the river.

146.01 Concrete waste weir for Levels 58–59. The river bend ends; the floodplain widens.

LOCK 59

146.56 (39.603639, -78.425820) Access: From I-68 take Exit 68. Follow Orleans Rd. NE 5.7 miles. Turn right onto Oldtown Orleans Rd. SE. Continue 6.1 miles and turn left onto Mertens Ave. Go 2.7 miles and make a slight left onto (unpaved) Kasecamp Rd. Continue 0.7 mile and park near the gate alongside the former railroad embankment. (Note: This portion of Kasecamp Road is very rough; SUVs or four-wheel drive is recommended.)

Lock 59 is the second of 13 composite locks. Little wood planking remains. The lock may have been one of the 16 extended in the winters of 1881–82 and 1882–83. It has a unique wooden quoin (which held the gate's heel post). A large part of the upstream berm wall collapsed in 1983. The stone foundation of a lockhouse is found on the berm.

146.92 Culvert #206, 12' span, built 1840–50, carries a stream from the extensive valley known as Devil's Alley. The canal bed can become swampy. The ruin on the berm downstream was known to boatmen as the Van House, Yellow House, or Pinkney House.

Canalling was often a family affair with wives and children working alongside the boat captain.

147.18 Pass under the Western Maryland Railway trestle where the track comes back across the river and enters a shortcut across the neck. Kasecamp Road parallels the canal for four miles.

147.73 The rough road across the canal bed leads to a large frame canal house once occupied by Joseph L. Higgins, a division foreman for the canal company, who also sold mules and boarded them for $3 a head per month. Mrs. Joseph Higgins was a cook on her father's work scow. When Joseph Higgins died in 1918 his remains were floated down to Little Orleans by canal boat.

148.24 Culvert #207, 8' span, built in 1850. The rows of rounded hills ahead beyond the river bend are the shoulders of the Purslane Mountain branch of Sideling Hill in West Virginia.

148.88 Begin a long 180° bend of the river.

149.36 Stickpile Hill Hiker–Biker Campsite. Nearest access is from Bonds Landing at mile 150.10.

149.45 Concrete waste weir for Levels 59–60.

LOCK 60

149.69 Access: Bonds Landing at mile 150.10.

Lock 60 still shows some of the wood construction characteristic of the 13 "economy" locks. Known as the "Upper Lock in the Seven-Mile Bottom," it was extended on the lower end to accommodate two boats. The lock has an 8.4' lift. Some of the lockhouse foundation remains. The lockhouses on the upper canal were also built economically and are less enduring than the substantial brick and stone houses downstream.

150.10 Bonds Landing (39.582848, -78.411246). Access: From I-68 take Exit 68. Follow Orleans Rd. NE 5.7 miles. Turn right onto Oldtown Orleans Rd. SE. Continue 6.1 miles and turn left onto Mertens Ave. Go 2.6 miles and make a sharp right onto (unpaved) Kasecamp Rd. Continue 1.4 miles and turn right onto (unpaved) Bonds Landing Rd. (Note: This part of Kasecamp Rd. is very rough and has two stream fords that are sometimes impassable for low-clearance vehicles.)

150.69 Informal overflow, 180' long.

150.83 The river comes into view as the long turn is completed; the towpath now bears west-north-west.

151.18 Culvert #208, 12' span, carries a substantial stream coming from Roby Hollow. The culvert was completed in 1849 "at head of 7-mile Bottom." The berm is a built-up levee. The culvert is a road culvert that was built to provide access to the towpath and river.

151.20 Roby Hollow. The Busey canal construction cabin was up the hollow from the canal. The cabin collapsed and little remains.

151.24 Pass under the Western Maryland Railway trestle, which emerges from Stickpile Tunnel on the berm side and crosses the river to follow the West Virginia side for three miles. CAUTION! DANGEROUS TUNNEL. DO NOT ENTER.

151.50 Towpath comes onto the riverbank. The berm becomes a rocky hillside with nice cliffs, rock folds, and an occasional shelter cave.

152.xx Lovely view of the river at a clearing 50 yards below NPS milepost 152. The river is not whitewater here but makes an excellent beginner's trip.

153.01 Concrete waste weir for the "Four Mile Level" between Locks 60 and 61; the actual distance is 3.4 miles.

LOCK 61

153.10 Access: Twigg Hollow at mile 153.28.

Lock 61 is another wood-lined lock almost entirely faced with concrete. The composite locks actually have less tilting inward than the masonry ones. The stone foundation of a lockhouse sits opposite the lock just off the towpath. According to canal legend, locktender Joe Davis and his wife were shot and killed here, and the lockhouse was burned to cover up the murder. Recent research, however, revealed that the coroner ruled the deaths accidental.

153.28 Twigg Hollow (39.58128, -78.46154) Access: From I-68 take Exit 68. Follow Orleans Rd. NE 5.7 miles. Turn right onto Oldtown Orleans Rd. SE. Continue 6.1 miles and turn left onto Mertens Ave. Go 0.4 mile and turn right onto Outdoor Club Rd. Continue 1.2 miles to parking at Green Ridge State Forest campsite 66. Follow the sign for the Great Eastern Trail to reach the towpath. Note: Outdoor Club Road is unpaved and in muddy conditions may not be suitable for certain vehicles.

Twigg Hollow is a deep ravine of special geographic interest, best appreciated with a topographic map of the area. For more than one mile it parallels the Potomac, but drains in the opposite direction. As seen from a spectacular viewpoint a half mile up Outdoor Club Road, at one point its valley comes within 150 yards of a river gorge, then swings away again. This curious arrangement results from the fact that the river, cutting away the hill on the outside of a sharp bend, has all but captured the Twigg Hollow stream and appropriated its valley. The region is well worth an exploratory side trip. The abutments of a former footbridge are present on the berm.

153.46 Culvert #210, 12' span, carries a stream from Gross Hollow. Ponds of the old Potomac River channel are still visible opposite the culvert.

153.76 Rock folds and cliffs. The cut exposes an anticlinal fold in shale, inter-bedded siltstones, and conglomeratic sandstones (rarely seen) of the Jennings Formation. Note the well-exposed, alternating weak and resistant beds, especially near the bottom. A small synclinal fold on the berm side is obscured by vegetation in the summer months. The cliffs reach heights of 20'–75' from this point to Sorrell Ridge. The entire cut is covered with a variety of ferns, lichen, small trees, and shrubs.

153.92 Another cut exposes interesting folds and faults. The towpath comes onto the riverbank. This stretch of the river is one of those considered for the location of Dam 7, which was proposed but never built. (Another site considered was near the mouth of the South Branch of the Potomac at mile 164.82.)

154.14 Sorrel Ridge Hiker–Biker Campsite. Nearest access is from Twigg Hollow at mile 153.28. This is a good landing for canoes after coming through the Potomac Goosenecks.

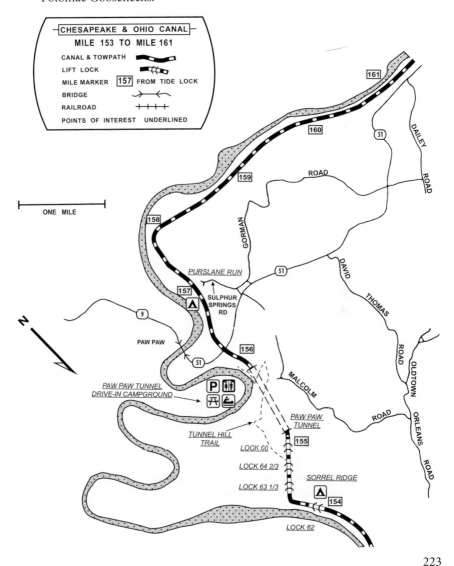

LOCK 62

154.16 Access: Paw Paw Tunnel at mile 156.10.

In an isolated setting at the bottom of Tunnel Hollow, Lock 62 is the fifth of 13 composite locks. The lock has a 10' lift. Some wood lining remains on the lock walls. The bypass flume running along the rock wall of the berm is in good condition. The concrete foundation of a 26' x 16' lockhouse is under a tree near the towpath. Shale cliffs on the berm are covered with a variety of ferns, wildflowers, lichen, small trees, and vines. Though the canal prism was cleared of vegetation in 1957, vegetation is now heavily re-established well into Tunnel Hollow.

154.21 The canal begins to turn away from the river into Tunnel Hollow, originally Athey's Hollow. Evidence of an old turning basin includes a small, swampy pond. The basin marks the foot of Sandy Flat Hollow, with traces of an old road leading up to Anthony Ridge.

154.28 Masses of wild blue flags bloom in the canal bed in May and June from here to the tunnel gorge. Where canal boats once waited their turn to enter the tunnel, cattails now grow, and red-winged blackbirds live where the canal bottom is a swamp.

154.29 The large, elaborate waste weir was rebuilt by the NPS in 1979. The structure—similar to those used on the Erie Canal—was designed to minimize erosion caused by water flowing out of the canal. It consists of two stone

A carpenter shop at Lock 66 burned in the 1960s. The creosote tank into which lumber was dipped survived the fire and is seen in the photo.

overflow channels that curve around to face each other and empty into a common stone central channel that carried water away from the canal.

LOCK 63 1/3

154.48 Access: Paw Paw Tunnel at mile 156.10.

Lock 63 1/3 has a 10' lift. The extensive concrete replacement on Lock 63 1/3 is dated 1910. The gate pockets are lined with concrete; only the bolts remain from the wooden sheathing. This is an excellent place to study the miter sill and upper gate pocket floor construction, as it is all in place and in excellent condition. Some stones of the lock chamber have shifted or are missing. There are no lockhouse remains.

The peculiar numbering of Locks 63 1/3 and 64 2/3 was adopted by the canal company to document the gap in the lift lock numbering system that resulted from the decision not to build Lock 65. All of these locks are in poor condition.

LOCK 64 2/3

154.60 Access: Paw Paw Tunnel at mile 156.10.

Lock 64 2/3, with a 10' lift, was once sheathed in wood, some of which remains on each side. The upstream and downstream lock gates are gone; the butt of a snubbing post remains on the towpath side of the lock. The bypass flume is rather rough; the lower berm wing wall is crumbling badly. Piles of sandstones on the bank across from the towpath at the upstream end of this lock (and at Lock 63 1/3) suggest that the stones may have been removed when the locks were repaired with concrete in 1919. Evidence of a lockhouse—the first to be identified in this section—is on a small plateau or bench (probably composed of tailings from construction of the deep cut and tunnel) about 10' above the towpath grade up a ravine at the upper part of the lock on the towpath side. The foundation remains can be found only in winter.

154.65 Missing Lock 65. Locks 62, 63 1/3, 64 2/3, and 66 all have a 10' lift—2' deeper than the average lock. The combined extra 2' comprised the 8' lift Lock 65 would have had if built.

LOCK 66

154.70 Access: Paw Paw Tunnel at mile 156.10.

The lock has a 10' lift; its walls have bolts to hold the sheathing in place, but no wood remains. A carpenter shop here burned in the 1960s. A creosote tank into which lumber was dipped survived the fire.

154.85 Two-mile Tunnel Hill Trail is an alternate route for those who do not wish to go through the Paw Paw Tunnel. In 2011 the NPS upgraded the trail and installed interpretive signs. Once the tunnel construction road, the trail leads over Tunnel Hill to the upstream portal of the Paw Paw Tunnel. Tailings from the tunnel construction were carried away via this road. This not only reduced tailings but reduced the runoff of surface water back down into the gorge, thus helping prevent landslides induced by water. Massive fills of broken rock are visible along the trail, providing evidence of the quantity of material that was moved. The canal company's 1879 telephone line ran over Tunnel Hill.

Tunnel Hill Trail

In 2011 park staff, volunteers, partners, and Maryland Eagle Scouts worked together to improve the Paw Paw Tunnel Hill Trail. Their project included the installation of 12 wayside exhibits—two trailhead markers and 10 informational markers with topics such as the life of the canal builders, the tremendous task of removing the stone from the mountain, the natural features of Sorrel Ridge, the Potomac River valley below, and Paw Paw, West Virginia, across the river. Six directional sign markers guide visitors along the two-mile trail.

The trail is a steep, strenuous hike, and comfortable, sturdy footwear is recommended. Bikes are not permitted on the trail. CAUTION: Copperheads have been spotted along the trail.

154.95 A 10'-high cliff over the towpath has a good deal of dripping water. Just overhead is a spring once used by passing boats as a water source. Stairs once led from the towpath to the spring. In winter the water flow creates massive and beautiful ice sheaths on the cliff.

At this point the towpath begins its passage through the 2,322'-long deep cut that is up to 79' deep and involved 213,229 cubic yards of excavation. As the ravine steepens, it creates a spectacular approach to the Paw Paw Tunnel's downstream portal. Very interesting examples of "slickenslides"—slip-jointing between the strata causing frequent rockslides—are visible, and iron rods serve to stabilize the rock. The tunnel axis follows an anticline, although somewhat off center.

Note horizontal rope burns at the first bend below the tunnel. This bend is sharp enough that boats coming upstream were unable to tell whether there was a boat in the tunnel until they rounded the curve. The canal was a single lane for a total of 4,212' in the tunnel and deep cut (over three-quarters of a mile). This forced boats waiting for traffic to clear to remain further back in the deep cut, where it was wide enough for two boats to pass. After 1872, crewmen in boats entering at the upstream end activated a semaphore signal in the deep cut to alert boats downstream of their presence in the tunnel.

Above: This January 20, 2013, rockslide blocked about 100' of the towpath. *(Image courtesy National Park Service)*
Below: View of the Paw Paw Tunnel Gorge looking down the canal from the downstream (north) portal of the tunnel, ca. early 1950s.

PAW PAW TUNNEL

155.20 North (downstream) portal. Access: Paw Paw Tunnel Drive-in Campground at mile 156.10.

A good deal of water falls down the cliffs on the berm side of the portal, possibly including genuine springs as well as runoff. In wintertime, the cliffs are covered with great frozen waterfalls. This has induced rock falls and slides from time to time; a massive slide that occurred in 1968 or 1969 engulfed the canal prism to the towpath level just at the portal. It did only minor damage to the towpath, but it did somewhat obscure the view of the portal.

The portal keystone is inscribed: "J. M. Coale, President, 1850." James Coale was president of the C&O Canal Company from August 1843 to February 1851 and was the primary person involved in the efforts to finance the completion of the canal to Cumberland.

A swinging boom on the berm was used to drop timbers into slots in the masonry of the portal to form a stop gate sealing off the canal and making it possible to drain the canal downstream for repairs and maintenance.

A flashlight, lantern, or headlamp should be taken into the tunnel as it gets dark. Note the hole in the wall beside the towpath a short distance into the tunnel where six layers of bricks have been removed to allow a view of the lining and mountain rock behind it. The locations of vertical shafts used during the tunnel construction can be identified by the increased presence of water and the fact that the weep holes are larger and closer together under the shafts. (The weep holes drain the groundwater that collects behind the brick lining, lessening its tendency to seep through the mortar and bricks.) At times, snow-like mineral deposits or small stalactites can be seen, which are caused by the seepage and evaporation of groundwater through the bricks and mortar.

At the tunnel entrance, the tunnel lining is dressed stone, and from there to 26' below the south portal it is four-course-thick brick, except under the vertical shafts, where it is six. The tunnel is 3,118' long, 24' wide (19' waterway, plus 5' towpath), and 25' high. The water depth averages 7'. The towpath is equipped with a stout railing approximately waist high. The top rail, which dates from the operating era, is a square stout beam, in many places showing deep ruts burned into it by the tow ropes of mule-drawn barges. The rail has been retained beginning at a point far enough in from the portals to be protected from the weather. There are wooden railings (or bumpers) on both inner sides of the tunnel to keep barges from scraping the brick walls. The volume of rock cut out of the tunnel was 82,000 cubic yards.

Building "A Wonder Of The World"

Construction of the Paw Paw Tunnel was an impressive feat. It involved not only 3,118' of tunnel, but also 200' of deep cut at the southern/upstream end and 890' at the northern/downstream end. While the deep cut was being excavated, two pairs of vertical shafts were dug through the hill overhead (two shafts per set to provide ventilation) until tunnel level was reached. The vertical shafts were 122' and 188' high, and were 8' in diameter, with 23' between the centers of each pair. Each pair was located in a ravine to shorten the vertical distance. One pair was about 370' in from the north portal, and the other about 900'. From the vertical shafts, digging proceeded along the tunnel line in each direction. This made a total of six active digging faces—although that in the downstream deep cut did not involve tunneling. Because of rockslides in the deep cut, the face at the north portal was not as active as the others. The shafts can be found inside the tunnel by the water dripping down them and through the brick lining, and also where weep holes in the brick walls at towpath level are much closer together and larger. Digging scars are still visible on the hill above.

Black powder was used to blast through large pieces of rock, which were further reduced by sledgehammers and picks. Waste was hoisted up the shafts by winches or hauled out of the portals by carts on rails. The waste was then carted to spoil heaps in the lower sections of Tunnel Hollow where it widened out, in nearby ravines, and on the river side of the canal. When not covered with plant growth, these heaps are still detectable, particularly above the towpath, downstream of the tunnel.

Other numbers:

- 14 years from start to finish but with varying levels of construction during only 10 of those years.
- $616,478.65 cost for the tunnel and deep cuts.
- 82,000 cubic yards of shale removed.
- 5,800,000 bricks line the tunnel walls.
- Millions of tons of coal, agricultural products, lumber, stones, and industrial goods passed through the tunnel between 1850 and 1924.

Approaching the tunnel entrance, boatmen would note things like the water line on the rocks of the deep cut. If there was a wet line above the water level, it meant a boat was ahead of them in the tunnel, as water tended to pile up in front of boats, lowering the level slightly behind the boat. Over the years several methods were tried to avoid problems at the tunnel, including using a watchman and a signal arm controlled with a pulley system that could be set for the opposite end of the tunnel when a boat entered. However, in oral histories most indicated that they had not had any problems at the tunnel.

Paw Paw Tunnel

The Paw Paw Tunnel is one of the finest features of the canal, built as a bypass to some very difficult terrain along the Potomac River. The route up Tunnel Hollow and through the deep cut and tunnel avoids six miles of the Paw Paw Bends, with steep slopes and cliffs that come right to the river. Following the river would have required either crossing to the West Virginia shore and back, hacking out the canal along the steep Maryland shore, or damming the river at the lower end of the bend to form a six-mile slackwater navigation stretch and then either cutting a towpath along the cliffs, or moving it to the West Virginia side.

All of these alternatives were thoroughly debated within the canal company. Eventually, the tunnel plan won out—due largely to the enthusiastic advocacy of the company's long-serving engineer, Charles B. Fisk. In the spring of 1836, Lee Montgomery, a Methodist minister whose previous experience included work on a tunnel in Pennsylvania, was awarded the contract to build the tunnel. Construction began in June 1836, and the tunnel was holed through in 1840. Work stopped here along with the general stoppage of work 1842–46 and continued in fits and starts until the final work on the brick lining was completed in late 1850 or early in 1851. Violent labor riots, strikes, sickness, and financial failures affected work at the tunnel until it finally opened for navigation on October 10, 1850.

Montgomery had a reputation of being a tough, energetic, and imaginative contractor. Bricks were scarce in the area, so he brought in a patented brick-making machine from Baltimore and set up his own brick works. Much of the tunneling work involved cutting through rock and constructing sophisticated brickwork and masonry. The Irish laborers who built much of the canal were not particularly skilled in these areas, so Montgomery hired English masons, English and Welsh miners, and local Pennsylvania and Maryland

Excursion Boat "Oak Spring" at the north portal of the Paw Paw Tunnel, ca. early 1900s.

"Dutch" miners and laborers. Those moves, rational as they seemed, later contributed to Montgomery's downfall.

Montgomery accepted the contract at a very low cost based on optimistic estimates that "a single hand can bore from seven to eight feet per day." In reality, a crew of up to 44 men progressed only 10'–12' per week. Frequent cave-ins of the soft shale rock formations slowed the work. Rising costs and unexpected expenses bedeviled Montgomery from the beginning; by the end of the first year he was already trying to renegotiate his contract.

One problem: the canal company paid Montgomery in monthly installments, according to how far work had progressed. However, to enforce the contractor's intention to fulfill the contract in its entirety, a certain percentage was retained by the canal company to be paid at the project's completion. While the company from time to time relinquished portions of the retained money to help keep Montgomery going, he was forced to invest more and more of his own resources. Eventually, Montgomery fell behind in payments to his laborers.

By early 1837, unrest among Montgomery's men over the pay situation and rivalries among the various national groups finally exploded into violence. The Irish terrorized work camps and drove off British workers for a time. More riots among the Irish, English, and "Dutch" occurred in 1838. In May of that year the failure of contractors to meet payrolls along the whole line of the canal forced a general strike. Local militia, who by this time strongly sympathized with workers, turned out reluctantly to restore order. Montgomery fired and blacklisted 130 men, and work was resumed. More rioting broke out in 1839, this time near Little Orleans. Once again the militia was called in to restore order.

South (upstream) portal of the Paw Paw Tunnel, 2012. *(Image courtesy Steve Dean)*

Despite failing finances and violent unrest, work on the tunnel continued through 1840 and 1841. In 1842, however, the canal company's legal and financial troubles forced work on the entire canal to halt. At the time, the canal was in operation up to Dam 6 (mile 134.1), about 20 miles below the tunnel. Additionally, much of the stretch above the tunnel to Cumberland had been finished. Montgomery—now bankrupt and pursued by creditors—had somehow managed to clear the tunnel from portal to portal. But a great deal of work remained. North of the tunnel, the rockslide-prone deep cut was not fully cleared, and the canal here had to be completed. The brick lining had yet to be installed in the tunnel. Montgomery's patented machine actually produced very poor brick. Fortunately for the canal, in 1847 enough funds were raised through the sale of 1844 state-backed construction bonds to resume work. The tunnel and canal were finally sufficiently finished under a series of contractors and opened to traffic on October 10, 1850.

Tales From The Tunnel

Like many spots along the C&O, the Paw Paw Tunnel abounds with tales and legends. One such tale involves an Irishman and his mule. During construction, the man operated a sort of elevator at one of the vertical shafts, bringing loads of rock to the surface and lowering men and supplies. The Irishman and mule shared one characteristic: a very short temper. Man and beast quarreled more and more as work progressed until one day the mule kicked the Irishman. Incensed, the Irishman kicked back. Unfortunately, the mule was standing on the edge of the shaft. Down he went, landing angry but unhurt at the bottom. As there was no way to get him to the top again, the Irishman, in addition to his other duties, had to lower bales of hay and buckets of water down the shaft to the mule until workers could bore through the rock and reach a portal to get him out.

A tunnel incident that grew to tunnel legend occurred after the tunnel opened to navigation. Typically, the first boat into the tunnel had the right-of-way, but if two boats ended up in the tunnel at the same time, the light boat would be the one to back out. On one occasion both captains (Gene Bower with a light boat and Clete Zimmerman with a loaded boat) refused to back up to allow the other through. In one version, both had a gun with which to make his point that he believed he was not the one who should have to give way. Eventually a canal superintendent appeared and talked one of them into backing up—most likely Bowers since his was the light boat.

In some re-tellings the standoff went so far as to result in a backlog of boats stretching for miles, with Capt. Zimmerman warning, "Anyone that's goin' to untie that line is going to die." In other versions the section superintendent (or, in some cases, the general superintendent during the receivership era, George L. Nicholson—traveling all the way from Georgetown) resorted to burning green corn at the upwind end of the tunnel to smoke out the stubborn captains.

155.78 The canal exits the south (upstream) portal. The volume cut at the upstream end was 10,000 cubic yards.

The engraved keystone is marked: "C. B. Fisk, Engineer" for Charles B. Fisk, the canal company engineer who pushed for the tunnel project, and was chief engineer when it was finished in 1850. Fisk was the only engineer to remain with the canal company throughout the construction years, having started in 1828 as an assistant engineer and not leaving until 1852.

In winter months the NPS may install a wooden wall to block the portal and prevent the tunnel's masonry and brick lining near the portal from alternately freezing and thawing. A small door in the wall at the towpath provides tunnel access.

Tunnel Hill Trail (see mile 154.85) descends the hill and rejoins the towpath here.

156.10 Paw Paw Tunnel Drive-in Campground. (39.544450, -78.460806) Access: From I-68 in Cumberland take Exit 43C/MD-51. If coming eastbound on I-68, the exit ramp for Exit 43C merges directly onto MD-51. If coming westbound on I-68, take Exit 43C; at the bottom of the exit ramp turn left onto Harrison St.; go one long block and turn left onto S. Mechanic St., which becomes MD-51 as it goes under I-68. Follow MD-51 south approximately 26 miles and turn left at the parking lot for the tunnel and campground. (If you come to the bridge over the Potomac River into West Virginia, you've gone too far.) Campsites include fire rings, grills, water, chemical toilets, and access to a canoe launch. Contact the park's Cumberland Visitor Center for current camping fees and information, 301-722-8226, www.nps.gov/choh.

156.2x Canal section superintendent's house. In 1970 thousands of broken bricks were turned up in a field between the section house and MD-51. The bricks were thought to be discards made by tunnel contractor Lee Montgomery using his portable brick-making machine from Baltimore. A report dated March 16, 1838, from engineer Elwood Morris to Charles B. Fisk stated that Montgomery's bricks were of poor quality. Montgomery's kiln may have been at the upstream end of the field where a large quantity of cinders and coal were also unearthed.

Across the river is the town of Paw Paw, West Virginia, once a stopping point on the B&O and a minor industrial center. A tannery here took advantage of the abundance of oak bark in the vicinity. The USGS river gaging station at the highway bridge may be of interest to students of the Potomac's flood history. Zero on the gauge equals 483' above sea level. Only the 1936 and 1985 floods crested the towpath level here, the first reaching 54' and the latter 53.58'. Low water is 2'; annual high-water probability is 24'. The flood stage is 40'. The 1877 and 1889 floods were at 45'—the same as the towpath level here.

156.24 Pass under the MD-51 bridge, built after the canal operating period. Prior to the creation of this route, Paw Paw was reached by ferry and ford one mile upstream.

156.43 Pass under the Western Maryland Railway bridge; the railroad parallels the berm for several miles. Beyond the railroad bridge the canal passes through the Mitchell's Neck Deep Cut, avoiding another bend in the river.

156.66 Deep masonry waste weir; adjacent is a buried masonry spillway. This is the upstream end of Mitchell's Neck Deep Cut.

156.75 There is a steep rock face above the railroad bed; the river is far below the towpath.

156.89 Purslane Run Hiker–Biker Campsite. The nearest access is the Paw Paw Tunnel at mile 156.10.

Canoeing The Paw Paw Bends

The stretch of river around the Paw Paw Tunnel is fine for the semi-skilled canoeist. There are several small but definite ledges to pass, but in normal summertime conditions the slow water requires only mild back paddling. Around the first bend (across which the tunnel cuts) are a number of spectacular cliffs overlooking the river. Here, severe rock folds typical of many Appalachian formations can be seen.

Canoeists can launch at the Paw Paw Tunnel campground at mile 156.20 or near the WV-9/MD-51 bridge in Paw Paw. One can also launch at Bonds Landing Boat Ramp, accessible from Kasecamp Rd. via a branch road that crosses the C&O Canal at mile 150.10. The first really convenient launch below Paw Paw is at the Fifteen Mile Creek Recreation Area near Little Orleans. At the end of a long bend after putting in from the campground at mile 156.20 and heading downstream is the upstream end of a long island separated from the riverbank by a narrow channel. This channel forms a delightful little woodland stream, heavily shaded and with several small rapids, negotiable but fun for the novice. Sorrel Ridge campsite at mile 154.10 is on the riverbank just after the channel, making this a convenient landing.

156.94 The floodplain—now a hayfield with abandoned machinery—was once the site of a shanty construction camp where approximately 200 men lived during the canal construction period.

157.17 An access road to the hayfield crosses the canal. A grassy road descends around the end of the field toward the river. This deeply entrenched route was the main road to the Paw Paw ferry and ford. The ferry was approximately in line with the road; the ford was somewhat upstream. A canal workers' cemetery lies ahead at mile 157.18, accessible by a short path from the river side of the towpath.

157.26 Culvert #211 (Purslane Run), 14' span, referred to in 1851 as the "road culvert at Greenwell's Hollow." The valley of Purslane Run represents a former channel of the Potomac River, reaching two miles inland from its present bed. Terrace gravels deposited along the way at levels far above the present channel attest to this dramatic change of course.

157.6x Large cottonwoods grow in the canal prism.

158.00 The canal swings away from the river, leaving a wide, wooded floodplain. On the far side of the river is the steep end of Devil's Nose with interesting ravines and waterfalls.

158.79 Culvert #212, 8' span, built in 1850. The culvert barrel is almost completely silted in. The stream comes from Reckley Flat, a valley that was the former Potomac channel.

158.8x A deep flood channel runs between the towpath and an embankment along the river. Tightly folded rock layers rise above the canal bed.

159.06 The towpath comes onto the riverbank.

159.41 The Western Maryland Railway runs close to the canal, with a concrete retaining wall. The inscription "1905" is clearly visible at the top of the retaining wall. The railroad constricts the canal in a place or two along here.

159.5x A greenish-gray rectangular stone is found 100' off the towpath toward the river. The 20" stone resembles a tombstone, but has no visible markings.

159.60 Across the Potomac is the mouth of the Little Cacapon River. The B&O (now CSX) railroad viaduct arches are visible from here during winter months.

159.72 Lost Culvert #213, built in 1850, carried Big Run.

160.xx A box culvert under the railroad bed drains water from an upland ravine into the canal during heavy rainfall.

160.26 A double masonry spillway/waste weir combination is intact except for stones at the river end of the spillway. Blockages of the box culvert at mile 160.xx have led to severe erosion of the railroad bed into the prism.

160.60 Most complete section of upper part of Jennings Formation seen in Maryland (Middle and Upper Devonian period).

160.7x Red stonework (15' high) on the berm side supports the railroad bed.

161.1x Rock rubble from the canal excavation is piled up along the river side of the towpath.

161.30 Prominent knobs and steep slopes across the river mark the end of Town Hill. This mountain rises again in Maryland to the north. Like Sideling Hill farther east, it is a syncline, rather than the more common anticline. Strata here reach the bottom of one of their folds, but harder formations in a trough of the fold have become the top of the mountain, while softer rocks of the lower strata have eroded into side valleys. Virtually all other ridges from this point west to Cumberland are anticlines.

The prism is completely watered here. The riverbank, towpath, canal, and railroad bed are within a 60-yard span.

LOCK 67

161.76 (39.52560, -78.53626) Access: From Cumberland follow MD-51 south approximately 19.6 miles. Turn right at NPS sign for Town Creek Aqueduct onto the former Western Maryland Railway right-of-way. (Limited parking—do not block gate.) A footpath crosses the canal prism.

Lock 67 at the head of the 6.5-mile-long "Tunnel Level" is another economy lock originally built of broken stone lined with kyanized (treated) wood and now largely replaced with concrete. The lower lock gates are gone. Above the lock a worn wheelway crosses to MD-51, which has descended the slope to parallel the far side of the railroad. Only the 16' x 22' foundation of a frame lockhouse remains.

According to Isaac Long, a long-time occupant of Lock 68, this was once known as "[Hughey] Darkey's Lock," and boasted a saloon by Gene Stumph, whose flirtatious red-headed daughters made this a favorite stop of canal boatmen.

161.82 Culvert #215, 16' span, built in 1850, brick-lined with exposed barrel, carries Big Run, which drains from the eastern slope of Green Ridge. An old road formerly ran diagonally back to Okonoko Ford, leading to a road up Miller Hollow on the West Virginia side. The culvert extends under MD-51, which parallels the canal here.

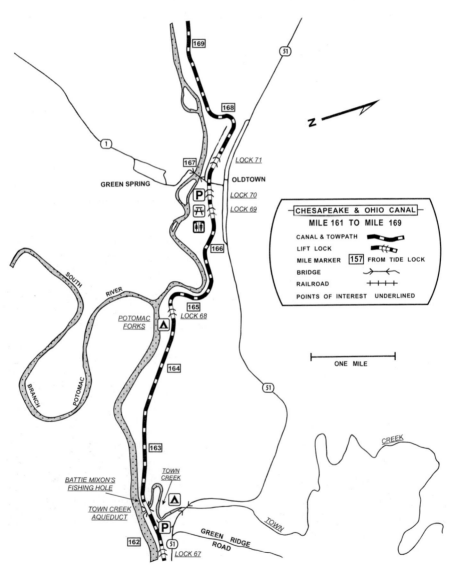

162.0x A 200'-tall bluff rises above the river and railroad tracks on the West Virginia side. A wooden observation deck sits at the top edge of the bluff.

162.1x Town Creek Hiker–Biker Campsite. Access by crossing the canal at the Town Creek Aqueduct parking.

TOWN CREEK AQUEDUCT

162.34 (39.523862, -78.543122) Access: From Cumberland follow MD-51 south approximately 20 miles. Turn right at the NPS sign for Town Creek Aqueduct, onto the former Western Maryland Railway right-of-way. (Limited parking—do not block gate.) Park at end of road and follow footpath down to aqueduct.

The tenth of 11 stone aqueducts carries the canal over Town Creek on a single 100' span. Much of the aqueduct was rebuilt in 1977. The stonework is in good condition except for the collapsed upstream wall; the missing stones are piled nearby.

Town Creek, one of the larger streams in Allegany County, exhibits a number of interesting geologic features, particularly its entrenched meanders, one of which may be observed just beyond the railroad tracks. From a vantage point on one of the nearby mountains, it is evident that the flat tops of lower ridges were once the floor of a broad, nearly-level valley, in which Town Creek swung back and forth in its changing meanders. As the valley floor was uplifted, the stream cut faster, and its bends became restricted by

Town Creek Aqueduct near Oldtown, Maryland. *(Library of Congress, Prints and Photographs Division, HABS, Reproduction Number HABS MD, 1-OLDTO.V.1--2)*

the rock structure resulting in today's entrenched meanders. A fine view of this condition can be found 3.5 miles north on Green Ridge Road, which starts from MD-51 just east of this point. Topographic maps reveal other interesting features, such as the erratic course of Sawpit Run, a tributary of Town Creek.

Craigs Mill operated here in the late 1700s, followed by a succession of water-powered mills. Some foundation ruins may be seen above the railroad trestle. NPS property includes a flat west of the Town Creek railroad embankment where canal workers are buried in unmarked graves.

162.38 A low concrete dam in the canal forms a fishing pond. This is the first of several levels of fishing pools extending to Lock 71 beyond Oldtown. The ponds were constructed in 1945 by volunteer groups of Western Maryland sportsmen in cooperation with the state. These ponds are called "Battie Mixon's Fishing Hole," after the Allegany County game warden who conceived the idea and directed the work of volunteers. The ponds are stocked with fish, one of which is reserved for children and hosts an annual fishing "rodeo." See http://battiemixoncatfishclub.webs.com.

Aside from fishing, the pools restore the canal to much of its original appearance. For the next two miles the floodplain consists of broad fields while the berm becomes a steep, wooded hillside with frequent cliffs.

164.7x A causeway across the canal provides NPS access to the towpath.

LOCK 68

164.82 Access: Lock 70 at mile 166.70 or from Town Creek Aqueduct parking lot at mile 162.34.

Lock 68, once known as "Crabtree's Lock" after two generations of locktenders, is opposite the mouth of the South Branch of the Potomac. This lock may have had a downstream extension to permit two boats to pass through the lock at one time. Parts of the lock gate lie on the towpath side of the canal about 30 yards below the lock, and again on the river side of the towpath just before one reaches the lock. A poorly defined, unlined bypass flume remains.

An old steel and wood bridge across the lower end of the lock has 12'-high piers that give the appearance of being tied into the lock. The bridge carries a road that once led from MD-51 one-half mile to the river ford and ferry to a settlement of the South Branch Depot (later French Station on the B&O). The bridge, rebuilt ca. 1865, was once a pivot bridge. The present bridge, built ca. 1918, is a modified Warren truss, 84'9" long x 12' wide. A concrete wall at the upper end of the lock serves to keep Level 68 watered as part of the Battie Mixon pool system. A footbridge across the lower end of the lock leads to a fine well, and a picnic and camping area.

Lockhouse at Lock 68 (Crabtree's Lock), 1961. The iron bridge in the background is a modified Warren Truss. It replaced a wood pivot bridge destroyed in the Civil War and rebuilt ca. 1865.

164.8x Potomac Forks Hiker–Biker Campsite. Nearest access is from Lock 70 at mile 166.70. The camping area is behind an unoccupied, wood frame lockhouse. Beyond the well on the berm, trails lead up a rocky hillside, affording a picturesque route with a rewarding view. Since the canal is normally watered, one must return here to re-cross. Numerous lock stones are located on the river side of the towpath upstream of the lockhouse.

165.08 During low water, stumps appear in the canal bed. The towpath comes onto the riverbank as the canal and river make a sharp curve known as Yorker Bend. Rhododendron-covered cliffs on the berm are locally called Falling Rocks—a very scenic area not duplicated elsewhere on the canal.

165.33 The sharp turn of the river and the canal continues. Cliffs here give way to a broad valley where an earlier course of the river swung one-half mile north. The canal becomes a wide basin, retained by a berm levee. A field begins here and continues almost into Oldtown. The lack of trees on the canal side of the towpath gives the drained canal an almost barren appearance.

165.45 Culvert #216, 6' span. This culvert and other culverts upstream were built in 1850. MD-51 is visible beyond the former Western Maryland Railway track.

In 2007 a large breach between the river bend and Culvert #216 forced the NPS to erect earthen dams and bypass pipes to control the water flow.

North vs. South

The division of the Potomac River here into the North and South Branches marks an important point in both the geography and history of the river. The North Branch carries more water, but the South Branch is longer. For many years, dispute continued as to which was the "main stem" of the river, and therefore stipulated the boundary between Maryland and Virginia (now West Virginia). The C&O Canal follows the North Branch, commonly referred to simply as the Potomac. Had not the spring marked by the Fairfax Stone been ultimately accepted as the Potomac River's source, present-day Maryland would have a significantly different shape.

The South Branch was long considered a potential source of water for the canal, and early proposed locations for Dam 7 (which was never built) included a site here that would have used its flow. Later, a steam pump was installed and was finally put into operation in 1858. It was used whenever low water required it. The pump proved unsatisfactory and was out of service by 1862. In 1873–74 the canal company built a new pump 10 miles upstream near Lock 72.

165.70 The canal swings away from the river to follow the valley of Mill Run, formerly Big Spring Run. This stream's valley drains the west side of Warrior Mountain and flows to within one mile of the Potomac, then suddenly swings east to parallel the river for nearly four miles before joining it. The canal route uses this side valley, passing through Oldtown and returning to parallel the Potomac through an interesting cut that may have been an early channel of Big Spring Run.

166.10 Culvert #217, 20' span, carries Cresap Mill and Seven Springs Run.

166.24 Concrete waste weir.

LOCK 69 (Twiggs Lock)

166.44 Access: Lock 70 at mile 166.70. There is a canoe ramp at the river.

Lock 69 is the first of three Oldtown locks, all of which were originally of broken stone sheathed with kyanized wood planking, now largely replaced with concrete. The lock was extended upstream and may have been extended downstream. A bypass flume runs from a basin above the lock and discharges through a sloping wall. A stop gate maintains the water level above, forming another pool of the Battie Mixon fishing area. Locks 68, 69, 70, and 71 were completed in the latter part of 1849 or in the early part of 1850. A path parallels the berm, separating the canal from the bed of Mill Run.

On the river side the towpath is a marsh, beyond which is the site where Union Fort Lininger once stood. The fort was located opposite South Branch Cliff or "Walnut Bottom." This marshy area was probably created by construction workers taking earth to build the canal berms.

LOCK 70, OLDTOWN

166.70 (39.540405, -78.611936) Access: From Cumberland follow MD-51 south approximately 14 miles. Turn right onto Oldtown Cemetery Rd. then make a left onto Opessa St. Continue 0.1 mile and turn right onto Green Spring Rd. SE. Follow to a parking lot on the right.

If you continue south a short distance on Green Spring Road, you come to a low-water one-lane bridge that is the only private toll bridge across the Potomac River.

A canal store once sat behind the two-story frame lockhouse. A 1906 photo shows a large barn-like structure across the canal. Above the lock is a broad basin and wharf for Oldtown. The canal follows the valley of the stream bed of Mill Run, formerly Big Spring Run, which is separated from the North Branch of the Potomac River by hills. In 1957 the towpath here was heavily cleared of the shade trees that had developed since the canal shut down in 1924. An NPS maintenance area is now behind the lockhouse area off Green Spring Road.

In 1850 a pivot bridge was built on Lock 70. At some later time it was replaced with a high covered bridge over the canal, leading to a river ford. The first wooden canal bridge (along with the lockhouse and store) burned in 1906. It was replaced with a high wood and steel bridge similar to the one at Lock 68.

Lockhouse at Lock 70. Note the canal basin in the foreground, once the dock area for Oldtown. *(Image courtesy Maria Keifer, 2012)*

Lock 70 near Oldtown, Maryland.

The McCausland–Johnson Raid

In August 1864 the canal at Lock 70 was the scene of a dramatic Civil War encounter. After burning Chambersburg, Pennsylvania, on July 30 and occupying Hancock the next day, Confederate troops threatened Cumberland on August 1. With Union cavalry approaching from the rear, Confederate Gen. John McCausland sent a force to secure the ford at Oldtown. There they discovered that Union troops had destroyed the bridge over the canal and were occupying the ridge (Alum Hill) between the canal and river, which blocked the Confederates from crossing the Potomac. After some fighting on August 2, the Confederates drove the Union forces across the Potomac to Green Spring, West Virginia, where they took refuge in a blockhouse, supported by a train of armored cars on the B&O tracks that had artillery pieces mounted upon it. A Confederate battery disabled the train's engine and one artillery piece. Gen. Bradley Johnson demanded the surrender of the Union force, to which the federals agreed. The Confederates then crossed the river to Green Spring and completed the capture, opening the way for McCausland's entire force to retire to Virginia.

The Oldtown area of the C&O Canal affords nature lovers an abundance of flora and fauna to observe and enjoy. The area is also popular for its large and varied dragonfly population. The C&O Canal Association occasionally hosts dragonfly nature walks on this level. For information on these walks call 301-983-0825 or visit www.candocanal.org.

LOCK 71

167.04 Access: Lock 70 at mile 166.70.

The third of the Oldtown locks, Lock 71 is another example of the "economy" locks of the upper canal, originally lined with treated wood, and now largely replaced with concrete. Lock 71, though largely overgrown, still shows some of the bolts used to hold the wooden sheathing in place. Vertical grooves in the crude stonework to hold stop planks are plainly visible. The 6" x 6" openings in the upper gate pockets held wooden posts that kept the gates from banging into the lock. A footbridge crosses the upper part of the lock to a path on the berm levee. Above the lock, the stretch of fishing pools ends, and the canal bed becomes a running stream. The two-and-a-half story lockhouse is now an NPS storage area. The Oldtown Sportsmen Club did much of the canal improvement in this area in 1957.

167.11 A masonry spillway/waste weir formerly discharged into Mill Run. Ahead, the stream comes into the canal through a hole in the berm levee made to provide the water supply for fishing pools.

167.51 According to the canal mileages of 1851, this is the site of "Cresap's Mill," built by James Cresap, grandson of Thomas, and son of Daniel, who had 11 children. When the canal was built, the company was required to provide a bridge to the Cresap mill. A temporary bridge was built in 1839, but it collapsed shortly after under a heavily loaded wagon, killing one man and a horse. Ultimately, the canal company concluded an arrangement with the Cresaps to pay them to build their own bridge and to accept all responsibility for its maintenance—thereby divesting the company of any connection with the road to the mill.

The canal makes a sharp left turn into Alum Hill Deep Cut. Sheer walls of shale rise on both sides; the towpath is a ledge cut into crumbly rock.

167.99 The deep cut ends as the canal reaches the river and makes another sharp turn.

168.42 A pool at the mouth of a ravine (at times dry) continues beyond the railroad fill; another pool is further west. The cleared section ends at mile 168.46, and the towpath becomes shaded again. Roads to fields cross the towpath from time to time.

168.95 The foundation of a bank barn and the remains of a wooden gate are visible.

169.10 Pigmans Ferry Hiker–Biker Campsite. The nearest access is at Oldtown at mile 166.70.

169.17 Culvert #221, 6' span, carries Pigmans Run from beyond the railroad embankment.

170.0x Approximate location for Shelhorn Tavern, which was operating in 1795.

170.37 Culvert #222, 6' span, brick-lined; the ringstones are 18" deep.

170.84 Culvert #223 (Kelly's Road Culvert), 10' span. This culvert is in much better condition than Culvert #222. Note the stonemasons' marks.

171.45 Masonry spillway, 250' long. Note the concrete piers that allowed mule tenders to cross on wooden planks.

Oldtown

Oldtown has a long and entrancing history. Here, some claim, the famed Warriors Path—Athiamiowee, Path of the Armed Ones—forded the Potomac. Others place the crossing at the mouth of the Conococheague or at McCoys Ferry. In any case, this site hosted the meetings of widely separated Native American tribes.

Several mountain ridges converge in Oldtown, bringing with them five Indian trails: Warriors Trail, Bear Hill Trail, Creek Road Trail, Dry Run Trail, and Mill or Big Spring Trail. Around 1715 a group of Shawnees settled here, and the village later became known as King Opessa's Town, after the local Shawnee chief.

When English pioneer Col. Thomas Cresap arrived sometime prior to 1746, the place was referred to as Shawnee Old Town, as the tribe had abandoned the area. Cresap acquired the patent known as Indian Seat in 1746, built a fortified house, and called it Fort Skipton after his birthplace in England.

During the following years, the main street of the village was a part of the old road to Ft. Cumberland, and until the shorter route (US–40) across the mountain ridges was built, this was a stopping place for the westbound stagecoach lines.

Nothing remains of Cresap's fort, which was in a hayfield south of Oldtown, on a high terrace about a thousand feet from the river. Cresap was active in exploration and trail building, and he acted as commissary for Gen. Edward Braddock's troops, who camped here before and after their fateful venture to the west in 1755. After Braddock's defeat, the early settlers took refuge in Cresap's "fort." When George Washington was a teenager, he visited Fort Skipton with a survey party and spent five nights here in March 1748, detained by high water on the Potomac. Although the surveys were actually performed by the more experienced members of the party, the trip was Washington's formal initiation into the field and led him to pursue surveying as a profession.

Cresap's son Michael built a stone house in Oldtown in 1764, which still stands on the main street through town. When Washington called for troops in 1775, Michael Cresap and perhaps as many as 130 riflemen met at this house in Oldtown before marching to Frederick and on to Boston. The house has been restored and is undoubtedly one of the historical treasures of Western Maryland. The brick addition to the original stone house was added by Rev. John Jacobs in 1781. The house is open by appointment and for selected events in the summer. 19015 Opessa Street, SE, Oldtown, MD 21555, 301-478-5848, www.michaelcresapmuseum.org.

In June 1863 Confederate cavalry under Gen. John Imboden cut the canal two miles above Oldtown and four miles below the town in high embankments, which caused significant damage from erosion. These actions, along with the railroad bridges his men burnt, screened Gen. Lee's advance into Maryland and Pennsylvania, ultimately to a confrontation with the Union army at Gettysburg.

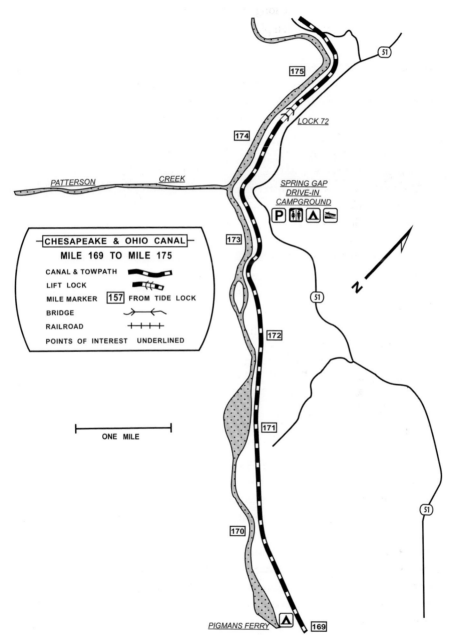

CHESAPEAKE & OHIO CANAL
MILE 169 TO MILE 175
CANAL & TOWPATH
LIFT LOCK
MILE MARKER 157 FROM TIDE LOCK
BRIDGE
RAILROAD
POINTS OF INTEREST UNDERLINED

ONE MILE

PATTERSON CREEK

LOCK 72

SPRING GAP
DRIVE-IN
CAMPGROUND

PIGMANS FERRY

Brick-lined Culvert #223, known as Kelly's Road Culvert. *(Image courtesy Maria Keifer, 2012)*

171.8x The canal is very close to the river here, allowing views of small islands from the towpath.

172.10 Culvert #228, 12' span, drains a large area, including Brice and Frog Hollows and the slopes of Collier and Martin Mountains. Dramatic rock folds are on the berm.

172.50 The canal widens into a dry basin, referred to in 1851 canal data as "Basin at Alkyre's House."

172.81 Location of an earlier washout, beyond which the canal follows the riverbank for 250 yards, curving around cliffs and interesting rock folds directly on the towpath.

173.37 Spring Gap Drive-In Campground. (39.564306, -78.719289) Access: From Cumberland follow MD-51 south 7.6 miles. Turn right into the campground. Campsites include grills, water, chemical toilets, and access to a boat ramp. The area is open to camping only during the summer. (For current fees see www.nps.gov/choh/planyourvisit/camping.htm.)

MD-51 parallels the canal on the berm side for the next two miles. Collier Mountain ends.

173.37 Culvert #230, 6' span.

173.47 A path leads through the woods to the river, where views of West Virginia include the sheer cliffs at the end of Patterson Creek Ridge and the adjacent Patterson Creek valley.

173.64 The overgrown, large stone bridge abutment carried a road bridge across the canal; a small portion of the abutments remains. The stonework is especially interesting, the individual stones having been cut out to fit jig-saw fashion rather than laid in straight-line courses.

173.72 Boat basin.

173.78 Culvert #231, 12' span, carries Collier Run. About 84,250 bricks were used in the culvert construction.

174.18 Site of canal water supply pumps. The unusual concrete trough and pump emplacements are interesting, but little of the original structures remain. A steam pump was installed here to maintain the water level in the canal, replacing the first one installed at Lock 68 in 1856. William R. Hutton, consulting engineer, described the newly installed steam pump in the June 7, 1875, Annual Stockholders' Report:

> A centrifugal pump guaranteed to raise 24 cubic feet of water per second to a height of 25 feet. Pump turns on vertical shaft in well of brick work 6 feet in diameter. Water rises in well, flowing over top into circular channel and then to canal by way of flume. Engine house, wood 23 feet by 23 feet and boiler room of brick 18 1/2 x 32 feet—floors of concrete. Water from river admitted by culvert 6 feet wide, 6 1/2 feet high. Cost $20,504.40.

Ruins of steam water pump used to pump water from the Potomac into the canal. *(Image courtesy Maria Keifer, 2012)*

Upper lock gate of Lock 72. *(Image courtesy Maria Keifer, 2012)*

174.32 Concrete waste weir. MD-51 continues along the berm.

174.40 A path to the left leads about 40 yards to Blue Spring, also known as "Blue Hole," described in earlier editions of this book as one of the largest springs in the Eastern United States, with an average temperature of 54 degrees in the summer. In recent years the spring has been very low.

LOCK 72 (The Narrows)

174.44 Access: Lock 74 at mile 175.47.

Lock 72 was finished in 1841 and was constructed of stone from a nearby quarry as a standard masonry lock (Lock 71 being the last of the composite locks). This lock design uses a "slope wall" at the lower end of the wing wall and bypass flume. One badly damaged upper lock gate is in place; the lower lock gate is in the canal bed. In canal operating days Lock 72 was known as "Ten Mile Lock" because it is almost exactly 10 miles below Cumberland. The lock has a 9' lift. The two-story frame lockhouse is in fairly good condition. The Douglas Hike began here (rather than in Cumberland) on the morning of March 20, 1954.

Ahead the canal, highway, and railroad are squeezed into a tight space between the Potomac and the ends of Nicholas Ridge and Irons Mountain—an area known in canal days as "The Narrows."

175.02 Lost Culvert #233 (Moores Hollow), 4' span.

175.30 Head of "The Narrows." The river and canal swing sharply into a long S-curve. A path on the berm side leads to MD-51. From here it is nine miles via the towpath to the center of Cumberland.

175.35 Culvert #234, 6' span.

LOCK 73, NORTH BRANCH

175.3x Irons Mountain Hiker–Biker Campsite. Access: Lock 74 at mile 175.47.

Lock 73 is the first of three locks at North Branch and was completed in 1840 but rebuilt in 1869. The view of the mountain wall along "The Narrows" is impressive. Limestone for Locks 73–75 came from Evitts Creek Quarry. Lock 73 has a 9' lift.

175.43 The CSX Railroad comes across the river from West Virginia, crossing first the Potomac and then the canal on steel bridges. The present bridge #65 was built in 1923; the original bridge at this site was built in 1842. The bridge is being torn down and replaced in 2014–15.

Locktender's shanty and Lock 74 drop gate, ca. early 1900s.

LOCK 74, NORTH BRANCH

175.47 (39.587733, -78.738143) Access: From Cumberland follow MD-51 south 5.5 miles. Turn right onto Pittsburgh Plate Glass Rd. Continue 0.4 mile and turn left onto River Rd. SE. Make slight right onto River Rd. SE and follow to parking lot, picnic area, and restrooms. River Rd. parallels the canal and dead ends at a farm.

Lock 74 was completed in 1841 but rebuilt in 1869. It has a 10' lift—a total lift of 599.193' above the tide lock. All three North Branch locks may have had drop gates installed in 1875 on the breast wall at the upper end, replacing the original swing-type gates. Part of the lock gate mechanism remains. Road indications are that there was a pivot bridge here.

Hardware from these locks (and perhaps even others along the canal) was given to a World War II scrap iron drive. The lockhouse burned in 1974.

175.58 Late period waste weir.

LOCK 75, NORTH BRANCH

175.60 Access: Lock 74 at mile 175.47.

The last lift lock of the C&O Canal, Lock 75 has a 10' lift—a total lift of 609.193' above the Georgetown tide lock. The nine-mile level beginning here extends to the guard lock at the head of the canal in Cumberland. This lock, rebuilt in 1869, is constructed of well-cut, laid and mortared gray limestone built in accordance with the 1836 specifications. Both lock walls were elevated 6" with wood. The two-story log lockhouse—17' x 29'3" over a full stone basement—was reconstructed in 1978. New gates were installed at the downstream end of the lock in the 1990s. During this time the lockhouse began to be open on weekends in the summer, staffed by C&O Canal Association volunteers.

176.00 The property line of the North Branch Pumping Station (formerly Pittsburgh Plate Glass) follows the berm for a considerable distance. Canoeists should avoid the Pittsburgh Plate Glass Dam. Instead of using the river at this point, put in at Spring Gap at mile 173. The buildings are now part of the Allegany County Industrial Park.

Lock 75 in the early 1900s. Note the log lockhouse to the left.

176.51 River Road (39.587303, -78.754629) Access: From Cumberland follow MD-51 south 5.5 miles. Turn right onto Pittsburgh Plate Glass Rd. Continue 0.4 mile and turn left onto River Rd. SE. Make a slight right onto River Rd. SE and continue 1.0 mile to small parking area.

On the riverside is the small, iron-fenced Pollock Cemetery where Confederate soldier James D. Pollock is buried. This was the vicinity of "Van Metre's Ferry." This site allows great views of Knobly Mountain ahead.

176.87 A former basin in the canal, now a marsh, attracts marsh birds (bitterns are seen here) and other wildlife.

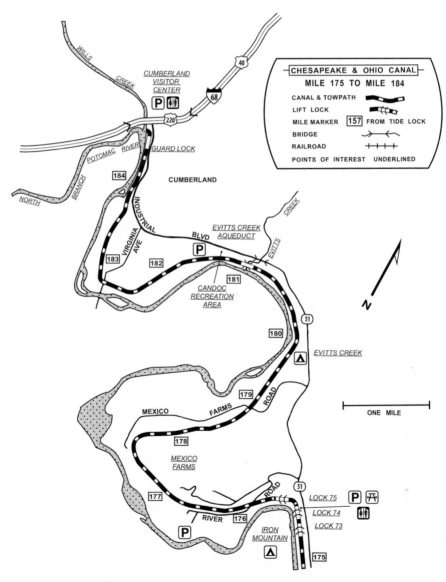

177.00 Federal Correctional Institution, Cumberland, comes into view.

177.67 Culvert #235, 4' span.

177.69 Remnants of a former Western Maryland Railway bridge are at the canal's intersection with Mexico Farms Road. The small landing field of Mexico Farms Airport lies between the canal and the river. Founded in 1923, it is one of the nation's oldest continually-operating airports. Across the river in West Virginia is the Greater Cumberland Regional Airport. A Native American village once located on the Mexico Farms subdivision was converted to a training airport for the Army Air Corps during World War II. Canal data of 1851 listed this as the area of the "Ferry on the Mexico Tract." The canal was watered here in the 1979 canal cleanup.

178.50 Triple-culvert Canal Road crosses the towpath. The towpath is very narrow and rutted in this area.

178.84 Brehm Road crosses the towpath, leading 0.8 mile to MD-51. Houses are right next to the towpath at this point. To the left was the location of Kirkendall Ferry.

179.10 Culvert #236, 4' span.

179.31 Culvert #237, 4' span, waste weir combination. Culvert #237 was built several feet high rather than near ground level. Across the canal the berm bank conceals a large wall to the left of the waste weir. Use CAUTION—the berm bank is very steep here.

179.99 Evitts Creek Hiker–Biker Campsite. Nearest access is at Candoc Recreation Area at mile 181.83. This is the last campsite if traveling upstream to Cumberland.

180.01 Culvert #239, 7' span. Originally a 10'-high road culvert, it is now blocked on the berm side by railroad debris dumped as fill; the downstream side shows some deterioration. (Up and down the canal from this point several culverts on the berm side drain waste water into the canal.) The canal is extremely narrow here.

180.35 The berm here is a marsh with aquatic plants and much bird life.

EVITTS CREEK AQUEDUCT

180.66 Evitts Creek Aqueduct is the last of the canal aqueducts. It is also the smallest, with a single 70' span. Completed around 1840, it has partially collapsed at both ends on the upper side. A nearby culvert carries Evitts Creek under the railroad yards. The MD-51 bridge, completed in 1958, is on the far side of the culvert. Stabilization work was done by the NPS in 1979 and 1983.

180.75 Cumberland city line.

180.86 Low cliffs exhibit interesting rock strata.

181.20 Culvert #240, 10' span.

Evitts Creek Aqueduct, 2012. *(Image courtesy Steve Dean)*

181.26 The canal emerges from woods and bears away from the railroad. This former basin area is choked with growth and downed trees.

181.30 Modern culvert, 4' span.

181.76 Cumberland Waste Water Treatment Plant. The flat top of the cliff across the river is the site of the Greater Cumberland Regional Airport.

181.83 Candoc Recreation Area (39.625274, -78.759307) Access: From Cumberland take MD-51 south 1.1 miles. Turn right onto Virginia Ave. After 0.3 mile make left at E. Offut St. Continue 0.5 mile to intersection with Candoc Ln. Continue straight on E. Offut to the recreation area. (Candoc is acronym for C and O Canal.) The canal is watered miles 181.80–183.39.

182.22 The Western Maryland Railway crosses the canal, having come from the Welton Tunnel across the river. The bridge (#1628) was built in 1904.

182.62 Wiley Ford Canal Bridge, built in 1997 to eliminate the at-grade crossing, is part of the approach and bridge that now carries the "Airport Parkway" (MD-61) across the Potomac. An earlier ford was somewhat downstream. Beyond is a small culvert, after which the canal curves into Cumberland's industrial district. The 1889, 1924, and 1936 floods were above the towpath level.

182.63 Former site of Culvert #241, lost to construction of the new Wiley Ford Bridge.

182.97 Pass under the Western Maryland Railway bridge built in 1904. The Carpendale Rail Trail connects with the towpath from Carpendale, West Virginia, by way of the bridge and Knobley Tunnel. The canal bed is cleared to the stop gate upstream.

253

A Daring Raid at Night

In the middle of the night, February 21, 1865, a unit of Confederates known as McNeill's Rangers slipped across the Potomac into Cumberland and surprised two Union generals in their beds at two different hotels.

Maj. Gen. Benjamin F. Kelley commanded the Second Infantry Division, Department of West Virginia, with headquarters in Cumberland. Maj. Gen. George C. Crook commanded the Department of West Virginia. At gunpoint, both generals were ordered to dress, were mounted on horses, and were led back across the river before the 7,000 Union troops occupying the town knew what had occurred.

General Crook reportedly said, "Gentlemen, this is the most brilliant exploit of the War." As part of their escape route, the Confederates used the canal towpath to Wiley's Ford below Cumberland. The generals were taken to Richmond, where they were well treated in captivity until exchanged a month later.

183.39 Masonry piers of an old stop gate. Built in 1849, the gate was designed to retain water in the Cumberland basins when the canal was drained for winter repairs. Across the canal was a small quarry from which the stone for the gate came.

183.55 Long concrete spillway. Note: the concrete was built around an earlier stone waste weir at the upper end; this weir was the drainage gate for the Cumberland Basin. Beyond, the towpath runs along a high flood-control embankment that slopes to the river. The berm is a cliff, with the Canal Parkway on top of it and the CSX Railroad yards beyond that. Ahead is a splendid view of Cumberland, with Wills Creek Narrows prominent behind the city. The flood-control project completed in 1959 eradicated the line of the original towpath and canal prism, radically altering the last mile from here to the guard lock terminus.

CUMBERLAND

184.1x The scene here has been vastly altered since canal days, for the entire area ahead was the busy complex of boat basins and railroad tracks on berms and trestles. During the operating era the number and location of basins, wharfs, loading areas, and boatyards for the construction and repair of canal boats changed frequently. The loading areas for coal consisted of rails on trestles above bays for the boats. Hatch covers were removed from the boats, and the coal was dropped into the holds, where men known as trimmers shoveled coal into the corners and distributed the cargo evenly.

Beyond the basin, the streets were busy with stores, blacksmiths, veterinarians, mule stables, and saloons catering to the canallers—many of whom lived on their boats here in the winter. The canal company steam dredge, one of two on the canal, and the repair scows were moored here. The scene is

The Cumberland Basin, ca. early 1900s.

difficult to visualize today, when Canal Place, Riverside Park, and the extensive reclamation and flood control levees along the river front have totally altered the landscape.

184.37 At the confluence of Wills Creek and North Branch is all that remains of Dam 8: a remnant of the stone abutment on the Maryland riverbank. The 400'-long, 17'-high Dam 8—the last of the canal supply dams—was blown up by the Corps of Engineers as part of their flood control project in 1958.

The canal passes the end of the dam and continues to a point at mile 184.5, where the guard lock and inlet gate mark the end of the canal. In 1954 the Douglas Hike began 10 miles down the canal at Lock 72 because of the chaotic and disrupted condition of the canal in Cumberland and for some distance below it.

In recent years the NPS erected a stone milepost marked as "Mile 184.5" in the grassy basin to the right, to symbolize the endpoint of the canal and towpath. Many through-hikers and bikers have a picture taken here, to mark the start or end of their journey.

A pedestrian bridge crosses the canal and provides access to a boat replica, *The Cumberland,* and other destinations in town, including the park's Cumberland Visitor Center. *The Cumberland* is occasionally open for tours—inquire at the NPS Visitor Center.

Canal Town, Cumberland

The terminus of the western end of the C&O is also the last town in the Canal Towns Partnership.

Cumberland was established as a town in 1787. The name came from Fort Cumberland built near Wills Creek and used by Gen. Edward Braddock in 1775. The town has been called the "Queen City of the Alleghenies," because it was for a time the second largest city in Maryland and the largest in the heart of the Allegheny region. Cumberland was also known as the "Gateway of the West," because of its strategic location in the gap of the Appalachian Mountain range through which passed both the National Road after 1818 and the B&O Railroad after 1852—major east–west transportation routes.

Prior to the arrival of the railroad and the canal, Cumberland was for many years an important town on the National Road. The Braddock Road went out what is now Greene Street and crossed the gap in Haystack Mountain, visible from the canal. The new National Road in 1821 followed this general route. When the macadamizing of the road was undertaken in 1834, the newer route up the valley of Wills Creek and through the Narrows was adopted. Competing stagecoach lines operated on frequent schedules, and Cumberland became a bustling metropolis of the route. The discovery of the rich coal vein in the George's Creek region gave impetus to the construction of both the railroad and the canal. The railroad reached Cumberland in 1842 and the canal in 1850, and use of the National Road began to decline. The last stage line ceased operation in 1853.

For much of the Civil War, Cumberland was headquarters to Union Gen. Benjamin Kelley, whose troops were charged with protecting the B&O Railroad and canal. On June 17, 1863,

Skyline view of Cumberland, Maryland.

A Sunday outing in Cumberland.

Confederate cavalry under Gen. John Imboden demanded the surrender of Cumberland and occupied the town for several hours before moving down the river to burn railroad bridges, including that over the canal east of town. During the McCausland-Johnson Raid, on August 1-2, 1864, the Confederates threatened Cumberland before withdrawing across the river at Oldtown.

The mountain ridges in the Cumberland region provided coal, iron ore, and timber, which helped supply the Industrial Revolution and turned the city into a key manufacturing center in the mid-nineteenth century. In addition to coal, industries in glass, breweries, fabrics, and tinplate flourished. Following World War II, however, industry in Cumberland began to decline and its population dwindled.

Today, Cumberland is a busy city that boasts small-town charm and a rich cultural life. Its Washington Street Historic District was listed on the National Register of Historic Places in 1973. Canal Place, Maryland's first certified heritage area, is home to the Western Maryland Scenic Railway Station, the C&O Canal Visitor Center, and a number of shops and restaurants. Downtown Cumberland is a short walk away, with a pedestrian mall filled with specialty shops, boutiques, art galleries, and eateries. This designated Main Street and Arts and Entertainment District hosts outdoor dining and a Summer in the City series that includes their well-known Friday After Five event.

Visit www.canaltowns.org for current listings of points of interest, services, bike rentals and service, restaurants, and lodging. Amtrak's *Capitol Limited* stops in Cumberland daily on the train's journey between Chicago and Washington, D.C.

The Canal Opens To Cumberland

An article in the Cumberland newspaper *The Alleganian* described the October 10, 1850, ceremonies formally opening the C&O Canal's 184.5 miles from Georgetown to Cumberland:

This great work, commencing nearly a quarter of a century ago, is at length so far completed as to be in a navigable condition from Cumberland to tide water. The opening was celebrated at Cumberland on Thursday last.

On Wednesday evening, the President and Directors of the Canal Company, the State's agents, and a number of guests from several counties of Maryland, Virginia, and the District cities, accompanied by the Independent Blues' Band of Baltimore, arrived in our city, via the railroad, to participate in the opening ceremonies.

On Thursday morning, at 8 o'clock, Col. Davidson's company of light artillerists, from the Eckhart mines, arrived and about one hour after a procession, made up of the military, the canal board, and guests, the corporate authorities and citizens, was formed in Baltimore Street, under the direction of Col. Pickell, of Baltimore, and marched to the head of the canal. On arriving at this point, and after the firing of a salute by the artillerists, Wm. Price, Esq., on behalf of the corporate authorities and citizens, in a neat speech, welcomed the canal board and their guests and congratulated them upon the occurrence of the event so long looked for—the opening of the canal to Cumberland. Gen. James M. Coale, President of the Canal Company, responded in appropriate terms, and embraced the occasion to briefly review the history of the progress of the work.

About 11 o'clock the several boats fitted up for the occasion, pretty well crowded, proceeded down the canal in the following order:

Way's excursion boat, *Jenny Lind*, having on board the Canal Board and their guests from abroad;

The *Charles B. Fisk*, with the Baltimore band and a large number of citizens;

Mr. Clarke's boat, with the Eckhart artillerists and the Mechanics' Band of Cumberland;

These were followed by the *Southampton, Delaware and Ohio*, of Mssrs. McCaig & Agnew's merchant line, and the *Freeman Rawdon*, of the Cumberland line, all bound for Alexandria, laden with coal; and Mr. Mong's *Elizabeth*, with coal, for Harper's Ferry.

The Canal Board and their guests landed about nine miles below Cumberland, where they partook of an abundant collation, prepared for the occasion, on board the *Charles B. Fisk*. The company returned to Cumberland in the evening, delighted with the excursion.

The proceedings of the day closed with a Supper and Ball in the evening, given by citizens at Heflefinger's hotel.

A compilation of Cumberland and other canal town newspaper articles from the era can be found at www.candocanal.org/histdocs/newspaper.html.

The Western Maryland Railway has an office in Cumberland where freight and cars are shipped over the C&O Canal to Williamsport, a distance of 100 miles, and thence by this railway to tidewater in Baltimore, the eastern terminus of the road. The first shipment from Baltimore to Cumberland over this road in connection with the canal was made August 5, 1876, when it reduced the tariff rates carried by the B&O Railway. The road has a regular line of boats to carry its freight on the Canal from Cumberland to Williamsport, where it is transferred to the cars. The railway has a warehouse at the head of the basin in Cumberland, where it receives freight from or for boats. –J. Thomas Scharf, History of Western Maryland, Vol. II, (Philadelphia, 1882).

Shanty Town

During the heyday of the canal one of the busiest areas of Cumberland was "Shanty Town," a popular, yet notorious spot among canallers, mule drivers, and boat builders—a place to "blow off steam" between round trips from Georgetown.

Approximately 25 buildings comprised this area, which started at the B&O underpass at the lower end of Wineow Street and ended near Footers Dye Works. Most of the houses were made of wood, two stories high with flat roofs. Some even had false fronts. The only brick house was Murphy's Grocery Store at the lower end near the underpass. Most of the other houses were saloons, pool halls, lunch rooms, gaming rooms, and disreputable establishments. All of the buildings were on one side of the narrow street facing the canal loading wharf and the boat-building yard, only a few hundred feet away. The B&O railroad went right through the back yards of these houses.

A boatyard and Shantytown, ca. 1890.

259

184.50 Cumberland Visitor Center. (39.649348, -78.762800) Access: Cumberland, Maryland, is approximately 130 miles by road from Washington, D.C. Take I-270 north to Frederick, then I-70 west to Hancock, and I-68 west to Cumberland. From I-68, take Exit 43C toward downtown Cumberland. At the bottom of the ramp make a left onto Harrison St. and follow Harrison to the visitor center in the Western Maryland Railway Museum. From the west take Exit 43C off I-68. At the bottom of the ramp make a left onto Queen City Dr. Cross under I-68, and at the traffic light make another left onto Harrison St., and follow it several short blocks to the visitor center.

The visitor center is open year-round, seven days a week, from 9 a.m. to 5 p.m. (Closed Thanksgiving, Christmas and New Year's Days.) Call ahead to confirm hours of operation. The exhibit area features interactive and educational displays about the history of the C&O Canal and Cumberland, a model of the Paw Paw Tunnel, and a life-size section of a canal boat. Exhibits highlight the canal's construction, cargo, mules, locks, and crew. Western Maryland Railway Station, 13 Canal St., Cumberland, MD 21502, 301-722-8226, www.nps.gov/choh/planyourvisit/cumberlandvisitorcenter.htm.

The Western Maryland Scenic Railroad offers train excursions from Cumberland to Frostburg, Maryland. Call 1-800-TRAIN-50 or visit www.wmsr.com.

A view of the Western Maryland Railway Station in Cumberland. The building now houses the C&O Canal National Historical Park Visitor Center.

Traces of the inlet gate and guard lock remain under the railroad trestle, which used the filled-in locks as solid building foundations. The locktender's house sat between the inlet gate and guard lock and was removed when flood control work was done. The flood control construction also eliminated the canal's terminal and filled in the locks.

Hikers and bikers who want to continue their adventure can join the Great Allegheny Passage (GAP), a trail that winds 150 miles between Cumberland and Point State Park in downtown Pittsburgh, Pennsylvania. Like the towpath, this nearly flat trail carries visitors along winding rivers, shaded valleys, and traditional small towns. For information call 888-282-BIKE, email atamail@atatrail.org, or visit www.atatrail.org.

The GAP extension finally achieves George Washington's vision of a continuous route 334.5 miles from Georgetown to the Ohio River. Though no longer the commercial waterway Washington envisioned, the Chesapeake and Ohio Canal remains a monument to nineteenth century ingenuity, human endurance, and natural wonders to be enjoyed for generations to come.

The End of the Line

There were plans and talk of extending the C&O Canal to Pittsburgh for a number of years after the canal opened to Cumberland in 1850. At an 1874 convention, an 8.4-mile tunnel was proposed through the mountains. This was the last major drive to push the canal to the Ohio River. In his book, *The Great National Project: A History of the Chesapeake and Ohio Canal* (John Hopkins Press, 1947), Walter Sanderlin wrote:

Of the projected western section, the best indication of its proposed course is the main line of the Baltimore and Ohio Railroad from Cumberland to Pittsburgh. According to the Army Engineers in 1874–1875, the railroad occupies the identical route surveyed for the canal, with the exception of the ambitious tunnel on the summit level.

By 1875 the canal operating period had reached its peak. That year more than 500 boats carried nearly 905,000 tons of coal down the canal. In the late 1870s, as rail technology and infrastructure improved, coal companies increased their shipments over the B&O Railroad, significantly impacting business on the canal. Major floods in 1877 and 1886 severely strained the canal company's finances. An 1889 damaging flood forced the company into receivership. Ironically, the B&O Railroad emerged as the majority owner of the 1844 and 1878 canal bonds, mortgaging the future profits and real property of the C&O Canal, which resulted in B&O representatives constituting the majority of the receivers.

During World War I the canal transported most of the coal used by the Naval Powder Factory at Indian Head, Maryland, and other government stations along the Potomac River. A swift decline in the postwar period, the 1922–23 strike at the George's Creek Coal Company, and the shift to coal supplies from sources outside the Potomac Basin further crippled the company. Another devastating flood struck in 1924, by which time the railroad had captured almost all of the carrying trade. This time the repairs necessary to resume operation were not required by the bankruptcy court. Instead, the court allowed the suspension of navigation with the understanding that the canal was not being legally abandoned. Finally, in 1936 the B&O attempted to sell the canal between Georgetown and Point of Rocks to the government, triggering a study of the complicated ownership question by the office of the U.S. Attorney General. The resultant opinion cleared the way for the B&O to sell the canal in its entirety, but not in parts, which is what ultimately happened in 1938. That "sale" however, served only to reduce the B&O's $80 million indebtedness to the Reconstruction Finance Corporation so that it could borrow more money.

Points of Interest

Note: GPS coordinates are included with each site that has vehicle parking available.

0.00	Georgetown Tide Lock (38.901107, -77.057467)
0.38	Lock 1 (38.904167, -77.060133)
0.42	Lock 2
0.49	Lock 3
0.54	Lock 4
1.07	Alexandria Canal Aqueduct
2.26	Georgetown Canal Incline
3.14	Fletcher's Cove/Abner Cloud House (38.918691, -77.102019)
4.17	Chain Bridge (38.932652, -77.113304)
5.02	Lock 5/Inlet Lock 1
5.40	Lock and Lockhouse 6 (Canal Quarters Brookmont) (38.944737, -77.123348)
5.64	Feeder Dam 1 (Little Falls Dam)
6.4x	Sycamore Island (38.95832, -77.131465)
7.00	Lock and Lockhouse 7 (38.964611, -77.138363)
8.33	Lock and Lockhouse 8 (38.971559, -77.160636)
8.70	Lock 9
8.79	Lock and Lockhouse 10 (Canal Quarters Bethesda) (38.972631, -77.169278)
8.97	Lock and Lockhouse 11
9.29	Lock 12
9.37	Lock 13
9.47	Lock 14
10.41	Carderock Recreational Area (38.974560, -77.201968)
11.52	Marsden Tract Group Campsite
12.28	Cropley/Old Angler's Inn (38.981897, -77.226205)
12.62	Widewater begins
13.45	Lock 15
13.63	Lock and Lockhouse 16
13.74	Guard Gate, Guard Wall, and Winch House
13.99	Lock 17
14.05	Side trail to Great Falls Overlook
14.09	Lock 18
14.17	Lock 19
14.30	Lock 20, Great Falls Tavern Visitor Center (NPS fee area) (39.001748, -77.246836)
16.64	Lock and Lockhouse 21 and Swains Lock Hiker-Biker Campsite (H-B) (39.031634, -77.243531)
19.63	Lock and Lockhouse 22 (Canal Quarters Pennyfield) (39.054972, -77.290334)
21.02	Blockhouse Point
22.12	Lock 23 (Violettes Lock) and Inlet Lock 2 (39.067226, -77.328483)
22.15	Feeder Dam 2

22.82	Lock and Lockhouse 24 (Rileys Lock) and Seneca Aqueduct (39.069167, -77.340877)
26.10	Horsepen Branch H-B
27.21	Sycamore Landing (39.074731, -77.420193)
30.5x	Chisel Branch H-B
30.64	Goose Creek River Lock
30.84	Lock and Lockhouse 25 (Canal Quarters Edwards Ferry) (39.103463, -77.472933)
31.94	Broad Run Trunk Aqueduct
33.27	Harrison Island (opposite Battle of Balls Bluff site)
34.43	Turtle Run H-B
35.50	Whites Ferry (39.154861, -77.518206)
38.2x	Marble Quarry H-B
39.37	Lock 26 (Woods Lock)
39.63	Dickerson Conservation Park (39.194685, -77.469402)
41.46	Lock and Lockhouse 27 (Spinks Ferry)
42.19	Monocacy Aqueduct (39.222563, -77.449987)
42.40	Indian Flats H-B
44.58	Nolands Ferry (39.249948, -77.482726)
47.65	Calico Rocks H-B
48.20	Point of Rocks (Canal Town) (39.273218, -77.540045)
48.93	Lock and Lockhouse 28 (Canal Quarters Point of Rocks)
50.31	Bald Eagle Island H-B
50.89	Lock and Lockhouse 29 (Lander) (39.306507, -77.558006)
51.53	Catoctin Creek Aqueduct
54.0x	Brunswick Family Campground
55.00	Lock 30, Brunswick (Canal Town) (39.311220, -77.630749)
58.01	Lock and Lockhouse 31, Weverton (39.329916, -77.681966)
58.07	Junction with the Appalachian Trail
60.23	Lock 32, Sandy Hook
60.62	Shenandoah River Lock
60.70	Lock 33, Harpers Ferry (Canal Town)
61.27	Harpers Ferry Road/Maryland Heights (39.329395, -77.731919)
61.57	Lock 34 (Goodhearts Lock) (39.333430, -77.738577)
62.27	Feeder Dam 3
62.33	Lock 35
62.44	Lock 36
62.90	Huckleberry Hill H-B
64.89	Dargan Bend Recreation Area (39.364182, -77.740073)
66.96	Lock and Lockhouse 37 (Mountain Lock) (39.385295, -77.734451)
69.36	Antietam Aqueduct and Antietam Drive-in Campground (39.419001, -77.746573)
72.4x	Railroad Bridge (Shepherdstown) (39.433927, -77.795512)
72.65	Shepherdstown River Lock
72.80	Lock 38, Shepherdstown (Canal Town) (39.436456, -77.799527)
72.82	Ferry Hill (39.438269, -77.798283)

74.00	Lock 39
75.29	Killiansburg Cave H-B
75.73	Killiansburg Cave
76.65	Snyders Landing (39.465270, -77.777313)
79.41	Lock 40
79.68	Horseshoe Bend H-B
81.0x	Taylors Landing (39.499645, -77.767866)
82.46	Big Woods H-B
83.30	Dam 4 Cave
84.40	Dam 4, Big Slackwater begins upstream (39.496001, -77.826266)
85.40	Big Slackwater Boat Ramp (39.501346, -77.845385)
85.62	Inlet Lock 4
88.10	McMahon's Mill (39.530654, -77.823522)
88.90	Lock 41
89.04	Lock 42
90.94	Opequon Junction H-B
92.96	Lock and Lockhouse 43
95.20	Cumberland Valley H-B
99.30	Lock and Lockhouse 44 (39.595037, -77.824712)
99.72	Cushwa Basin, Conococheague Aqueduct, Williamsport (39.600996, -77.826927)
101.28	Jordan Junction H-B
103.26	Gift Road (39.616863, -77.888503)
106.80	Dam 5, Inlet Lock 5, and Lockhouse (39.607079, -77.921117)
107.27	Lock 45
107.42	Lock and Lockhouse 46 (39.615866, -77.926626)
108.13	Charles Mill Ruins
108.64	Lock 47
108.70	Lock 48
108.80	Lock and Lockhouse 49 (Canal Quarters Four Locks) (39.615311, -77.947494)
108.87	Lock 50
110.00	North Mountain H-B
110.42	McCoys Ferry Drive-in Campground (39.609261, -77.970065)
112.40	Fort Frederick State Park (39.605391, -78.005041)
112.50	Big Pool, lower end
114.52	Ernstville Road (39.632970, -78.028951)
116.30	Licking Creek Aqueduct and H-B (39.655987, -78.053946)
119.84	Little Pool, lower end (39.684430, -78.103796)
120.60	Little Pool H-B
122.59	Lock 51 (39.695110, -78.153670)
122.85	Bowles House (Hancock Visitor Center)
122.89	Lock 52
122.96	Tonoloway Creek Aqueduct
124.10	Hancock (Canal Town) (39.698253, -78.181036)

126.43	White Rock H-B
127.24	Devil's Eyebrow
127.40	Round Top Cement Mill
129.88	Leopards Mill H-B
129.96	Lock 53
130.70	Cohill Station (39.645446, -78.251711)
133.6x	Cacapon Junction H-B
133.96	Lock 54
134.06	Dam 6, Guard Lock 6, and Lock 55 (39.628174, -78.298262)
135.90	Western Maryland Rail Trail Terminus (39.636480, -78.323262)
136.21	Lock and Lockhouse 56 (39.637868, -78.328302)
136.56	Sideling Hill Creek Aqueduct
138.06	East Portal of Indigo Tunnel
139.22	Lock 57
139.2x	Indigo Neck H-B
140.77	Fifteen Mile Creek Drive-in Campground and Little Orleans (39.625648, -78.385868)
140.90	Fifteenmile Creek Aqueduct
143.96	Lock 58
144.54	Devils Alley H-B
146.56	Lock 59 (39.603639, -78.425820)
149.36	Stickpile Hill H-B
149.69	Lock 60
150.10	Bonds Landing (39.582848, -78.411246)
153.10	Lock 61
153.28	Twigg Hollow (39.58128, -78.46154)
154.14	Sorrel Ridge H-B
154.16	Lock 62
154.29	Large Waste Weir Ruins
154.48	Lock 63 1/3
154.60	Lock 64 2/3
154.70	Lock 66
154.85	Tunnel Hill Trail
155.20	North (Downstream) Portal Paw Paw Tunnel
155.78	South (Upstream) Portal Paw Paw Tunnel
156.10	Paw Paw Tunnel Drive-in Campground (39.544450, -78.460806)
156.89	Purslane Run H-B
161.76	Lock 67 (39.52560, -78.53626)
162.1x	Town Creek H-B
162.34	Town Creek Aqueduct (39.523862, -78.543122)
164.82	Lock and Lockhouse 68
164.8x	Potomac Forks H-B
166.44	Lock 69 (Twiggs Lock)
166.70	Lock and Lockhouse 70, Oldtown (39.540405, -78.611936)

Coal being moved from railcars to canal boats at Consolidation Coal Company boatyard in Cumberland, ca. early 1900s.

Campsites

Drive-In Campsites (Fee area)

69.36	Antietam Creek
110.42	McCoys Ferry
140.77	Fifteenmile Creek
156.10	Paw Paw Tunnel
173.37	Spring Gap

Group Campsites (Fee area)

11.52	Marsden Tract
	(by reservation only)
140.77	Fifteenmile Creek

Hiker–Biker Campsites

16.64	Swains Lock
26.10	Horsepen Branch
30.5x	Chisel Branch
34.43	Turtle Run
38.2x	Marble Quarry
42.40	Indian Flats
47.65	Calico Rocks
50.31	Bald Eagle Island
62.90	Huckleberry Hill
75.29	Killiansburg Cave

Hiker–Biker Campsites, continued

79.68	Horseshoe Bend
82.46	Big Woods
90.94	Opequon Junction
95.20	Cumberland Valley
101.28	Jordan Junction
110.00	North Mountain
116.30	Licking Creek
120.60	Little Pool
126.43	White Rock
129.88	Leopards Mill
133.6x	Cacapon Junction
139.2x	Indigo Neck
144.54	Devils Alley
149.36	Stickpile Hill
154.14	Sorrel Ridge
156.89	Purslane Run
162.1x	Town Creek
164.8x	Potomac Forks
169.10	Pigmans Ferry
175.3x	Irons Mountain
179.99	Evitts Creek

The following campgrounds are near the towpath but are not operated or maintained by the National Park Service. Call or visit each campground for availability and regulations.

54.0x	Brunswick Family Campground
	40 Canal Towpath Road, Brunswick, MD 21716, 888-491-6615, www.potomacrivercampground.com
112.40	Fort Frederick State Park
	11100 Fort Frederick Rd., Big Pool, MD 21711, 301-842-2155, dnr2.maryland.gov/publiclands/Pages/western/fortfrederick.aspx
129.88	Happy Hills Camp Ground
	12617 Seavolt Rd., Hancock, MD 21750, 301-678-7760 www.happyhillscampground-md.net
140.77	Little Orleans Campground & Park Area
	31661 Green Forest Dr., SE., Little Orleans, MD 21766, 301-478-2325, www.littleorleanscampground.com
153.28	Green Ridge State Forest, 28700 Headquarters Dr, NE, Flintstone, MD 21530-9525, 301-478-3124, http://www.dnr.state.md.us/forests/StateForests/greenridgeforest.asp

Canal Towns

The Canal Towns Partnership is a collaboration of nine historic communities between Point of Rocks and Cumberland that offer services and amenities to visitors along the canal. Visit www.canaltowns.org to learn about points of interest, services, lodging, and food sources in these towns.

48.20	Point of Rocks
55.00	Brunswick
60.70	Harpers Ferry & Bolivar
72.80	Shepherdstown
72.80	Sharpsburg (From the towpath at mile 72.80 go 3 miles east on MD-34 to Sharpsburg)
99.30	Williamsport
124.10	Hancock
184.50	Cumberland

Canal Quarters

In 2009 the National Park Service and its partner, the C&O Canal Trust, began a program to restore and furnish lockhouses and make them available to the public for overnight stays. Currently, six lockhouses with varying amenities provide visitors with a unique interpretive experience. Photographs, maps, and books in the houses help visitors step back in time and relive the locktender's life on the canal. Fees range from $100 to $150. Each house is equipped with beds, dishes, and utensils; visitors must provide their own linens; maximum occupancy is eight. For information or reservations contact the C&O Canal Trust at 1850 Dual Highway, Suite 100, Hagerstown, MD 21740, 301-714-2233, www.canaltrust.org/quarters.

5.40	Lockhouse 6, Brookmont
8.79	Lockhouse 10, Bethesda
19.63	Lockhouse 22, Pennyfield
30.84	Lockhouse 25, Edwards Ferry
48.93	Lockhouse 28, Point of Rocks
108.80	Lockhouse 49, Four Locks

Lockhouse 22, Pennyfield, 2014 *(HFHA image)*

Towpath Glossary

abutment. The part of a structure anchoring it to the land, such as the ends of a dam, canal lock chamber, bridge, culvert, or aqueduct.

aqueduct. Freestanding structure that carries a canal and towpath across a stream, river, road, etc.

balance beam. Long, large timber on top of and extending from the lock gate that is pushed to open and close the gate; it also serves to counter-balance the weight of the gate and pull it into the quoin stones against which the heel post swings as the gate pivots.

barrel. The interior arched structure of a culvert or tunnel.

bateau. Shallow-draft, flat-bottom boat designed to transport goods on the shallow, rocky rivers above tidewater. Also known as a flat boat or gundalow.

berm. A raised bank or earthen ridge. Also used for the side of the canal opposite to the towpath, usually referring to the land vs. the river side.

> Canal terminology is frequently interchanged or misapplied when used to discuss or describe structures. This glossary includes alternately used terms wherever applicable.

breast wall. Wall at the upstream end of a lift lock. It steps the canal bottom from the floor of the lock to the bottom of the canal upstream and represents elevation change.

bypass flume. Ditch or culvert that allows water to flow around a lock from the upper to lower level. More elaborate versions had gates that allowed the locktender to control the amount of water flowing around the lock.

canal. A man-made waterway.

coping stone. Stone that forms the top of a masonry wall, such as that of a lock or aqueduct.

crib. Box-like structure of heavy timbers, generally filled with rubble stone. Rubble-stone-filled cribs were used to make dams and other types of walls and were covered with heavy planking.

crossover bridge. (also called a **mule bridge**) Bridge that transfers the towpath from one side of the canal to the other.

culvert. Structure carrying a waterway, path or road under the canal. Culverts pass under the earthen canal prism and towpath and, unlike aqueducts, are not freestanding structures. The canal passes over more than 150 culverts.

drop gate. Upstream lock gate that pivots at the bottom to lie flat and allow boats to pass over it. Drop gates and their gate pocket were on the breast wall that constituted the upper end of the lock chamber. One person on one side could operate it using a mechanism that raised and lowered it.

dry dock. Lock-like structure into which boats could be taken for repair. Once a boat was in the dock, it was drained, allowing the boat to settle on supports that permitted work under and around the sides of the boat.

feeder canal. Canal that carries water from the river to the canal. On some canals the feeder was built from a natural or artificial reservoir. On the C&O Canal a feeder extended from the guard lock behind a dam to the main channel of the canal at Dam 1, Dam 3, and Dam 6.

feeder dam. Dam built across a river to create a reliable pool from which water could be drawn to supply water to the canal.

feeder lock. See **guard lock**.

flood gate. See **guard gate**.

flume. See **bypass flume**.

freshet. Flood or overflowing of a river, due to heavy rains or melted snow; an inundation.

gate collar. An iron strap around the heel post at top of the lock, the ends of which connect with the gooseneck straps in a manner that locks the heel post into an upright position against the quoin stones, but loosely enough that the gate can swing open and closed.

gate pocket. (also called **lock pocket** or **gate/lock recess**) A recess in a lock wall into which a gate fits when it is open, thus not impeding boats entering or leaving the lock.

gooseneck strap. (also called **gate strap**) A curved metal bar anchored to coping stones and forming part of the mechanism for locking

Detail of gate hinge at Lock 35 showing **gooseneck straps** bolted into the **quoin stone**, and the **gate collar** around the **heel post**. Note also the staple-like iron cramp securing two **coping stones**. *(Library of Congress, Prints & Photographs Division, HABS Reproduction number HABS MD, 22-HARF. V, 9--3)*

the gate collar around the heel post. It also serves to distribute the stress of the heavy gate as it is swung open and closed.

guard gate. Gate in the opening of a guard wall that protects the canal from high water in the river. The gate and its abutments on both sides are the same height as the guard wall. Compare with **stop gate** (see below).

guard lock. Lock that feeds water into the canal and provides access to or from the reservoir of water behind a feeder dam. The upstream end of the guard lock

270

has abutments and a gate as high as the guard wall, thus making it possible to close the opening in the guard wall created by the lock.

guard wall. High wall or berm that protects the canal from flooding. Guard walls existed in various configurations at all the dams and guard locks, as the canal was at river level at these locations and thus vulnerable to high water and floods.

gudgeon. A cast-iron type of plate with a bearing or pin at the bottom of a lock gate heel post. The pin fits into and rotates in the gudgeon, keeping the lock gate in place while allowing it to freely rotate.

Lock gate shown open fully and fitted in the **lock pocket** at Lock 38. The **heel post** (left side of gate) rotates on a **gudgeon** at the bottom and is held in place by a **gate collar** at the top. Iron **wicket stems** run vertically through the gate, and are used to open or close **wicket gates**.

heel post. The post in a miter gate that fits into the quoin stones and pivots on a gudgeon as the gate is swung open or closed. At the top it is held in place by the gate collar that locks into the gooseneck straps set in the coping stones on the top of the lock. See also **toe post**.

hydraulic cement. Cement that hardens under water and withstands exposure to water far longer than lime mortars.

incline plane. An alternative system to lift locks for raising and lowering boats. It usually consisted of a caisson filled with water, into which the canal boat could be sealed as the caisson moved up/down the incline on rails (similar to those of a railroad). On some canals, boats would be floated onto flat cars that were then pulled up and down the incline.

informal overflow. (also called **overfall** or **mule drink**) Section of towpath approximately two feet lower than that of the adjacent towpath, allowing excess water to flow out of the canal, thus preventing it from overtopping and breeching a vulnerable part of the towpath berm. The recessed towpath surface and the river side of the towpath berm were well rip-rapped to prevent washout. Canallers referred to these as "mule drinks" due to the tendencies of the mules to stop and drink when water was flowing over one.

inlet lock. (also called **guard lock**) Lock that provides water to the canal from a pool behind a dam. Because water is lost by seepage, evaporation, the slow current in the canal, and the operation of locks, it was necessary to maintain the depth of the canal by adding water at various points. The inlet locks at the lower ends of the slackwater navigation stretches were also initial sources of water for the canal below them.

level. Section of the canal between locks that is level. Canals were flat bodies of water with minimal current, and their elevation was changed by means of lift locks or, on some canals, by incline planes.

lock. Structure with gates at both ends that allows boats to be raised or lowered to adjust for differences in water level or the elevation of the pool or waterway at each end. Locks were designed in different ways to serve different purposes, such as lift locks that changed the elevation of the canal and river locks that raised and lowered boats between the level of the canal and that of the river, below the canal. See also **inlet** and **outlet locks**.

lock culvert. (also called **sidewall culvert**) A culvert with an opening in the lock wall just above the upper lock gate to take in water, and with three openings in the lock walls proper to discharge the water. These culverts were used to fill the locks and to provide a continuous flow of water to the canal below the lock when the upstream gates were closed. This method was used on the original locks in the lower section of the canal (Locks 1 through 26, except for 20 and possibly 13) before bypass flumes were adopted to maintain water flow around a lock. See also **bypass flume**.

lock gate. (also called **swing** or **miter gate**) Gate that opens or closes as it swings on a pivot at the bottom of the heel post. These gates were typically in a pair, with the toe posts mitered so that they fit tightly against each other when both gates were closed. Each lock had upper and lower lock gates. Compare with **drop gate**.

lock recess. See **gate pocket**.

lockhouse. House provided to a locktender for living quarters. When locks were in close proximity and one tender might be responsible for more than one lock, only one lockhouse was constructed. On the C&O Canal the lockhouse numbering system was different from the numbering system for the lift locks, but the current popular practice is to give a lockhouse the same number as the lock nearest to it.

lock pocket. See **gate pocket**.

locktender. (also called **lockkeeper**) Person employed to operate a lock.

milepost. (also called **mile marker**) A post set at approximately one mile intervals showing the number of miles above tide lock.

miter sill. Timbers in a triangular shape against which the bottom of the lock gates rested when closed to form a water-tight seal and provide support against the water pressure when the level of the water on the downstream side of the gate was lower than that on the upstream side.

mule bridge. See **crossover bridge.**

mule drink. See **informal overflow.**

mule rise. Part of the towpath that slopes at the downstream end of a lock to change the towpath to the elevation of the new level. The mule rise accommodates the difference in height (or lift) of the lock at its upper end. All other points on the towpath were level when the canal was operating. (The historic level of the towpath is not always maintained at present, as for example below Lock 33 at Harpers Ferry where it has been lowered to allow flood waters from above to more readily flow into the river, limiting their damage.)

outlet lock. Lock through which water leaves a canal. On the C&O Canal the locks at the upper end of the slackwater navigation stretches and the tide lock are outlet locks.

overflow. (also called **overfall**) See **informal overflow.**

parapet. The upper extension of a culvert or aqueduct above the level of the arch(es). It impounds earth in a culvert and water in an aqueduct. On an aqueduct the parapet extends from the top of the water table, which extends from the base of the canal prism.

pivot bridge. Bridge that is swung when needed across a lock, stop gate, or the canal by pivoting on a pier in the canal or on a pivot device on a lock or stop gate wall.

prism. (also called **canal trunk**) The channel of the canal that holds water. Typically it is created by water-retaining berms unless the terrain constitutes a natural wall on one or both sides, or the prism is formed by ditching. To maintain a level between locks where the canal must be above the level of the surrounding land, the floor of the canal and its berms are built on a substantial supporting berm across the low area, with a culvert under the canal to provide drainage. This is the case wherever the canal crosses a small valley.

quoin stone. A curved stone at the downstream end of the gate pocket into which the round heel post of the gate fits.

rope burns. Grooves worn in snubbing posts, railings, and masonry, etc. by the tow ropes.

silt. Fine sand, clay, organic, or other material carried by moving or running water and deposited as sediment.

skirting canal. Canal built to pass boats around an obstruction in the river such as rapids or waterfalls.

slackwater. Quiet water with little current such as that impounded behind a dam.

sluice. Channel along the riverbank with a protective wall to carry boats around a section of river that is difficult to navigate, such as where there are rapids. The term is also used for the bypass culverts that carry water around a lock when the lock gates are closed.

snubbing post. (also called **strapping post**) A post placed on the towpath side of a lock around which snubbing ropes from the boat were wrapped, and tightened or loosened as the boat was raised or lowered with the change of the water level when locking through. Snubbing was also essential as the boat entered the lock, to keep it from hitting the closed gate in front of it or hitting either gate due to turbulence as the water was flowing into or out of the lock. Snubbing posts were about 12" in diameter by 30" in height.

spillway. Drainage channel or structure designed to carry excess water flowing out of the canal from an overflow or waste weir to the river or other natural watercourse.

stop gate. Short masonry structure through which the canal passes with a single gate or slots in both walls for heavy planks, either of which would allow the canal to be closed off at that point and water held back on the upstream side of the gate. Stop gates were used in the winter to keep water in large reservoirs that would not be completely drained, such as the basins in Cumberland and Big and Little Pools below Hancock. They were also used to keep long sections of the canal from draining during repairs or when the integrity of the canal was lost in some location, causing water to flow out of the canal. Stop gates were only as high as the sides of the canal. Compare with **guard gate** (see above).

tidal basin. Artificial body of water open to a tidal river, stream, inlet or bay, etc. The water level in the basin rises or falls with the tide.

tidal canal. Canal between two tidal points that remains at tidal level. Typically there would be tide locks at both ends.

tide lock. Lock between a basin or level of a canal at one end and tidal waters at the other end. The tide lock on the C&O passed boats between the Rock Creek basin (created by the dam across the mouth of the creek) and the tidal Potomac. Because the level of the river fluctuated with the tide, the vertical difference between the river and the basin also fluctuated, and thus the lift of the lock would vary with the water level in the river. If the canal or basin level on the land side of the lock was not designed to be different from that on the tidal side, the lock would serve only to compensate for normal tidal fluctuation between the two sides. However, on the C&O, the Rock Creek Basin was designed to be three feet higher than the mean high tide of the river.

tidewater. Water affected by the flow and ebb of the tide. The upper limit of tidewater, which on the Potomac is at the base of Little Falls, is related to sea level—the level halfway between high and low tide.

toe post. The post of a lock gate that is mitered so that, when closed, it forms a tight seal with the toe post of the gate on the other side of the lock.

towline. Rope connecting the towing animals and the boat. On the C&O Canal the towlines were 9/16" Plymouth rope and as much as 225' long.

towpath. Path for the towing animals and the person walking with them. The tow-path was typically the top of the canal's river side berm. Exceptions were in Georgetown where the towpath was moved to the land side of the canal to keep boats passing up and down the canal away from boats tied up along the wharfs on the river side, and along the slackwater navigation stretches as far as the crossover bridge where the canal resumes. A crossover bridge was used at such locations, where the towpath was transferred back to the canal's river side berm.

turning basin. Place in the canal wide enough for a boat to turn around. Wharves here allowed for the transshipment of cargoes or served as the home base for boats operating in either direction, such as those used by canal administrators or maintenance personnel.

waste weir. Structure in the side of the canal that opens at various levels to allow the water level in the canal to be lowered or entirely drained. Except where locks were close together, each level had at least one waste weir. Heavy planks were dropped into slots in the abutments on either side. The number of planks determined how much the canal water was lowered in that weir's section. The weirs were normally in the towpath berm with a towpath bridge over them and a spillway from the weir to the river or a natural watercourse flowing toward the river. In a few cases the weir is on the land-side berm, and sometimes in the wing wall of an aqueduct.

wharf. (also called **quay**) Structure alongside the canal with a vertical wall that allows boats to tie up directly against it for loading and unloading.

wicket gates. (also called **butterfly** or **sluice valves**) Gates located at the bottom of miter gates that open to allow water to enter or leave the lock depending on whether they are in the upper or lower gates, respectively.

wicket stem. Rod extending from the wicket gates up through the gates and for several feet at the top. An iron rod known as the lock key fits on top of the squared heads of the wicket stems and was used to crank the wicket gates open or closed.

winch house. Building on top of a guard gate containing the planks used to close the gate. A winch mechanism lowers the planks into place across the gate opening with their ends in a vertical notch in the gate abutment.

wing wall. Masonry walls at the upper and lower end of locks, aqueducts, culverts, and other masonry structures along the canal. Wing walls typically curve away from the line of the lock walls and serve to guide boats into the lock. Culvert wing walls hold the earthen banks to the sides of the culvert arch back from the waterway or path.

Additional Reading

Achenbach, Joel. *The Grand Idea: George Washington's Potomac and the Race to the West.* New York: Simon and Schuster, 2005.

Allegheny Trail Alliance. *Trailbook 2014–15: Official Guide to the C&O Canal and the Great Allegheny Passage.* Pittsburgh/Cumberland: Great Allegheny Press, 2014.

Anthes, Gary. *The Chesapeake and Ohio Canal.* Atglen, PA: Schiffer Publishing, 2013.

Davies, William E. *The Geology and Engineering Structures of the Chesapeake & Ohio Canal.* Glen Echo, Maryland: C&O Canal Association, 1999. www.candocanal.org/histdocs/Davies-book.pdf

High, Mike. *The C&O Canal Companion: A Journey through Potomac History*, 2nd ed. Baltimore: The John Hopkins University Press, 2015.

Jex, Garnet W. *The Upper Potomac in the Civil War.* Harpers Ferry: Harpers Ferry Historical Association, 2012.

Kapsch, Robert J. and Elizabeth Perry Kapsch. *Monocacy Aqueduct on the Chesapeake and Ohio Canal.* Poolesville, MD: Medley Press, 2005.

Kapsch, Robert J. *The Potomac Canal: George Washington and the Waterway West.* Morgantown, WV: West Virginia University Press, 2007.

Kytle, Elizabeth. *Home on the Canal.* Baltimore: The John Hopkins University Press, 1996.

National Park Service. *Chesapeake and Ohio Canal: A Guide to Chesapeake and Ohio Canal National Historical Park, Maryland, District of Columbia, and West Virginia.* Washington DC: U.S. Government Printing Office, 1991.

Peck, Garrett. *The Potomac River: A History & Guide.* Charleston, SC: The History Press, 2012.

Sanderlin, Walter S. *The Great National Project: A History of the Chesapeake and Ohio Canal.* Baltimore: The John Hopkins University Press, 1947.

Shelton, Napier. *Potomac Pathway: A Nature Guide to the C&O Canal.* Atglen, PA: Schiffer Publishing, 2011.

Snyder, Timothy R. *Trembling in the Balance: The Chesapeake and Ohio Canal During the Civil War.* Boston: Blue Mustang Press, 2011.

Unrau, Harlan D. *Historic Resource Study: Chesapeake and Ohio Canal.* Prepared by Karen Gray. Hagerstown, MD: U.S. Department of the Interior, National Park Service, Chesapeake & Ohio Canal National Historical Park, 2007. www.nps.gov/parkhistory/online_books/choh/unrau_hrs.pdf

Way, Peter. *Common Labor: Workers and the Digging of North American Canals, 1780–1860.* Baltimore: The John Hopkins University Press, 1997.